THE RHETORICAL WORD

This book offers a bold reading of Protestant tradition from a rhetorical and literary perspective. Arguing that Protestant thought is based in a rhetorical performance of authority, Hobson draws on a wide range of modern and postmodern thought to defend this account of rhetorical authority from various charges of authoritarianism.

With close readings of Augustine, Luther, Kierkegaard and Barth, this book develops a new 'rhetorical theology of the Word' and also a new critique of secular modernity, with particular reference to modern literature and the thought of Nietzsche. Confronting the related issues of rhetoric and authority, Hobson provides a provocative account of modern theology which offers new perspectives on theology's relationship to literature and postmodern thought.

ASHGATE NEW CRITICAL THINKING IN THEOLOGY & BIBLICAL STUDIES

Ashgate New Critical Thinking in Theology & Biblical Studies presents an open-ended series of quality research drawn from an international field of scholarship. The series aims to bring monograph publishing back into focus for authors, the international library market, and student, academic and research readers. Headed by an international editorial advisory board of acclaimed scholars, this series presents cutting-edge research from established as well as exciting new authors in the field. With specialist focus, yet clear contextual presentation, books in the series aim to take theological and biblical research into new directions; opening the field to new critical debate within the traditions, into areas of related study, and into important topics for contemporary society.

Other Titles in the Series:

Charismatic Glossolalia
Mark J. Cartledge
God in the Act of Reference
Erica Appelros
A Poetics of Jesus
Jeffrey F. Keuss
Feminist Biblical Interpretation in Theological Context
J'annine Jobling

The Rhetorical Word

Protestant theology and the rhetoric of authority

THEO HOBSON

Ashgate

Published by
Ashgate Publishing Limited
Gower House
Croft Road
Aldershot
Hampshire GU11 3HR
England

Ashgate Publishing Company
131 Main Street
Burlington, VT 05401-5600 USA

Ashgate website: http://www.ashgate.com

British Library Cataloguing in Publication Data
Hobson, Theo
    The rhetorical word : Protestant theology and the rhetoric
    of authority. - (Ashgate new critical thinking in theology
    & biblical studies)
    1. Protestant churches - Doctrines 2. Rhetoric - Religious
    aspects - Protestantism 3. Authority - Religious aspects -
    Protestantism
    I. Title
    230'.044

Library of Congress Control Number: 2002100382

ISBN 0 7546 0655 4

Printed and bound in Great Britain by MPG Books Ltd, Bodmin, Cornwall

Contents

Preface

This book is well aware that it tries to do too much, and that experts in various fields will look upon the endeavour with suspicion, should they look upon it at all. The breadth of cope has a corrective intention, in an academic culture of minute specialism and thickening jargon. Theology ought to have some difficulty with such a culture: it is concerned with communication. It ought to fear obfuscation more than over-simplification, and solipsism more than solecisms.

It is aimed at students (of literature as well as theology) and the intelligent general reader who would be interested to see what a contemporary defence of Protestant tradition might look like. It is also aimed at experts who can tolerate the occasional broad brushstroke.

My thanks to those who helped with the original thesis from which this sprang, especially Graham Ward, whose patient guidance was just what the doctorate ordered. Thanks also to George Pattison, John Milbank, David Ford and many others who helped me to sustain and order my enthusiasm. My thanks also go to my family (especially my parents for their supplementation of the British Academy's limited generosity), to friends and housemates, and to Tess, my excellent wife.

For Tess and Martha

Introduction

Academic Protestant theology is like a man who tries to teach French without ever slipping out of English, or who tries to teach dance through words alone. It inhabits an inappropriate medium. It is fascinating to watch, and fun, though frustrating, to try. The appropriate medium of Protestant theology is the language of faith, a language rooted in acknowledgement and re-performance of divine authority. This language is intolerable to academic discourse, whose only authority is the spirit of inquiry. Academic theology's prime task is to accept the contradiction in which it finds itself, to admit that its proper concern is a language it cannot speak. Otherwise, it begins to believe in itself, and to reinvent its subject-matter accordingly. Above all, it will want to efface or devalue this other, purer, bolder rhetorical performance, which haunts its seminar table like some bloody ghost.

This book is about the role of authoritative rhetoric in Christian thought, particularly Protestantism. It argues that this role can hardly be overstated; that a rhetorical performance of authority is what Protestant Christianity essentially *is*. The case for the relevance of authoritative rhetoric to Christian theology surely need not be made. And yet, the issue has become so intellectually problematic that its centrality is not easily approached. Contemporary thought, most of theology included, is evasive of the question of rhetorical authority, 'in denial' about it, perhaps. It wants to wish it away, or deconstruct it away. It knows on the one hand that it is dangerous, the germ of fascism, perhaps; yet it also has a strong hunch that it is the essential ingredient of any account of 'truth'. It prefers not to dwell on the contradiction. Yet precisely this contradiction is where contemporary theology should be situating itself.

Protestantism very largely consists in rhetorical forms intended to communicate the authority of God in Jesus Christ. It is also a practice, or a 'form of life', which is to say that it goes beyond the verbal and rhetorical, but its social and practical existence is determined by its rhetorical basis. It invests more in the rhetorical than any other religious tradition. ('The rhetorical' is obviously a problematic category, whose complexities will emerge gradually. For now it is sufficient to define it as any form of discourse with claims to truth; speech with teeth.) The Protestant account of truth is uniquely bound up with the idea of authoritative rhetoric. This is its contemporary crisis and its hope. Its crisis because authority, including rhetorical authority, stands, rightly, under the severest modern suspicion. Its hope for two reasons: postmodernity and Protestant tradition itself. Postmodern thought suggests that 'truth' can never be anything other than an authoritative rhetoric, a persuasive performance, a powerful story. And Protestant tradition knows how to perform a very peculiar rhetoric of authority, one in which human claims to authority are challenged and broken, and space is cleared for the possibility of an utterance wholly other.

In my account of it, Protestant discourse is openly and consciously grounded in a rhetorical performance of authority. It shuns any other account of truth or authority. It does not seek to base itself in a claim of reasonability, whether historical or philosophical, nor does it appeal to the innate authority of an institution. As recent theologians have suggested, this makes it fully nonfoundationalist, fully postmodern. The postmodern climate is a very favourable for one for theology, yet it is slow to exploit it. It is *fascinated* by postmodern thought in a negative way, like a rabbit caught in headlights. It is so caught up in rediscovering its own complexity that it is in danger of neglecting the urgent simplicity of its calling.

My concern, then, is with the role of authority in Protestant thought. The received wisdom is that the Bible is the locus of Protestant authority; but this is not quite right. Authority lies in the rhetorical tradition instituted in the Bible, and in the process of its repetition. (In religious terms, authority lies in the Word of God as living event.) In every appeal to the authority of the text, authority has to be reconstructed in a new rhetorical performance. Consequently, faith is understood in rhetorical terms: as the performative acknowledgement of the authority of this rhetorical idiom. Faith is rhetorical praxis. To 'have' faith is to speak this rhetorical language, to propagate the pathos of 'God'. It is to re-perform prophetic speech; to re-endow this speech-form with authority. According to Protestant thought, Christianity's claim to truth must be answered with reference to the rhetorical practice of prophet and apostle: its claim to truth is its claim to mediate divine utterance. A philosophical understanding of truth can only be marginally relevant to such an account – as we shall see, it is generally inimical to it.

The tradition that I seek to uncover is a theology of the Word; more particularly, a rhetorical theology of the Word's authority – more particularly still, a *dialogical* rhetorical theology of the Word's authority. 'Dialogical' because direct, single-voiced communication is inadequate to the task of Christian discourse. The starting-point of Protestant theology is that *God speaks*. It is burdened with a claim to communicate this speech and to reflect on God in terms of it. This claim could hardly be more problematic; politically, morally, aesthetically – and, perhaps above all, theologically. In Luther, Kierkegaard, Barth and others, Protestant thought finds its foundation in the same basic rhetorical movement: the 'question' of theological truth is settled by the intrusion of an authoritative voice. (As we shall see this precludes *other* foundations.) This 'voice', known through scripture and its cultural ripples, must be re-performed, given new rhetorical life. It bids us speak it, demands we lend it new verbal life. According to Karl Barth, this sense of rhetorical obligation is the foundation of the church. The church exists to imitate prophet and apostle; it 'dares to do what they dared. Or rather, it does *not* dare *not* to do so'.[1]

---

[1] Karl Barth, *The Göttingen Dogmatics: Instruction in the Christian Religion*, vol. 1., ed. by H. Reifen, trans. by G. W. Bromiley, W. B. Eerdmans, Michigan, 1991, p.53.

Yet it is also Barth who most fully confronts the massive problem entailed in this formula. The problem is the seemingly inevitable confusion of the Word of God with its contingent human expression. I aim to show that, even since Luther, the Protestant enthusiasm for rhetorical authority is accompanied by a particular mechanism of self-criticism, which is best summed up in Barth's phrase 'dialectical theology'. Without this dialectical, or dialogical, element, which means the presence of two points of view, two voices, 'the Protestant rhetoric of authority' would have only negative connotations. It would only be further evidence of historical hubris, another stick with which to beat religion. Yet dialectical theology enables us to think again about 'the Protestant rhetoric of authority' – more critically, more sympathetically. It insists upon the *otherness* of the Word of God from all human rhetoric. Instead of claiming to communicate the Word directly, its discourse becomes a dramatic performance, a staging of faith's agonistic apprehension of the Word's authority.

As a result, the Protestant idiom is unlike any other point of view, or system, or account of 'truth'. For it always needs more than one voice, it never stops arguing with itself. But this does not detract from the singular force of its truth-claim; rather the opposite. At root it is the performance of a rhetoric of absolute authority, the Word of God; this is the form its truth-claim takes. But here is the surprising thing: this absoluteness demands to be represented in the context of a conversation with what it is not. For this alone preserves its lofty otherness. Faith lives through being contradicted, and so it is in its interest to have a voice, or various voices, of contradiction present, as its foil and fuel. Faith, then, is like a king who wants his fool in constant attendance.

My first chapter discusses the biblical basis of my rhetorical theme. It shows how authoritative speech is at the root of the Semitic apprehension of God, and briefly inquires into the anthropological origins of this religious conception. The next chapter consists in theoretical reflection into the concepts of rhetoric and authority as they relate to my theme. In particular it considers the work of René Girard and of Mikhail Bakhtin. The former's critique of religious violence affords a useful perspective from which to account for the rhetorical force, even violence, of Christian tradition. In relation to Bakhtin's critique of the 'monologism' of authoritative discourse, I begin to show how Christian rhetoric contains its own 'dialogical' structure which seeks to preserve the otherness of God's speech – this dynamic will surface repeatedly in my account of Protestant rhetoric. Chapter 3 continues my chronological reading of Christian thought. It is predominantly concerned with Augustine, whose writings anticipate some basic Protestant concerns. Through his *Confessions* I show how his account of faith is based in agonistic polyphony, and apprehension of the rhetorical authority of the Word of God. I trace the development of these themes in *The City of God*: revelation is God's authoritative speech-act, in which theological discourse participates. Here, as in his Protestant followers, this performance of the Word's authority is a crucial resource against Pelagianism.

I begin my review of Protestant tradition with a re-reading of Luther. I show how he puts a form of rhetorical authority at the heart of the Christian idiom, and how this 'rhetorical militancy' refers to the violence of Satan's defeat. Yet, amidst the seeming excess of this rhetoric, I also want to suggest that Luther's theology has self-critical potential by virtue of its dialogic structure. I finally propose a distinction between 'internal dialogism', which is intrinsic to Christian faith, and dialogism as a general principle.

The next chapter turns from theology to religious literature. Here and in Chapter Seven I consider the ambiguous relationship of poetic discourse to Protestant thought: I suggest that this relationship is fundamental to the Protestant story. I first show how my reading of Reformation theology, with its dramatic dialogism, is reflected in the work of Herbert and then Milton. Chapter Six returns to theology in the stricter sense. It discusses Kierkegaard's response to the Enlightenment-based theology of his day, which is a new understanding, and presentation, of the Christian rhetoric of authority. His opposition to liberal Protestantism anticipates that of Barth, as does his rhetoric of crisis and obedience. My literary 'sub-plot' then continues with a reading of Romantic and Modernist literature. Here, I argue, an alternative rhetoric of authority is being forged from the body of Christian prophetic tradition, with dangerous consequences. This process of abstraction therefore helps us to appreciate the uniqueness of the Christian rhetorical idiom; its capacity to resist ideological abuse.

Now I turn to Karl Barth, in whose early work my reading of Protestantism finds perhaps its clearest expression. His theology presents Christian faith in rhetorical terms; as participation in a rhetoric of authority, in *the* rhetoric of authority; the Word of God. But Barth bases this theology of affirmation in a cautionary, critical principle; a radical suspicion of all human claims to authority. Through a reading of his early thought, I show how this theology of the Word is rooted in the 'internal dialogism' that we have already encountered. I then consider Barth in relation to Nietzsche, whose philosophy is heavily influenced by prophetic and preaching rhetoric, and seeks to out-do it in secular terms. The Nietzschean construction of an authoritative voice serves to remind Protestantism of its own rhetorical basis. Finally I consider Barth's 'postliberal' legacy; a major form of his academic reception. In response I suggest that the dialectical tradition at the heart of Protestantism is a neglected resource for contemporary theology.

The nub of my thesis is this: Protestant faith need not be ashamed of itself; of its basis in a rhetoric of authority. It need not cower under charges such as monologism, logocentrism, totalising, absolutism, authoritarianism. Why not? Because Protestant faith, properly understood, has at its heart a principle of self-criticism, of openness to otherness, that is co-existent with its truth-claim, and intrinsic to it. By this means, it emerges from modernity as the truly different discourse of authority.

PART ONE: RHETORICAL ORIGINS

Chapter 1

The Rhetorical Gospel (I): Biblical and Anthropological Roots

'Only desire speaks. Satisfaction is silence.' [1]

At the basis of the biblical conception of God is his character as authoritative speaker. Thus does he create; by commanding, declaring, summoning. Thus does he relate to the first humans; by injunction and veto, and then by announcing a new deal which takes their transgression into account. Thus does he dispense merciful justice to the first murderer. (Administering justice and law-giving are of course central and recurring functions of his authoritative speech.) Other examples abound: thus does he frustrate the arrogance of Babel – with a literal 'put-down'. Whenever he intervenes in the human realm, it is always with telling words. His words are never 'only' words, but are charged with 'performative' force.[2] He decrees and forbids, promises and warns, curses and blesses.

And so begins the story of his dealings in human history. He calls Noah, then Abraham and the rest. '[T]his direct and unexplained confrontation – a verbal assault on a given person by God – is not the sort of thing one meets with in Greek or other nonbiblical traditions'.[3] He commands them and they stammeringly assent. He makes promises about the future; he excites Abraham with the prospect of his descendants outnumbering the shining stars, and so talks him into signing a covenant. (It is signed not in ink, of course, but in blood: with the sign of circumcision. Throughout Hebrew religion God is revealed through the human signing of commitment to him.)

He is not just a God of words. He shows Moses his strength as a God of political liberation (and of military violence). But first he speaks to him, calling him by name, explaining his plan of deliverance. He wills to be known to Israel through words; remembered in stories and songs about his mighty deeds. In Deuteronomy he explicitly prescribes such speech-forms, whereby future generations are to be engrafted into the narrative. Also of course, Hebrew law is presented as his (written) utterance. (This is in common with the tendency of early law-codes to retain the direct authority of the ruler's voice.)

---

[1] Jacques Ellul, *The Humiliation of the Word*, trans. by J. Main Hanks, W. B. Eerdmans, Michigan 1985, p.53.

[2] J. L. Austin coins the term (J. L. Austin, *How to Do Things with Words*, Oxford University Press, 1975, *passim*).

[3] Walter Ong, *The Presence of the Word: Some Prolegomena for Cultural and Religious History*, Yale University Press, New Haven, 1967, p.12.

The narrative of the Hebrew Bible is the narrative of Jahweh's voice, and of his word's problematic reception. Alongside the stories of his speaking, the Jews develop a rhetoric of prayerful response, which praises his deeds and appeals for their repetition, often in tones of near desperation. These verbal means of relating to God – narrative and poetic – are gradually exalted over older religious habits, though they of course develop in the context of religious ritual. The authoritative voice becomes God's primary medium, and the explicit authoriser of ritual practice – most obviously in the presentation of the law, but also in the 'private rituals' of certain prophets, and in the prophetic criticism of empty worship. And it is the *voice* of God which underlies the emergence of textual authority: despite the role of writing in securing religious orthodoxy, these religious texts remain dominated by the power of the speaking voice.[4]

The notion of idolatry, so crucial to the differentness of the Jews, relies upon this vocal conception of God. It is only because God is essentially a voice of authority that he can, and logically *must*, veto the worship of other gods and even images of himself. A strong association between divinity and vocal authority works against the seemingly natural tendencies of polytheism and syncretism. Theism only becomes wedded to ideas of absoluteness, authority and exclusivity (i.e., henotheism becomes monotheism) when God is known as voice. (This dynamic is very consciously revived in the Reformation: the Roman church is charged with idolatry, with being a new 'Babylonian captivity' from which only God's pure Word can deliver.)

Why is this? Why does a God of exclusive authority have to be a speaking God, known for the commanding power of his voice? The reason seems to lie in the vocal basis of political authority. An authoritarian regime constructs and projects a single voice, generally identified with the sovereign ruler. Mere force of arms is insufficient to sustain power; its rule must become internal to its subjects' minds – it must exist in the aural guts of the people. The word 'dictator' points to a link between strength of speech and strength of rule. It may then be objected that, in its exaltation of the authoritative voice, this religion occupies the natural territory of political authoritarianism; it resembles an ideal, transcendent form of 'dictatorship'. But this need not be an objection. Though it resembles authoritarian politics, or rather precisely *because* it does, this voice may be used against all worldly claims to authority. (Admittedly, as we shall also discuss further on, it may also be used for the opposite, i.e. to hypostasize worldly rule.)

The Semitic exaltation of vocal authority should also be understood in terms of religious and linguistic anthropology. For it is a common trait of primitive religion to associate strong speech with both natural and supernatural power. In oral-aural cultures, words are intimately related to the exercise of power, as Walter Ong, among others, has shown. Before writing, words exist exclusively in the realm of sound. Unlike vision, sound always relates to an event occurring now, to something happening. Early man experiences words as 'powerful, effective, of a

---

[4] See Susan Niditch, *Oral World and Written Word; Ancient Israelite Literature*, John Knox Press, Kentucky, 1996, p.88.

piece with other actuality far more than later visualist man is likely to do'.[5] This helps to explain the dual reference of the Hebrew word *dabar* to both word and deed. And whereas vision is selective and optional (one can look somewhere in particular or nowhere at all), 'I not only can but must hear all the sounds around me at once. Sound thus situates me in the midst of a world'.[6] Hearing is thus related to our reception of another's *presence*: When we speak of a presence in its fullest sense...we speak of something that surrounds us, in which we are situated...'.[7] As we shall soon see, vocal power is also associated with demonic and spiritual possession.

From this association between words and dynamic power arises the magical belief in the intrinsic power of certain words and speech-forms. Perhaps the clearest example of this is the phenomenon of cursing (and of oaths, which are conditional curses directed against oneself: 'If I am lying, may the gods punish me...'). Here words become the quasi-physical bearers of hostility; a certain formalised speech-form is deemed magically efficacious, like a spell. Indeed a spell is itself essentially linguistic. The claim to control one's environment through magic generally entails a claim about the efficacy of language. Ritualised language is deemed to have authority over the material and spiritual world. Healings and exorcisms performed by shaman and witchdoctor figures offer further examples of this. Here, as in Christian tradition, demons are expelled by a ritual form of speech which bids them depart. 'Exorcism' literally means 'out-oath-ing'; i.e., the special exercise of *verbal* force. Intruding spirits are often taunted and abused, and the demons' voices may be represented by the shaman in a sort of ventriloquism.[8] At the centre of such rituals is a linguistic performance of authority over the spirit-world. (A form of this abides in psychoanalysis: in Freud's 'talking-cure' the neurosis-causing childhood memory must be verbally acknowledged, or named, for its dark power to be vanquished.) Another, related, area of linguistic magic relates to names. It is a common primitive belief that a person's name is a source of their vulnerability to hostile magic. This applies to spirits as well: the act of naming is often central to the spiritual combat of exorcism. And repeatedly in the Bible the divine name is the locus of divine power.

All such belief is rooted in the ability of speech to communicate authority and, even more basically, to perform hostility. Classical epic narrative is a useful resource here: it celebrates verbal as well as physical force; the power of rhetoric as well as of arms. *The Iliad* very largely consists of speeches – one of its central concerns is the power of rhetoric to move, to change minds, to affect reality at least as much as physical force. Even gods are open to the 'winged words' of humans.

---

[5] Ong, 1967, p.111.

[6] Ibid., p.129.

[7] Ibid., p.130.

[8] See e.g. Evans Pritchard, on the rhetorical exorcisms of the Azande witchdoctors (Evans Pritchard, A., *Witchcraft, Oracles and Magic Among the Azande*, Clarendon, London, 1976, pp.87-89). Frazer also records the role of mocking and aggressive speech in the process of exorcism (James Frazer, *The Golden Bough: a Study in Magic and Religion*, Penguin, Middlesex, 1996, ch. 55, p.658).

And it is here that humans most closely resemble gods – in their ability to instil pathos through rhetoric, to inspire or 'possess' other souls with their words.[9] The ability of words to instil courage and so affect military action is the classic 'proof' of the power of rhetoric, in which human and divine capability merge. (One of the most famous speeches in English literature – the one that Shakespeare writes for Henry V before Agincourt – fulfills the same function.) Such is a basic ingredient of heroism (which also entails the ability to *resist* rhetoric: thus Achilles' refusal to be persuaded to join the fray).

Speech and force are related in other ways in Homer. Every duel between rival heroes is preceded by vaunting and taunting, boasts and threats; a form of verbal sparring known as 'fliting'. Though on one level these speeches are unrealistic embellishments to the action, they may hint at the very origins of rhetoric. Like rival stags or bulls, the heroes first attempt to avoid fighting by scaring the other off.[10] The verbal violence of boasting and taunting is ambiguous: it can either prevent actual bloodshed or provoke it, constitute a sort of foreplay to fighting. Something similar is still part of the ritual of boxing: every big fight is preceded by televised boasts and threats in which the opposition is strongly advised to back down. (Interestingly, the bragging of the greatest boxer of modern times, Mohammad Ali, has entered the rhetorical lexicon; for instance his poetic threat to 'float like a butterfly and sting like a bee', and his simple assertion, 'I am the greatest'. He remains lauded for his rhetorically expressed attitude as well as his actual success – perhaps an echo of the Homeric ideal of heroism.) Ong argues that this polemical duelling, or 'fliting', has a profound influence on all arenas of ancient discourse, most notably classical rhetoric, and even philosophical dialectics (despite its claim to transcend such origins). Even well after the advent of writing, public discourse remains related to the assertion of claims to authority: 'the history of the word, at least in the West, is intimately tied up with the history of certain kinds of polemic'.[11] Oral cultures are steeped in agonistic performance; writing, on the other hand, 'fosters abstractions that disengage knowledge from the arena where human beings struggle with one another... . By keeping knowledge embedded in the human lifeworld, orality situates knowledge within a context of struggle'.[12]

The formalisation of strong speech is thus at the heart of the magico-religious. Spells, curses and prayers are forms of verbal power. Such belief is not entirely alien to us. In a sense primitive cultures are only more explicit than us in endowing words with such power. The power of words and the verbal creation of sense is something we cannot fully make sense of either. The nursery rhyme insistence that, unlike sticks and stones, words cannot hurt us is mere wishful

---

[9] 'Athena swept through the armies, lashing the fighting fury/in each Achaean's heart' (Homer, *The Iliad*, trans. by R. Fagles, Penguin, Middlesex, 1990, bk. 2, ll.524-5, p.114). Hector, among others, does the same (bk. 13, l.186, p. 346).

[10] Ibid., bk. 20, l.233, p.510.

[11] Ong, 1967, p.194.

[12] Ong, *Orality and Literacy: the Technologizing of the Word*, Methuen, London, 1982, pp.43-44.

thinking (indeed it is an incantation against their power; and thus a contradictory attempt to use verbal power against verbal power). Words can and do hurt and we have many expressions which know it: they can be scathing, cutting, crushing, venomous, vitriolic etc. Words, for us as well, can 'contain' authority: your word is my command; his word is his bond. Speech can be called 'mere words' or 'empty' because it is not expected to be.

These 'primitive' dynamics surrounding language are crucial and will recur throughout my study. Religion never outgrows its primitive linguistic roots. It endows certain forms of speech with a power and significance that ultimately defies sober analysis. (Sober analysis is always weaker than religious speech: this is theology's methodological problem.) Religion stubbornly does things with words that should not be possible; things which scandalise the wider verbal community. In relation to language, religion never stops believing in magic. And secular thought remains marked by this belief: as proponents of 'deconstruction' have insisted (or complained), a magical and religious aura still surrounds the spokenness of langauge. More abstract and conceptual models of truth have less popular currency than the model based in utterance. Truth, like lies, is something spoken. The traditional rival of the oral-aural model is of course the visual model, based in the Greek concept of truth as the unveiling of what is hidden (*aletheia*), which dominates metaphysics from Plato's cave to Heidegger's Being.

To return to the Bible, the Jewish conception of God reflects some of these aspects of early linguistic thought in its 'dynamistic' conception of language. We have already noted the Hebrew word *dabar* and the role of 'performative' speech-acts. Perhaps most central to the Old Testament is the magical belief in the power of blessing and cursing. Blessing is the whole point of Israel's involvement with God; this 'speech-act' is the source of fertility and order, and so of all good things. (Blessing is not exclusively verbal, it has a ritual basis; yet it becomes predominately so, as is later suggested by the Latin *benedicere*, from which 'benediction'.) Blessing is accompanied by the possibility of cursing. In Deuteronomy God's blessing is made conditional on obedience to the divine voice (as mediated by the Mosaic law), and a series of curses is threatened as the alternative (Deut. 28.15-16). The language of blessing and cursing is the natural accompaniment of the biblical assertion of vocal authority; it illustrates the power of God's word.

This theme of obedience to the voice of God – and of curses as punishment – extends back into Genesis chapter three. In his post-mortem cross-examination of the guilty couple, God makes sure that they know what they did wrong. Eve's fault is that she listened to the serpent rather than to God's commandment; Adam's is that he listened to Eve instead of God. The prototype of disobedience is neglect of the divine voice, and the preference of other voices, other accounts of authority. For obedience derives from hearing (including etymologically: *ob-audire*). The error provokes a string of curses from God: his first extended speech. Previously all his speech, in creation and instruction to humanity, had been in the mode of blessing. The result of the Fall is that divine rhetoric is also, or primarily, known as negative in its power. (Incidentally we note that the word 'negative', like 'affirmative', refers to the power of speech to confer value.)

In the book of Proverbs the theme appears in a very different form. Divine wisdom is personified as a virtuous woman advising the young man in the marketplace. His attention is distracted by her antitype, the scarlet woman Folly, who calls out from her seedy doorway, promising sensual delights. Here is a rhetorical understanding of morality and faith: as adherence to one form of rhetoric over another. Idolatry is consequently conceived in rhetorical terms: it is to yield to seductive voices, false rhetorics of authority. (Similarly, the first commandment implies a diagnosis of idolatry as refusal to heed the divine voice.) As we shall see throughout this study, this dynamic becomes absolutely basic to Christian thought and literature.

Further evidence of the rhetorical character of early Hebrew faith is afforded by the briefest glance at the Psalms. (To talk of *looking* at the Psalms is of course a modern anomaly: they are traditionally spoken, sung, heard.) 'Blessed is the man', says the first psalm, 'who walks not in the counsel of the wicked,/…nor sits in the seat of scoffers'(1:1). The 'wicked' are defined by their counsel and their scoffing; both functions of their speech. In the Psalms idolatry and sin are consistently depicted in rhetorical terms; as speech which threatens God's reality and power. The second psalm, which has its basis in an enthronement ritual,[13] warns that 'the kings of the earth take counsel together,/against the Lord and his anointed, saying,/"Let us burst their bonds asunder"'(2:2-3). At their conspiracy God laughs and 'has them in derision' and 'will speak to them in his wrath' (2:4-5). This 'voice' of political hubris is answered by God's superior speech-act, which is ritually re-performed.

One of the most common themes of the Psalms is the indignant protest that there are ungodly speech-forms in the world creating aural chaos and dissonance and deception: 'the wicked boasts of the desires of his heart,/and the man greedy for gain curses and renounces the Lord' (10.3); 'The fool says in his heart,/'There is no God' (14:1); 'They scoff and speak with malice;/loftily they threaten oppression./They set their mouths against the heavens,/ and their tongue struts through the earth'(73:8-9). To these verbal affronts God must and will respond, answer back; he will judge and rebuke them, and even 'cut off all flattering lips, the tongue that makes great boasts'(12:3), and 'break the teeth in their mouths'(58:6). (Mouths are both physically and verbally dangerous; the wicked are ascribed the mouths of lions (57:4) and snakes (58:2).) Often the speaker cites, or imitates, evil speech, such as the above conspiring of kings, or the fool's unbelief. Evil and arrogant speech must be reproduced in the context of the assurance of its defeat; only thus is its power overcome, or exorcised. It also seems that God must be reminded of the outrage and so provoked into action. In their need to perform the defeat of these voices, the Psalms take on a dialogic and polyphonic complexity.

Just as sin is depicted in rhetorical terms so, largely, are both faith and the divine action it looks to. Like Job, the speaker appeals to God as his advocate, the one who pleads his cause (9:4), and his judge (7:11). He has faith in the power of

---

[13] Many psalms reflect the 'victory-enthronement pattern', also found in other Near Eastern literature (see e.g. Niditch, 1996, p.21).

divine speech, and remembers its chaos-taming power: 'The Lord also thundered in the heavens,/and the Most High uttered his voice/…Then the foundations of the world were laid bare,/at thy rebuke, O Lord,/at the blast of the breath of thy nostrils'(18:13-15). God orders the cosmos through his 'rebuke' (*ger*) of the chaotic powers, an echo of his creation by his word. This is one of the clearest biblical surfacings of 'the combat myth'; a pattern common throughout ancient Mesopotamian religion in which divine power is exerted against some form of bestial or demonic opposition.[14] Through a sustained emphasis upon linguistic power, this mythical pattern becomes moulded into something distinctively Semitic. God triumphs over cosmic chaos through a *verbal* blow. (Incidentally, does the noun 'blow' remember the power of divine word-breath?) Verbalised combat-myth recurs in the New Testament. Jesus 'rebukes' his first unclean spirit (Mk. 1:25); later he 'rebukes' the storm (Mt. 4:39) in an echo of Psalm 107:25-30; and also 'rebukes' Peter with the words 'Get thee behind me, Satan!' (Mk. 8:33).

In the Psalms it is through faithful speech that the speaker relates to God, corresponds to him: God's chosen is he who 'speaks truth from his heart;/who does not slander with his tongue'(15:2), and who refuses to breathe the names of other gods (16:4). Again and again, faith in God consists in its linguistic expression: 'I say to the Lord, "Thou art my Lord;/I have no good apart from thee…"'(16:2); 'But I trust in thee, O Lord,/I say, "Thou art my God"' (31:14). The speech-act of faith is the reality of faith; it is a matter of rhetorical performance. God's power must be stated, affirmed, reasserted; almost as if its repetition has the power to make it come true. This dynamic reflects the social and liturgical setting: according to Kraus, 'the basic experience of the Psalms is that Yahweh speaks in the sanctuary'.[15]

Narratives of God's direct vocal agency, which dominate the early books of the Pentateuch, gradually give way to the prophetic claim to divine inspiration. The transition begins with Moses, the prophetic secretary of the Law. It continues throughout the history of Israel's uneasy achievement of political stability. Saul, the first king, is reprimanded by Samuel, his prophetic minister and critic (and his predecessor in power – an intimidating combination). What disqualifies Saul's rule is his failure to listen to 'the voice of the Lord' – what we have seen to be the essence of all sin. He neglects a command from God (via Samuel) to wipe out the Amalekites without mercy. Confronted by Samuel, Saul admits his error, explaining that he 'feared the people and obeyed their voice'(1 Sam. 15:24). His sin is also to have trusted in sacrifice, Samuel points out: 'Has the Lord as great delight in burnt offerings and sacrifices,/as in obeying the voice of the Lord?'(1 Sam. 15:22). He is thus guilty of confounding this religion of vocal authority with political expediency and pagan generality.

Israel's political history is thus told in relation to the drama of God's voice. The Deuteronomic History is largely the story of prophetic opposition to political absolutism. The origins of monarchy are ambiguous: in creating the first king,

---

[14] See Forsyth, N., *The Old Enemy: Satan and the Combat Myth*, Princeton University Press, New Jersey, 1987, *passim*.
[15] Kraus, H., *Theology of the Psalms*, trans. by K. Crim, Augsburg Press, Mass., 1986, p.33.

Samuel gives in to the voice of the people (1 Sam. 12:1), but with God's assent as it were; and Saul experiences a sort of temporary prophetic calling. The monarchy becomes semi-detached from the divine voice: kings need prophets to remind them of their calling. Nathan dares to confront David with his scandalous transgression, telling the parable with the famous punch-line, 'Thou art the man!' The use of parable anticipates the preaching ministry of Jesus; it shows that there is more to 'the prophetic voice' than grandiose ranting and austere commanding: it can also challenge more subtly, more gently – and more *strangely*.[16]

But the mark of most prophetic speech is boldness rather than subtlety. 'Prophet' (*nabi*) means mouthpiece, in the sense of a ruler's spokesman or herald. This is often foregrounded in the introductory 'messenger formula', 'Thus says the Lord', which seems to be lifted from royal decrees of the time. Though Christianity borrows the Greek word – *prophetes* (literally: 'one who speaks out') – biblical prophecy has little in common with the classical emphasis upon divination. The emphasis is upon speaking with divine authority, being compelled to deliver a 'royal' message. Despite some common ground with classical prophecy – both are rooted in an idea of rhetorical possession – only here is authoritative speech a sustained representation of the divine essence.

From a human perspective, those who become known as canonical prophets are those whose rhetorical performance is credited with perpetuating the narrative of Jahweh's voice. This is also a matter of reinterpreting this narrative, and even of subverting its conventional reception – as in Amos' threat that 'the Day of the Lord' will be one of darkness, not of light (Amos 5:18). There is no mark of authenticity by which a prophet can satisfy the religious authorities of his day, except fidelity to the narrative and rhetorical tradition. The prophetic principle – that God may choose to speak through a lone human voice – becomes crucial to the distinctiveness of this tradition. It makes rhetorical performance a new locus of religious authority and entails the relativisation of all other loci of authority, religious and political. The tradition's incorporation of prophetic voices creates an instability, an openness to reinvention by new claims. Although prophetic discourse is subject to certain rules (its representation of God must be in accordance with the textual tradition), it is subversive of religious hegemony. (Christianity discovers this in the Reformation, which revives the prophetic principle at the cost of ecclesial unity.)

In common with what we have already seen, prophetic speech very largely consists of blessings and curses. The latter often predominate to such an extent that the blessings come as rather a surprise. The blessing typically takes the form of God's promise to establish a new intimacy with his people, despite their past error. In one formulation it is announced that he will give them a new heart, and that he will write his law directly thereon. Interestingly, this image precludes the need for speaking and hearing, as if the present means of revelation will be improved upon.

[16.] Parable also raises the tricky question of wilful obscurity within proclamation. See Frank Kermode, *The Genesis of Secrecy: On the Interpretation of Narrative*, Harvard University Press, New Jersey, 1979, p.47.

Writing is often seen by the biblical writers as an intensification of the magical power of speech.[17]

Prophetic writing constitutes a very particular form of poetic discourse. Its core aim is to inspire fear, in the sense of holy reverence. Through the vividness of their representation, the threatened curses and promised blessings are intended to affect attitudes and conduct; to *move* the audience in the most extreme sense. To this end, God's power is poetically reasserted, for instance in Isaiah's image of the divine warrior: 'like a man of war [the Lord] stirs up his fury;/he cries out, he shouts aloud,/he shows himself mighty against his foes' (Isaiah 42:13). Here God's 'speech' is a war-cry; the speech-form closest to physical power (this also relates to our discussion of epic 'fliting' and fighting-talk). The innate power of God's word, and the danger of false rhetoric, are central prophetic themes. Because it is a verbal depiction of God's verbal power, prophetic discourse participates in its subject matter. It demands to be read (heard) as a direct expression of divine power. The renewal of God's blessing is dependent on Israel's reaction to this rhetoric of authority: God will 'look to' whomever is 'humble and contrite in spirit,/and trembles at my word' (Isaiah 66:2). Blessing comes through Israel's acknowledgement of being called; indeed redemption is rooted in vocation: 'Fear not for I have redeemed you;/I have called you by name, you are mine...' (43:1).[18] Prophetic writing of course contains various ('local') moral, political and legal stipulations, but the overarching and abiding 'message' relates to its own rhetoric as a repetition of divine speech: the blessing depends upon Israel's ability to acknowledge supreme authority in this rhetorical idiom, now reperformed for it.

Jesus Christ is understood as the culmination of this prophetic tradition. He represents God more fully, in his person and his flesh as well as in his words and works, yet he too conforms to the prophetic drama. His primary method of representing God is verbal, or rhetorical (until his death, which is *the* sign, yet it of course relies on reference to his teaching to signify). He creates interest (and faith) and provokes hostility through a new rhetoric of God, or the kingdom, or rule, of God. Yet he takes the prophetic office further in that his own life and death are central to the drama he narrates. His prophetic rhetoric relates to the question of his own messianism, and the cosmic crisis it entails.

In his gospel-portraits, Jesus is a powerful speaker. Historical likelihood suggests that he indeed was, but for the evangelists his rhetorical power is more than human. In his wilderness testing he dispels the seductive rhetoric of Satan with his citation of scripture. Like the 'rebuking' that we have already noted, this pericope may be seen as a rhetorical reworking of the combat myth (we shall return to this rhetorical bout in relation to Milton's *Paradise Regained*). He calls the first disciples with the cursory assurance of a higher being. He gets angry, satirising Pharisees, cussing Herod. He heals and casts out demons merely by the power of his speech (other exorcists tended to rely on complex spells).[19] In John's account, the ethereal boldness of his speech about himself is the principal mark of

---

[17] See Niditch, *Oral World and Written Word, passim.*

[18] Cf. Hosea 11:1: 'Out of Egypt have I called my son'.

[19] See Susan R. Garrett, *The Demise of the Devil*, Fortress Press, Mass., 1989, *passim.*

his divinity: here he echoes the God of Moses through the phrase *ego eimi* ('I am').

The first chapter of Mark emphasises his authoritative-rhetorical presence. He begins his ministry by announcing the Kingdom of God's imminence; he then summons his disciples from their fishing to follow him; he then teaches in the synagogue, astonishing his audience with his authority; he then rebukes and expels an unclean spirit, again astonishing with the authority of his technique. His first four actions are authoritative speech-acts, which of course allude to scriptural tradition.[20] He also develops the psalmic identification of sin with false speech, for example when charging the Pharisees with hypocrisy (e.g. Mk. 7:6). Indeed his run-ins with the Pharisees constitute an important arena of his rhetorical activity; they echo his testing by Satan in the wilderness. (It must be admitted that Mark's gospel combines this proclamatory force, intentionally or not, with an unsettling degree of obscurity.)[21]

This very brief account of the Gospels runs the risk of implying that Christ can be reduced to his function of rhetorical force, impressive speech. Instead, through his practice, suffering and death he reinvents the role of rhetoric in revelation. His bodily presence and suffering are fully central to his significance (which is his signifying of God). His ministry thus requires an account of 'rhetoric' which transcends the merely verbal. Also, of course, he reinvents the notion of authority. While he speaks 'with authority' he renounces all worldly power. He thus effects an absolute separation of the spiritual and the worldly senses of 'authority'. He establishes an authoritative-rhetorical tradition explicitly and uniquely distinct from human violence. This coexistence of rhetorical authority and nonviolence is something that I want to draw particular attention to. My entire study is Christological in that it seeks to expound this dialectical tension, wherein rhetorical force coexists with practical nonviolence. The Christian rhetoric of authority is *Christian* in as far as it exists to exalt the Christic refusal of power. (We shall return to this in the next chapter.)

To talk of Christ as linguistic event, as the Word, runs the risk of presenting him as a high form of human rhetoric, a uniquely powerful human announcement – and therefore of divinising rhetorical force. What gives the lie to this is the cross, which is the opposite of all human power, including the rhetorical. This idea is already present in some of the earliest 'theology of the Word'. For Ignatius of Antioch, Christ is 'a faithful mouthpiece, by which the Father's words of truth find utterance'.[22] Yet the difference of this speech is maintained by a (perhaps Gnostic-influenced) notion of the Word's emanation from divine silence. Christ's birth, baptism and passion are 'three trumpet-tongued secrets [literally: mysteries of a loud shout] brought to pass in the deep silence of God'.[23]

---

[20] See also e.g. Luke 4:21, 4:32, 4:36.

[21] See Kermode, 1979, pp.56-57.

[22] Ignatius of Antioch, 'Epistle to the Romans', 8, in *Early Christian Writings: the Apostolic Fathers*, trans. by M. Staniforth, ed. by A. Louth, Penguin, Middlesex, 1987, p.88.

[23] Ignatius of Antioch, 'The Epistle to the Ephesians', 19, in ibid., p.66.

In Paul's epistles the Christ-event inspires a new form of prophetic rhetoric which extends God's interest beyond the Jews, to all humanity. In Jesus Christ (he tells the Roman Christians) God has spoken. The judge has pronounced sentence, given his favourable verdict. Elsewhere the good news is characterised as God's 'Yes' to humanity (2 Cor. 1:20). Paul's rhetorical conception of revelation is of course derived from scriptural tradition, as he himself makes clear from his quotation of scripture.[24] The Gospel is understood as both God's speech-act and man's. We participate in God through telling his news. We join his 'Yes' with our 'Amen', uttered 'through him' (2 Cor. 1:20). Our proclamation creates new faith, as 'faith comes through hearing' (Rom. 10:17). As I shall presently argue in more detail, this *rhetorical* connection between God and man may be seen as Christianity's unique core (and banging on about it may be Protestant theology's main duty).

It should also be noted that a rhetorical understanding of the Christ-event entails an insistence on the Jewishness of it. The God revealed here is the one who has *already* established a dialogue with Israel. 'Christianity does not make full sense in its own terms without belief that the trial and execution of Jesus are the focal moment of God's own 'controversy' (*rib* in the Hebrew of the OT) with the chosen people, that the summons of Jesus is the creative utterance of God in respect of the people'.[25] This Word is not uttered out of the cultural blue (as John's hellenistic Prologue is in danger of suggesting) but as part of a cultural conversation.

The function of the emerging church is thus rhetorical: to communicate the good news in the world's end-time. It is a community whose existence is outside of itself; in the act of communicating to those beyond. And it is founded in God's speech-act: it is chosen, or called out (the root meaning of *ekklesia*) from the world by him, in order to be his voice, his agent of persuasion. Faith (*pistis*) means a conviction of trust engendered by rhetoric.

But already in Paul the Christian rhetoric of authority is open to suspicion. His neo-prophetic tone of authority is in seeming contradiction to a gospel of dispossession and inclusion. He seems dangerously intent upon controlling the ethical conduct of others. The problem of ethics already seems to threaten Christianity's unique rejection of authoritarianism. But what is also clear is that Paul seeks to base Christian ethics in a prophetic and rhetorical criterion. He addresses the Corinthian debate as to Christian dietary practice with a reminder of the 'bottom line': all Christian conduct should signify God: 'whatever you do, do all to the glory of God' (1 Cor. 10:31). This reflects the Gospel accounts of 'the ethics of Jesus', which cannot not be separated from their revelatory role: to manifest (or signify, announce) God's gracious will. The gospel's *ethical* novelty therefore brings us back to rhetoric, albeit in a wider sense than we are accustomed to Christian ethics has a proclamatory logic.

As the term 'Gospel' indicates, then, Christianity is a religion based in a particular form of rhetoric. Authority is essential to this rhetorical mode. For the

---

[24] See e.g. Rom. 3:13-14.
[25] Williams, R., *On Christian Theology*, Blackwell, Oxford, 1999, p.103.

good news concerns the triumph of divine authority over spurious authorities. And this triumphant authority is present *in* the message; it is made present in its re-presentation. In this message the distinction between form and content is uniquely fluid. It not only expresses (in a secondary sense) the triumph of divine authority; instead it is the very *expression* of this triumph.

This dynamic of rhetorical participation in the event attested may be further elucidated by probing the word 'triumph'. It means both victory and its celebratory representation. A military victory is announced in an appropriate style of grandeur and 'triumphalism'. Roman emperors brought home victorious armies from distant colonies to parade them through the streets of Rome – a practice copied by strong states ever since. The announcement and show of victory becomes part of the victory itself, maybe even the main point of it. This dynamic is taken further in Christianity. In the case of God's victory over Satan, the fact of victory is inseparable from the announcement of it. The triumph of divine authority relies on the 'victory parade' of Christian speech to give it reality.

Similarly, the Gospel may be called an *assertion* of authority – in both senses; an exercise of power (by God) and the declaration of this (by God and man). 'Assertion' is thus another enlightening word; like 'expression' and 'triumph' it confuses event with representation. Christianity inhabits this area of ambiguity between words and deeds, the actual and the represented, the rhetorical and the real. It involves a uniquely strong, or participatory, account of representation (*mimesis*). As previously hinted, it finds great use for those verbs known as 'performatives', which relate to both speaking and doing: asserting, denying, affirming, negating, declaring, promising, blessing, cursing, defending, attacking, ordering, etc. It undermines the distinction between 'reality' and the verbal report of it. For what is most real – the event of God's gracious authority – is only knowable through its proclamation. We are here touching on the knotty problems of 'realism' and 'reference'. Does our religious language refer to anything that *really exists*? One answer to this problem lies in the field of linguistic action, in the ability of words to create meaning.

In this first chapter I have widened the scope rather further than the rest of my study can justify. Though I have admitted that Christian rhetoric is not reducible to language, I am largely passing over the wider sense of 'rhetoric' to include all of Christian existence; sacramental, ecclesiastical, ethical. I am concerned with Christian discourse in the stricter sense of speech and writing (primarily writing of course); with how it attempts to communicate God. Though this is an almost absurdly large issue, it must also be admitted that it is too narrow. God is not communicated in speech or writing in isolation from life; the lives of individuals and communities. (But practical and ethical witness is also *witness*, communication, rhetoric. Both sides require each other if they are to signify.) Christianity is the communication of God in *word and deed*. Yet the literary-rhetorical arena remains strangely privileged, especially in communicating divine *authority*. Divine authority is eschatological, known only to faith, as yet unseen. It is as yet only present in verbal-rhetorical form. The eschatological nature of

Christian authority is thus a function of rhetoric – more specifically, of the rhetorical form of *promise* (this is explored further in the next chapter).

Christian rhetoric, then, is rooted in the communication of divine authority. Yet it uses a surprising variety of forms. Most obvious among these is the performance of a voice of divine authority: prophetic speech. Yet prophets also use their own voices to the same end; they testify to their passive reception of the Word, their experience of calling: this is another form. It relates to the dominant psalmic modes of imprecation, petition, prayer and praise. A desperate appeal for the Word is also an expression of the Word's authority. Another form is biblical narrative. To tell stories about God is actually a form of prophetic discourse. To represent God as a 'character' is similar to claiming to speak God's mind. It is a divinely inspired form of speech, or it is the greatest blasphemy. There is thus a logic in ascribing the Pentateuch to Moses, a kosher prophet. (Similarly there is a logic, however objectionable, in the Islamic reaction to Salman Rushdie's fictional depiction of Allah in *The Satanic Verses*.) In the New Testament we have a new form of inspired narrative, in this case from four perspectives, included in which is the supra-prophetic speech of Jesus. And in the epistles we have adaptations of psalmic and prophetic forms. And these various forms often feature internal dialogism, the interaction of two voices, or polyphony, a variety of voices. In the Psalms, as we have seen, the speech of the wicked is imitated, or parodied, necessitating a response; pious phrases are re-asserted, words attributed to God are quoted, re-cited. The New Testament writers are similarly polyphonic. The evangelists often resemble modern novelists in their terse sketches of other voices and their depiction of character through speech. For instance Peter; his errant enthusiasm, and later his denial, elicited by the accusations of bystanders. In a phrase or two, a character with a walk-on role expresses a whole world-view. The rich young man with his unhappy question; Nicodemus; the good centurion, who offers Jesus a sketch of military discipline; Pilate, and his question about truth. Often these other voices relate to other accounts of authority.

Even Paul incorporates other voices. Most obviously in his reference to scripture, yet more subtly through his imitation of scriptural polyphony. For example he tells the Corinthians that belief in the resurrection of the dead is crucial: 'If the dead are not raised, "Let us eat and drink, for tomorrow we die"' (1 Cor. 15:32). This quotation from Isaiah 22:13 is already a quotation in Isaiah, presumably of a popular phrase. It is again used, though in a different context, to signify an attitude of hedonistic fatalism. Now, as in the Psalms, this voice is erected as a challenge to the Word. The prophets often quote popular sayings, whether approvingly or not, and Paul does the same. In the very next verse he says: 'Do not be deceived: "Bad company ruins good morals"', a contemporary moral maxim.

In Bakhtin's terms (to be discussed shortly), Paul's rhetoric is not simply monologic. Indeed a form of dialogism is entailed in his famous dialectical conception of struggle between the flesh and the spirit. A single voice is insufficient for communicating the drama of revelation. An extreme example occurs in 2 Corinthians 11:16: in commending himself, boasting of his own virtues, he has to speak in another voice, as a 'fool'. The point emerging from these reflections is that the biblical 'rhetoric of authority' is not a single, homogenous thing. It is not just a matter of standing on a high platform, wearing a long beard, and 'doing' God. Divine authority is communicated by various rhetorical strategies, and often through the dramatisation of conflicting voices. It is communicated *through* dialogue, not at the expense of it. This is basic to Martin Buber's influential exegesis. The insight has recently been reaffirmed by Pattison, who argues that 'the Bible is itself profoundly dialogical, constantly arguing with itself, constantly presenting diverse and shifting perspectives on the ongoing and multi-faceted debate between God and humanity'; he points to Abraham's suasion of God to mercy, Job's complaint, multiple perspectives on Jesus.[26] My own account of biblical dialogism has a rather different agenda from Buber's and Pattison's: it wants to reaffirm 'the rhetoric of divine authority'; to clear it of monologic authoritarianism. (I shall return to the distinction later, in relation to both Bakhtin and Luther.)

I have referred to 'the Christian rhetoric of authority' as the form which Christian truth takes, as that which Christianity basically *is*. But is it adequately clear what its *content* is? We have seen that the Hebrew Bible establishes a strong association between divine truth and authoritative speech, between God and his word. What is the content of this word? This has no simple answer: it is creation, it is blessing for humanity, it is the calling of the Jews, the promise made to them, the covenant made with them; it is also the narratives in which these speech-acts figure. And it is the Mosaic law, in all its local complexity – and it is also a wider moral law of social justice, and perhaps a principle of hope for human history. It is a perplexing mixture of vagueness and over-particularity.

In the New Testament, Christian faith asserts, the content of God's word becomes adequately clear (though hardly without further difficulties!). It is Christ, his ministry and especially his death – understood in radically positive terms, through such metaphors as victory, redemption, salvation. The justification and the purpose of the Christian rhetoric of authority is the assertion of Christ; in a traditional phrase, the magnifying of his name. Yet here the problems begin. For from this 'core' Christian rhetoric builds, extrapolates, glosses. For it must strive to understand and to communicate this core. In doing so it claims divine authority for particular doctrinal formulations and historically contingent ethical and ecclesiastical stands – and it gets its fingers (and its enemies) burned. It commits the inevitable sin of straying into human authoritarianism. Which is why secular thought is so averse to the whole business. And why liberal theology has largely wearied of the claim at its heart; the claim to finally authoritative speech. But Christianity depends on the insistence that nevertheless there is an absolutely authoritative proclamation, identifiable with truth. It makes this claim even in the knowledge of the utter fallibility of all human rhetoric. To communicate Christianity's core idea – that God definitively speaks in Christ – is also to compromise it. In order to signify divine authority, human voices must imitate it, parody it. When human words make this proclamation they falsify it, for it is

---

[26] George Pattison, *The End of Theology – and the Task of Thinking about God*, SCM, London, 1998, p.33.

Christ himself. Put thus, Christianity sounds hopelessly self-defeating. Or, to put the matter slightly differently, it relies upon the constant miracle of God.

Chapter 2

The Rhetorical Gospel (II): Theoretical Questions

'Knowing what it means to fear God, we persuade men.' (2 Corinthians 5:11)

This chapter is concerned with theoretical reflection on the particular 'rhetoric of authority' in which I argue that Protestant faith and theology are based. First I consider the concept of authority from the perspective of my thesis, suggesting that the Christian rhetoric of authority need be seen as neither 'ideological' nor authoritarian. Then, in critical response to the work of René Girard, I offer a defence of the role of rhetorical violence in Christianity. I then consider the distinctive nature of Christian rhetoric in relation to the classical tradition, and challenge the approaches of two recent studies of this area. Finally, I briefly consider the thought of Mikhail Bakhtin, an influential critic of 'authoritative discourse'. In response to his theory of 'dialogism' I suggest that faith's rhetoric of authority has its own dialogic structure. This chapter as a whole may be seen as an attempt to defend Christianity's basis in a rhetoric of authority against the suspicions of recent secular (and theological) thought.

Reflections on the Christian Concept of Authority

Authority is a notoriously large and various concept – in this sense at least, it remains worthy of fear. I am by-passing many of its meanings and uses, for example its complex role in epistemology: my account of it is therefore far from comprehensive (or authoritative).

The main reference of the term 'authority' is political in a very wide sense. Authority implies power, yet not mere material power, in the physicist's sense. Lash provides a useful example: 'I may have power to kick a stone, or a donkey, but it would be odd to speak of my having authority over them. Moreover, to speak of authority is usually to speak of moral entitlement. From the mere fact that I have another person "in my power", it does not necessarily suggest that they are subject to my authority'.[1] Yet in one sense this is precisely the meaning of the word. Those in power are said to be 'in authority', or to 'have authority': we do not say that Hitler *claimed to be* the supreme authority in the German state, but that he *was*. In the political sense, authority is power that is exercised through being obeyed, whether willingly or not.

---

[1] Nicholas Lash, *Voices of Authority*, Sheed and Ward, London, 1976, p.16.

In one sense, then, authority refers to a human power relation, irrespective of its moral status. Yet the term is not synonymous with socio-political power. In another sense, authority means that which has *a right to be in power*, and in the religious context this means the divine power which is originative, creative and redemptive. As Lash says, '[o]ur conception of authority should not lose sight of the etymology of the word, according to which "authority" would have something to do with "authorship", and thus with the source of reality, life and growth'.[2]

There would seem to be two poles to the concept of authority where it relates to power. On the one hand, it is *sheer power*; on the other hand, it is *that which has an absolute right to power*. The ambiguity is expressed in the dictionary definition: 'authority' is 'the power or right to enforce obedience...'; 'authoritative' is 'possessing or claiming authority...'.[3] The complex religious significance of the word is expressed in the 'or'. This polarisation entails a crisis at the heart of the concept of authority. The authoritarian state denies such a crisis, claiming that its power directly corresponds to the divine good, or a secular form of it. In reality however it would seem that the first 'pole', political power, necessarily excludes the other. No political power is the power that created the world and redeems it. And the second pole excludes the first: that which we posit as having perfect right to power does not exist in the way that rulers and armies, or even parents, do.

It could be argued that the two poles are uniquely held together in Judeo-Christian thought. For here the Good is fully associated with actual historical power. In this it differs from the philosophical conception of the Good, which is conceived as an abstract ideal worthy of political embodiment (as in Plato's *Republic*) rather than as an actual historical agent. In the Old Testament, on the other hand, Yahweh corresponds to both 'poles' of authority, the ideal and the actual. It is not only held that he ought to rule but that he has, does and will (though the present tense is especially problematic). The actuality of his power precedes its ideality. Due to the witness of the Old Testament, authority in Christianity retains reference to the actual-political. Actual power is essential to God's nature: creation and redemption are essentially acts of power over the contrary powers of chaos and death. In stark contrast to philosophy, we refer to God by telling stories of his actual power, or, in worship, by speaking as if in its presence.

Yet in Jesus Christ divine power is manifest in the form of weakness: the cross would seem to abolish all identification of God with actual power. Jesus is simply devoid of authority in the first sense of tangible political power. In calling Jesus the Christ do we worship weakness and defeat then (as Nietzsche would have it), and accept the impotence of the Good? No: God is still known as power, though in the form of weakness. After Christ too, power remains basic to God's nature, though its full revelation is now strictly eschatological.

---

[2] Ibid.
[3] *The Concise Oxford English Dictionary*, 1982.

For the time being, God's authority, in the full sense which unites the two 'poles' and thus includes the actual-political, is *only a matter of memory and expectation*. Memory and expectation (or hope) are functions of rhetoric, of speech – which is also to say that they are textually constructed. God's authority, in the full sense, exists for us only as *a rhetoric of authority*. Faith is the rhetorical apprehension of what is not directly present, 'the conviction of things not seen' (Hebrews 11:1). Christian discourse is founded in this 'rhetoric of authority' which seeks to communicate the eschatological reality of divine authority.

Rhetoric and Power

We must now explore the relationship between rhetoric, in its widest sense of truth-concerning language, and power.

Language can of course be a manifestation of political power. The decree of a king is 'only words' yet has real force by virtue of its context. (Biblical prophecy, as we have seen, derives from such utterance.) Or a certain form of literary discourse can be an implicit manifestation of social power, as Marxist literary criticism attests. For example, the Augustan style of poetry of the eighteenth century in England reflects the power of the aristocracy. There is also a form of rhetoric which is powerfully opposed to the dominant political power, e.g., *The Communist Manifesto*. This is a complex example, for in heralding a new form of political power it invokes the authority of science, and also takes on prophetic tones. Its authoritative rhetoric is in the service of a putative political authority, just as the rhetoric of political legitimacy (e.g., Burke's *Reflections*) invokes the existing authority of the state.

These examples of 'rhetorics of power' are functions of political power, whether existing or putative, and from the secular perspective all such discourse is reducible to its political function. Yet it is the insistence of theology that there exists in Christianity a rhetoric of power which is not primarily the reflection of any existing or envisaged political power. It must first be admitted that *every* form of discourse is related to socio-political power in as far as it is printed, established, institutionalised. The pamphlet of a small rebel movement speaks of some degree of actual power, even if it is just that which gets it printed. Judaeo-Christian discourse is no exception (Bibles, for example, do not print or disseminate themselves): indeed it has obviously been hugely politically privileged. Yet it cannot be dismissed as the 'ideology' of political power. Of course Christian rhetoric *can* function ideologically, as Marx helped to show. Yet this possibility has been too readily equated with necessity in recent thought, not excepting theology.

Two of the most important modern critiques of Christianity consist in exposing its rhetoric of power as a function of political power. For Marx, it is the ideology of the ruling class. For Nietzsche, its ideological function works in the opposite direction. Judaeo-Christian rhetoric (reborn in socialism and democracy) is the 'subterfuge' for a form of power, which insidiously emasculates the 'natural' power of the strong. (In Chapter Nine we shall see how Nietzsche's rhetoric is itself indebted to the logic of Christian discourse.) In a sense, these two critiques of Christianity cancel each other out. The Christian rhetoric of authority is accused by secular modernity of being ideological in two directions at once. Unless we fully take sides with one of these thinkers, the secular attempt to expose Christianity's rhetoric of power begins to seem flawed.

Christian discourse is a rhetoric of authority which is conscious of *not* being essentially the reflection of any political power. It can bolster political authority and it can oppose it, and it necessarily does one or the other (or a bit of both), in that its rhetoric exists in the *polis*, but it does not necessarily serve any worldly authority, existing or putative. (To say that it serves the material power of the church is to make the same charge of political ideology, whether from the left or the right.) Christian rhetoric serves a power which has no tangible existence outside of the forms of speech which testify to it. Our concern in theology is the unique phenomenon of a rhetoric of power whose referent has no demonstrable extra-rhetorical reality. God is known to faith as actual power only in the form of the *rhetoric* of his actual power. Were God's power known in any other way, whether through reason or inner experience, or identification with some natural or political reality, it would be an idol. The one thing that holds together the paradox of God's power being revealed in the form of weakness is the rhetoric of divine authority. The cosmic victory over death, though entirely eschatological, can be represented rhetorically; and faith consists in seeing this 'rhetorical victory' as adequate for us, for the time being. The one form of worldly power that Christianity has never eschewed is rhetorical. God reveals himself in political weakness but in rhetorical strength. For Paul, Christian strength takes the form of weakness, but his discourse can hardly be called weak. He abjures 'eloquence' only to establish a new unleashing of prophetic power-speech. This appropriation, and reperformance, of prophetic power becomes normative for Protestant faith, as I shall argue in Part Two.

My entire approach locates the essence of the Christian idiom, and its truth-claim, in its rhetoric of divine authority. Again it must be asked: is there a danger of this emphasis promoting a form of theological authoritarianism? The dictionary defines authoritarian as 'favouring obedience to authority as opp[osed] to individual liberty...', and then offers the words 'tyrannical' and 'dictatorship'.[4] In relation to politics, this makes perfect sense. Yet according to the grammar of Christian theology, the definition is nonsense, its opposition is false. Obedience to God is the *definition* of the individual's spiritual freedom; all else means captivity to sin. In relation to divine authority, there is no such word as 'authoritarianism'. To call God tyrannical on account of his absolute authority is therefore a category error.

Yet such a defence of divine authority will hardly satisfy religion's critics, for whom the real issue is whether the *human* religious rhetoric of divine authority is in practice authoritarian. We have admitted that it may be. Yet this rhetoric is also able to oppose human authoritarianism. The image of the sovereign

---

[4] *The Concise Oxford English Dictionary*, 1982.

and powerful God has often been used to oppose rather than to undergird political power. The revolutionary zeal of Diggers and Puritan parliamentarians was fuelled by such an image of God; and in the same way Barth's opposition to National Socialism was inspired by his appeal to God as 'transcendent Commander' ['*Überlegener Gebieter*'].[5] He also refers to God as Leader (*Führer*), and insists that *this* Führer–principle is the basis of the Church.[6] Authoritarian imagery in theology has thus been responsible for some of the most decisive blows *against* political hegemony.

On another level, faith's adherence to the biblical rhetoric of authority might be called intellectually authoritarian in its identification of truth with the idiom claiming to represent divine authority. There are, I suggest, two responses to this. First, if faith renounces socio-political power, on the Christic model, it cannot be accused of authoritarianism in the normative, political sense. Its basis in nonviolence thus renders the Christian rhetoric of power unique – at least in theory. Also, as I shall subsequently argue, faith's intrinsic dialogic structure is anti-authoritarian: it ensures the ongoing presence of other voices, and places all rhetoric under suspicion. It thus becomes possible for theology to celebrate, rather than apologise for, the rhetorical force contained in the Gospel.

Response to Girard: Faith and Rhetorical Violence

The thought of René Girard has had significant influence upon theology; in the words of one critic, he 'has undertaken to construct…a new apologia for Christian religion'.[7] His central theological claim is that the truth of the Christian narrative lies in its unique critique of human violence.

This subsection argues that Girard's thesis makes a crucial oversight. There is a form of violence indispensable to the Gospel: rhetorical violence. This is an area left largely uncharted by Girard, and where he does touch upon it he seems to treat it as a suspect validation of actual, physical violence. I argue instead that rhetorical violence may be seen as central to the Christian *alternative* to actual human violence. The nonviolent praxis exalted in the New Testament cannot be separated from a rhetoric of divine authority and victory; the image of Christ's defeat of Satan, so central to the early church and later to Luther, can be seen as a form of counter-violence in which faith participates. In this account, as opposed to Girard's, Christianity emerges not so much as an Enlightenment-style critique of all religious violence but as a new form of religion in which the violent impulse is overcome through its translation into the purely rhetorical sphere.

Though this account contradicts Girard's later theory, it has some basis in his initial study of the roots of religion, *Violence and the Sacred*. This book boldly locates the 'meaning' of religion in its paradoxical relationship to violence,

---

[5] Barth, *CD* 2.2, p.665.

[6] See Gorringe, 1999, p.21.

[7] Scubla, Lucien, 'The Christianity of René Girard and the Nature of Religion', trans. by M. R. Anspach, in Dumouchel, 1987, p.160.

which is ordered in the 'special violence' of religious ritual.[8] The origins of sacrifice are traced to the universal proscription against retributive violence: because the logic of vengeance 'threatens to engulf all of society', the selection of an alternative victim saves the community from bloody anarchy. Primitive sacrificial rituals emerge as techniques for subverting the violent impulse: 'The function of ritual is to..."trick" violence into spending itself on victims whose death will provide no reprisals.... Ritual is nothing more than the regular exercise of "good" violence'.[9] Despite its seeming barbarism, then, primitive sacrificial religion provides the 'vent' for violence upon which the emergence of civilisation depends.

Though *Violence and the Sacred* does not apply itself to Judaeo-Christian tradition, I suggest that an original apologetic could be constructed from its core thesis. Religion's 'tricking' of violence by means of violence could be seen as taking a new and higher form in Christianity, in which a *rhetoric* of cosmic violence replaces actual sacrificial violence. Yet Girard's subsequent work constitutes an espousal of Christian revelation on rather different lines. His claim is that in Christianity the primitive religious mechanism is directly countered rather than transcended through rhetorical sublimation.

In *Things Hidden Since the Foundation of the World*, first published in 1978, the purpose of the sacrificial system is restated.[10] At the heart of primitive ritual is the 'scapegoat mechanism' which provides an outlet for civil strife: 'suddenly the opposition of all against all is replaced by the opposition of all against one'(24). It is essential to the efficacy of this mechanism that it is not understood by its agents; a principle Girard calls 'misrecognition'. Girard also explores the roots of this mechanism in 'mimesis', by which he means the tendency towards violent conformity that underlies all human culture.

Despite its 'good intentions', Girard argues, sacrificial religion remains helplessly implicated in violence. He now unleashes his central claim: the insufficiency of such religion is exposed and denounced in Christian revelation, and there alone. Girard's theology may be seen as a successor to Kant's; what we are now offered is 'Revelation within the limits of *nonviolence* alone': 'To recognise Christ as God is to recognize him as the only being capable of rising above the violence that had, up to that point, absolutely transcended mankind'(219).

In contrast to the popular view of the Old Testament as a chronicle of violence, Girard reads it as an account of the arduous rejection of violence: 'In the prophetic books, [the conception of deity] tends to be increasingly divested of the violence characteristic of primitive deities'(157). The Servant Song in Isaiah, for

---

[8] René Girard, *Violence and the Sacred*, trans. by P. Gregory, The Johns Hopkins University Press, Baltimore, 1977, p.23.

[9] Ibid., p.36-37.

[10] Girard, *Things Hidden Since the Foundation of the World*, with Jean-Michel Oughoulianand and Guy Lefort, trans. from *Des Choses Cachées Depuis la Fondation   du Monde* by S. Bann and M. Metteer, The Athlone Press, London, 1987. Page references supplied in main text.

example, emphasises the innocence of the 'scapegoat' victim. The Book of Job (to which Girard devotes a separate study) contains a similar logic. In contrast to the standard scapegoat myth (of which Oedipus is exemplary), the victim's point of view is here fully expressed. Job's stand effects a reinvention of the concept of God: 'he embraces the concept of a God of victims'.[11] Yet the final section of the book betrays this insight, reverting to a tyrannical concept of God. This ambiguity is typical of the Old Testament: 'it still remains sufficiently wedded to violence for people to be able brand it as violent without appearing totally implausible...' (268).

This revolution becomes explicit in the New Testament. In placing himself in explicit opposition to 'the Prince and principle of this world', Jesus forces the 'victimage mechanism' to the surface, which leads to his own death. Girard anticipates the objection that a sacrifice, albeit an entirely unique one, lies at the heart of this religion also. '[T]he sacrificial interpretation of the Passion must be criticised and exposed as a most enormous and paradoxical misunderstanding'(180): it promotes an ethic of retribution as opposed to forgiveness, thus giving free rein to the scapegoat mechanism.

Girard's exegesis has, unsurprisingly, been contested.[12] Yet I suggest that the real theological problems begin when we ask precisely *how* and *in what sense* violence is overcome by revelation. Girard's consistent implication is that Christ overcomes it through exposing its falsity: he thus saves us through *enlightening* us. 'After Christ, for the first time, people are capable of escaping from the misunderstanding and ignorance that have surrounded mankind throughout its history'(201). His theology is basically Pelagian in its implication that, once the revelation has occurred, our redemption depends upon our historical appropriation of it. It also seems to bear the marks of Kant and Hegel in its insistence that the historical unfolding of truth has now become fully intelligible: 'For the first time, we have acquired the capacity to understand the [biblical] text in [its] most radical implications'(260). Christ is credited with founding this 'critical praxis' but not with fully *effecting* it: such, it seems, is the task of modern history.

In contrast to Girard's Enlightenment-based trajectory, I suggest that Christianity is not so much the 'unmasking' of violence as the *assertion* of its overcoming, or defeat – to which a certain form of violence remains indispensable. Rhetorical violence is, in a dual sense, at the heart of the Gospel. The kerygma consists in a forceful mode of speech which lays claim to supra-human authority. And its content, as we shall see, requires to be expressed in correspondingly violent imagery. Girard thus shuns one of the central paradoxes with which theology must wrestle: the nonviolence of Christian praxis coexists with a rhetoric of divine authority. To proclaim *Christus Victor* is to celebrate a form of violence, though such violence is, in this world, confined to the rhetoric of our proclamation.

---

[11] Girard, *Job, The Enemy of his People*, trans. by Y. Freccero, The Athlone Press, London, 1987, p.139.

[12] See e.g., Scubla, 1987, p.161.

Instead of making this separation between worldly and eschatological violence (or actual and rhetorical violence), Girard sees the latter as inadmissable: 'the notion of a divine violence has no place in the inspiration of the Gospels' (189). The violence that some of Jesus' parables seem to attribute to God, he explains, is a tactical necessity: 'In order to secure the attention of his listeners, Jesus is obliged to speak their language up to a certain point and take into account illusions that cannot yet be eradicated'(189). He supplies a similar disclaimer to the apocalyptic imagery pervading the New Testament: 'the authors of the Gospels cannot stop themselves from reverting, in describing these powers, to expressions contaminated by the symbolism of violence, even when they are really announcing the complete and full deconstruction of violence...'(191). Girard thus subscribes to a specialised form of demythologising. To borrow Harnack's famous image, we can now reject the 'husk' of violent imagery and retain the entirely nonviolent kernel. Yet this position is plagued by inconsistency. For even now, in his own prose, the language of triumph and victory (and thus of violence) remains: 'As the Gospels tell us, Jesus engages in decisive struggle with these particular powers' ('*...Jésus engage la lutte décisive*'); though in the Crucifixion they believe 'themselves to be victorious once again, [they] have in fact been vanquished' ('*...en réalité sont déjà vaincues*') (191/215);[13] Christ 'wins the struggle against violence' ('*...il gagne...contre la violence...la bataille paradoxale...* ') (223/246). A close reading of his work shows that Girard's own thesis of the 'unmasking' of all violence has recourse to the traditional rhetoric of violent power-struggle.[14] Nowhere does he really acknowledge the abiding contradiction that a form of violence is necessarily entailed in the notion of the *overcoming* of violence; that redemption *still* cannot be envisaged in entirely nonviolent terms.

Against Girard's exegesis it may be argued that Christ's defeat of the devil (or the 'godless powers') is the foundational image of Christian faith. The Book of Revelation, for example, defines Christian witness as participation in this victory. As Bauckham observes in his recent commentary, 'Revelation's key concept of conquering...is applied both to the Messiah himself and to his people, who share his victory'.[15] Just as Jesus conquered through his death, it is through martyrdom that his followers join in the victory: 'They have conquered him [Satan] by the blood of the Lamb and by the word of their testimony, for they did not cling to life even in the face of death'(12:11). As Bauckham says, 'the call to Revelation's readers or hearers to 'conquer' is fundamental to the structure and theme of the book'.[16] Further evidence for the centrality of this theme is supplied in Gustaf Aulen's study *Christus Victor*. Aulen argues that the basis of the 'classic' or 'dramatic' view of the Atonement is the idea of 'divine conflict and

---

[13] The second page number refers to the original text: Girard, René, *Des Choses Cachées Depuis la Fondation du Monde*, Grasset, Paris, 1978.
[14] Further examples in *The Scapegoat*, p.194, p.206, p.207, and *Job, the Victim of his People*, p.159.
[15.] Bauckham, *A Commentary on the Book of Revelation*, Cambridge University Press 1993, p.69.
[16] Ibid., p.88.

victory; Christ – *Christus Victor* – fights against and triumphs over the evil powers of the world, the "tyrants" under which mankind is in bondage and suffering, and in Him God reconciles the world to Himself'.[17] He shows how this emphasis is central to patristic theology and later obscured by scholasticism, culminating in the legalistic theory of Anselm. However it is rediscovered by Luther, as we shall see.

The New Testament imagery of divine victory, as of divine authority, entails a form of violence, albeit an utterly unique form. The fact that its subject is God rather than man, and its object is Satan rather than man, means that it can have no extra-rhetorical reality, and that it is entirely other than actual human violence, which is unequivocally denounced. (The image of anti-Satanic violence is a *fully legitimate* expression of the scapegoat mechanism.) Because it is so instrumental to the actual practice of Christian witness (from the theology of Revelation to that of Luther – and, I would argue, that of Barth),[18] this violent image cannot be demythologised out of the Christian idiom, as Girard seems to demand. Instead it remains foundational to Christian rhetoric.

The Distinctiveness of Christian Rhetoric

I have so far used the term *rhetoric* fairly loosely; largely in relation to the linguistic expression of faith. This subsection offers a brief account of the relationship of Christian discourse to classical rhetoric.

The classical world understood rhetoric as discourse which functions in formal situations where some sort of truth is at stake, and a decision is required. Such discourse of course remains central to the arenas of politics, law and the academy. The question soon arose (which is perhaps the longest running intellectual issue of them all) as to whether this is *the* mode of discourse which relates to all questions of truth, or whether it should be held in check by another which is more objective. Socrates and Plato insisted upon the latter, of course; and philosophical discourse largely emerges in opposition to the lure of rhetoric. The Sophists were denounced as pseudo-philosophers who used rational argument as a cover for the pursuit of power through persuasion. In reaction, Socratic thought is wary of strongly persuasive speech: oratory is not deemed a true art, like medicine, which achieves something on the basis of knowledge, but a useful knack, like cooking or cosmetics; indeed this is a knack related to flattery and to 'seeming'. It is 'a way of directing the soul by means of speech, not only in the lawcourts and on other public occasions, but also in private',[19] and it is more likely than not to lead astray. The proper means to the truth is dialectic: asking questions, testing received opinion. And in this endeavour the power of linguistic persuasion is declared an irrelevance, even a hindrance. Yet some modern critics are sceptical of

---

[17] Aulen, Gustaf, *Christus Victor*, trans. by A.G. Herbert, SPCK, London, 1931, p.20.

[18] In Chapter Eight we shall see the importance to Barth of Blumhardt's motto, or mantra, 'He is Victor!'. As we shall also see, Barth is influenced by Luther's 'dialogical' violence.

[19] Plato, *Phaedrus* 261 a, in ibid., p.537.

the rigid distinction. Kennedy argues that philosophy itself can never be free of rhetoric; it should be referred to as 'philosophical rhetoric'.[20]

Aristotle inherited Plato's wariness yet treated rhetoric seriously, as an indispensable tool in the quest for truth. The rhetorical method applies in practical situations where the truth cannot be empirically demonstrated, and so where the most probable account of truth must be ascertained. To such an end it is right that various hypotheses (or, in deliberative rhetoric, various possible courses of action) should be persuasively presented, usually for the deliberation of an audience or jury. Aristotle thus dignifies rhetoric as a special area of science: it is 'an ability, in each [particular] case, to see the available means of persuasion'.[21] Rhetoric is thus subjected to a rational criterion; it is re-conceived as the rational pursuit of truth in cases where it cannot be logically verified. That which persuades (aside from the actual facts of a case) is *comprehended*: Aristotle discusses the role of *ethos* (the speaker's character), of *pathos* (the emotional response of the audience) and of *logos* (argument). He primarily seeks to highlight the role of rational argument in oratory, complaining that previous studies of 'the art of speech' 'had all neglected the argumentative element in oratory and had attended to extraneous matters instead'.[22] Unlike Plato, then, Aristotle recognises the legitimacy of the rhetorical realm. '[P]hilosophy was never in a position either to destroy rhetoric or to absorb it... . One possibility remained open: to delimit the legitimate uses of forceful speech, to draw the line between use and abuse... . Aristotle's *Rhetoric* constitutes the most brilliant of these attempts to institutionalise rhetoric from the point of view of philosophy'.[23]

Quite apart from its complex relationship to Christianity, then, its relationship to philosophy makes rhetoric a rather confusing term. It relates both to the 'beast' of powerfully persuasive speech, and to the philosophical attempt to control it, to ride it.

Christian discourse is not based in the realm of civic adjudication (on the classical, 'democratic' model), yet it too is a mode of speech with claims to truth which are not amenable to empirical demonstration. In his study of the history of rhetoric, Kennedy declares that, though the Old Testament precedes rhetorical consciousness, 'it seems fairly obvious that both as a whole and in its various books there are signs of oral, persuasive intent'.[24] Any account of biblical rhetoric must begin with the Hebrew notion that God's word is the locus of his power. Kennedy observes that the first chapter of Genesis describes God's action in terms

---

[20] Kennedy, G. A., *Classical Rhetoric and its Christian and Secular Tradition from Ancient to Modern Times*, University of North Carolina Press, Chapel Hill, 1980, p.67.

[21] Aristotle, *On Rhetoric: a Theory of Civil Discourse*, trans. by Kennedy, G. A., Oxford University Press, 1991, p.36.

[22] Ibid., Preface.

[23] Ricoeur, P., *The Rule of Metaphor: Multi-disciplinary Studies in the Creation of Meaning in Language*, trans. by R. Czerny, K. McLaughlin and J. Costello, Routledge and Kegan Paul, London, 1986, p.11.

[24] Kennedy, 1980, p.120.

of his speech, whereas in the second he acts nonverbally. On this Kennedy comments:

> Whoever put the first chapter first had a strong sense of the power of speech and in particular of the authoritative speech of God. The essential rhetorical quality of the Old Testament is this assertion of authority... . Authority is analogous to ethos in classical rhetoric, but at a different metaphysical level. It is bolstered by something like pathos in the remembrance of the past suffering of people and by their fears of future punishment or hopes of future reward. In its purest form Judaeo-Christian rhetoric shows similarity to philosophical rhetoric: it is the simple enunciation of God's truth, uncontaminated by adornment, flattery, or sophistic argumentation; it differs from philosophical rhetoric in that this truth is known from revelation or established by signs sent from God, not discovered by dialectic through men's efforts.[25]

He explains that 'the basic modes of proof of Judeo-Christian rhetoric are grace, authority, and logos, the divine message which can be understood by man. These correspond in a very incomplete way to the pathos, ethos, and rational logos of Aristotelian rhetoric'.[26] The typical rhetorical context in the Old Testament is identified as the covenant speech, which reminds people of what they theoretically know, and are already disposed to believe. The Old Testament 'as a whole constitutes a vast covenant speech, consisting of the narrative of God's actions toward the people of Israel, his commandments to them, and the warnings of the prophets when the people fall away from their duty'.[27] He also notes that Wisdom's speech in Proverbs resembles the classical form of 'prosopopoeia', yet contains 'no logical argument nor any definition of what is meant by wisdom or knowledge, only assertions delivered with authority'.[28]

In relation to the New Testament Kennedy shows how the Gospels emphasise the authority of Christ's words, and insists that the task of preaching is *not* that of classical rhetorical persuasion: 'The word for "preach" in Mark 13:10 and commonly in the New Testament is *kerusso*, which literally means "proclaim". It is what a herald (*keryx*) does with a message, a law, or a commandment. The message is a *kerygma*, or proclamation, and constitutes the gospel ('good news', *euangelion*). Christian preaching is thus not persuasion, but proclamation, and is based on authority and grace, not on proof'.[29] It thus emerges that Judaeo-Christian rhetoric substitutes conventional attempts at rational persuasion for assertions of authority. Paul provides the clearest evidence of this difference: in 1 Cor 1: 17-2:5 he objects to being judged as a rhetorician, for the task of inducing belief is

---

[25] Ibid., p.121.
[26] Ibid., p.123.
[27] Ibid.
[28] Ibid., p.125.
[29] Ibid., p.127.

ascribed to the Spirit. Like a herald, Paul's purpose is merely to announce, or to 'placard' Christ crucified. [30]

The affinities between classical and Christian rhetoric should thus not obscure the essential logical difference. I suggest that this distinction may be seen as essential to Reformation theology and its renewals. In Part Two we shall trace it in Luther's rebuke to Erasmus and in Kierkegaard's rejection of the logic of Enlightenment discourse.

The category of rhetoric has long been in vogue with a whole range of disciplines, including theology. Yet when Christianity is talked of as essentially rhetorical, there is a danger of losing sight of the essential distinction outlined by Kennedy. I suggest that this danger is evident in recent works by Cunningham and Jasper.

In *Faithful Persuasion*, Cunningham uses 'rhetoric' as an apophatic resource which reminds theology of its contingency: '[T]heology must employ language that takes account of contingency and uncertainty. Composed neither of propositions, nor of directives, nor even primarily of narratives, exhortations, or prophecies, Christian theology is instead – and above all – a form of persuasive argument'.[31] Because theology's arguments and assertions are human and contingent, '[t]hey can thus be analysed with the same tools that are used to analyse other attempts at persuasion. The most important tool for this enterprise is the ancient faculty of rhetoric'.[32] Without even citing Kennedy's distinction, he alleges that 'the classical rhetorical tradition is both compatible with, and complementary to, the enterprise of Christian theology', and so proposes that 'theological method should make a rhetorical turn'.[33]

> Theology and rhetoric are both tentative, permanently unfinished, and essentially unstable and destabilising endeavors. Both must admit the inherently revisability of their own assumptions and conclusions. Rhetoric concerns matters that might be otherwise; and theology concerns matters to which, this side of the beatific vision, human beings can gain no final and definitive access...[34]

Cunningham's point is that theological discourse is as relative and contingent as all else. Yet such scepticism only becomes theologically interesting when it is coupled, as it is in dialectical theology, with the need to proclaim the objective and certain truth of revelation. He concludes that 'the absence of...conclusiveness is a feature common both to ancient rhetoric and Christian theology',[35] and that the 'theological task is a yearning for truth, a longing for truth; but this side of the

---

[30] See Liftin, D., *St. Paul's Theology of Proclamation: 1 Corinthians 1-4 and Greco-Roman Rhetoric*, Cambridge University Press, 1994, *passim*. See also Levison, Barry, 'Did the Spirit Inspire Rhetoric?', in Watson, 1991.

[31] Cunningham, David S., *Faithful Persuasion: In Aid of a Rhetoric of Christian Theology*, Notre Dame University Press, Indiana, 1990, p.xv.

[32] Ibid.

[33] Ibid., p.31.

[34] Ibid., p.40.

[35] Ibid., p.254.

beatific vision, theology discovers ultimate truth to be elusive'.[36] But the element of uncertainty in theology is diametrically different from that in rhetoric. Rhetoric starts in uncertainty and works, through the power of reason, towards an adequate account of the truth. Theology starts with revealed truth and ends in the confusion of human thought. Cunningham makes much of the rather trivial similarities between the classical and Christian rhetorical situations: both involve speakers, audiences, etc. His aim seems to be to fit Christian discourse into general rhetorical categories. On one level this is a sensible enough endeavour; for Christian discourse is of this world, and can usefully be seen in terms of all other discourse. Yet a constructive theological approach would surely want to say something else as well.

In *Rhetoric, Power and Community*, David Jasper does acknowledge the difference of Christian rhetoric: 'modern scholars of rhetoric seem to be generally agreed that at the heart of religious rhetoric, quite distinctively, lies in [*sic*] authoritative proclamation and not in rational persuasion'; he even adds that 'the consequences of this absolute, rhetorical demand have not been properly recognised'.[37] Yet he cannot endorse this difference. On supposedly theological grounds he is concerned to warn against the 'radical' tendency of Christian rhetoric (identified by Kennedy) as dangerously authoritarian. 'In short', he explains, 'rhetoric is concerned with persuasion, power and authority';[38] and biblical rhetoric is hardly an exception. Indeed here we may be faced with rhetoric at its most dangerous:

> For it is my contention that in the New Testament we have erred grievously in our failure to heed Socrates and his warnings against rhetoric, since in the New Testament, so obsessed with theology, we are playing with power in the ultimate degree, and rhetoric is in its element, playing its subtle games with a freedom that eludes authorial or even rational demands.[39]

Rhetorical criticism of Paul uncovers a technique of persuasion and control that is 'a profound problem for Pauline studies, if not Christian theology as a whole'.[40] He observes that Paul's rhetoric hectors and bullies the community into alignment with his views, and threatens dissenters with exclusion. In his early letters Paul seems almost pathologically insecure: 'Paul's doctrine, it seems, cannot be distinguished from the political and personal motives of his writing, or the uneasiness of his relation to his readers. The assertion of authority and the exercise of personal power are dominant themes of these letters'.[41] Jasper implies that Paul's rhetoric of divine authority is entirely reducible to his dubious personal situation. Yet, as I have argued earlier in this chapter, theology must insist

---

[36] Ibid., p.257.
[37] Jasper, David, *Rhetoric, Power and Community: an Exercise in Reserve*, Macmillan, London, 1993, p.51.
[38] Ibid., p.17.
[39] Ibid., p.18.
[40] Ibid., p.45-46.
[41] Ibid., p.46.

otherwise; that the biblical rhetoric of authority is never reducible to any authority of this world (or to any psychological contingency). Paul's authoritarian personality need not invalidate his rhetoric of divine authority (instead, as we shall see in relation to Barth's commentary, it may serve as a parable of it). Similarly, Jasper observes that the language of Mark's gospel 'tends toward an absolute claim to truth without evidence and without recourse to logical argument';[42] from the first its tone is 'assertive, absolute, pitched without compromise'.[43] The aim of such rhetoric is again to enforce the consent of the community, to discourage variant opinion. In another chapter, Jasper considers Cranmer's Act of Uniformity: the rhetoric of the prayer-book should be seen 'not only as a discipline linking man with God, but more darkly as an instrument of mass persuasion and control'.[44]

Jasper is entirely right to stress the danger of authoritarianism intrinsic to Christian rhetoric. But in the age of postmodern suspicion this danger requires less emphasis than the other side of the coin: despite its all too apparent dangers, a rhetoric of authority is foundational to Christian witness. Christian theology must deny that such rhetoric is reducible to worldly power, showing how it tries to negotiate its difference. Instead Jasper implies that its potential political abuse renders all religious rhetoric innately suspect.

These suspicions of authoritative rhetoric are consonant with much secular postmodern thought: names such as Foucault and Derrida threaten to demand discussion. Instead, finally in this chapter, we turn to another influential analyst of language and power: Mikhail Bakhtin.

Hearing Voices: Bakhtin and Theology

In their critiques of religious rhetoric, both Cunningham and Jasper appeal to the insights of the Russian theorist Mikhail Bakhtin (1895-1975). Cunningham's case, he says, 'draw[s] upon the work of Mikhail Bakhtin, who distinguishes single-voiced, "monologic" discourse from multilayered, "polyphonic" discourse... . Bakhtin's praise of polyphony challenges us to speak about Christian theology in a way that does not reduce its multiform character to a tedious monotone. Here, the faculty of rhetoric can be of great assistance; for it underscores the complexity of all acts of human communication'.[45] The similarity of Jasper's theological approach is evident in his appeal to Bakhtin: his deconstruction of discourse that bolsters 'vertical' hierarchy can help us rediscover theology as 'a horizontal, comic and ironic discourse, without fixity...'.[46]

---

[42] Ibid., p.51.
[43] Ibid.
[44] Ibid., p.77.
[45] Ibid., p.205.
[46] Jasper, 1993, p.102.

For the remainder of this chapter I shall suggest that Bakhtin's preference of dialogism to 'authoritative discourse' is not necessarily an indictment of the Christian rhetoric of authority, which contains its own 'dialogic' structure.

Bakhtin is relevant to theology primarily as an analyst of the voice, and of the interaction of different voices, as the locus of meaning and truth. He has been influential in alerting the human sciences to the role of conflicting voices in the construction of textual and social meaning. All discourse, he insists, is invariably *dialogic*: words cannot but refer beyond themselves – to other words, to the tradition in which they stand, to their contemporary social context and even to the future responses that they anticipate. Every 'text', every utterance, is thus in dialogue with others, and its authorship conceals a myriad of conflicting voices. This 'polyphony' is the locus of all meaning: like words, ideas are not isolated, self-sufficient entities, but are brought to life in the process of dialogical interaction: 'At that point of contact between voice-consciousnesses the idea is born and lives'.[47] As we shall see, this also has implications for the self as an open, unfinalisable participant in a wider dialogic structure.

Theology has much cause to attend to such a theory of meaning. At the root of its discourse is the Word of God, and faith is understood as the apprehension of this Word, or 'voice' in relation to others. Faith is the ongoing argument, within the believer, between the revealed voice of God and the voices of the 'powers of this world'. It is a conception of meaning in terms of conflicting voices, or rhetorics, of authority. Bakhtin offers a new perspective on the theme of verbal *psychomachia* that, as we shall see, is central to Protestant theology and literature. Admittedly, this does not seem to be Bakhtin's starting-point or presupposition. Despite a well-documented interest in theology,[48] he does not see the expression of faith as paradigmatic for an analysis of meaning (as theology does, or should). His starting-point is the relationship of literature to society. From this perspective he develops a general philosophy of discourse and meaning.

Bakhtin's early works (whose authorship is disputed) claim to serve the socialist science of the Soviet regime, though with what sincerity it is difficult to tell. They address social psychology from a linguistic perspective and in turn treat language as an irreducibly social phenomenon. In *Marxism and the Philosophy of Language*, the currently dominant linguistic theory, that of Saussure, is accused of isolating language from social reality. Though Saussure claims to treat the specific speech-act (*parole*) as well as language in general (*langue*), his method is doomed to abstraction; it will always prefer system to reality. Formalism, the dominant school of literary thought, is similarly evasive of language's basis in social reality; it creates a gulf between artistic and 'ordinary' language, thus failing to see that true art is based in the reality of social exchange, in the 'constant struggle of accents'.[49] It fosters the myth of a special class of poetic language with authority

---

[47] Bakhtin, *The Dialogic Imagination: Four Essays*, ed. by Michael Holquist, trans. by Caryl Emerson and Michael Holquist, University of Texas Press, Austin, 1986, p.88.

[48] See Holquist and Clark, 1984, pp.84-85; Morson and Emerson, 1990, pp.61-62.

[49] From *Marxism and the Philosophy and Language* (1929), a work signed by Voloshinov but attributed to Bakhtin. In Bakhtin, 1994, p.37.

over the realm of the prosaic, thus indirectly endorsing authoritarian ideology, whether of Church or state.

Bakhtin's mature and undisputed authorship is concerned with the dialogical depth of all utterance, largely in relation to the modern novel. He explores the way in which everyday speech conceals references to various disparate linguistic styles, and to associated ideological viewpoints. The interaction of these different styles, or 'stylistic auras', is basic to consciousness and to the development of character. In contrast to Idealism, inner experience is not separate from social reality but is constituted by social forces, social voices. Ancient thinkers rightly saw inner speech as inner *dialogue*. In the words of Morson and Emerson: 'Bakhtin imagines the self as a conversation, often a struggle, of discrepant voices with each other, voices (and words) speaking from different positions and invested with different degrees and kinds of *authority*'.[50]

The discovery of the dialogic structure of language and meaning is attributed to Dostoyevsky, whose novels are declared its supreme representation. A concise example is that 'the consciousness of the solitary Raskolnikov becomes a field of battle for others' voices'.[51] Dostoyevsky is unprecedentedly sensitive to the location of meaning in different voices, and bases the novel form around this idea. He grants his characters the freedom to speak in their own voice: 'A character's word...possesses extraordinary independence in the structure of the work – it sounds as it were *alongside* the author's word...'.[52] His novels are meeting-places for the different 'languages' or viewpoints (*heteroglossia*) of his time. And Dostoyevsky himself was psychologically equipped for the portrayal of this new world: 'Dostoyevsky thought not in thoughts but in points of view, consciousnesses, voices... In each thought a whole person is expressed – this is his entire worldview, from alpha to omega'.[53] The freedom that Dostoyevsky gives to his characters constitutes the 'small-scale Copernican revolution' of his authorship.[54] It is a revolution not only in literary style but, Bakhtin insists, in the nature of truth.

In the essay 'Epic and the Novel' the polyphonic novel is seen as arising from a long tradition of literary discourse that questions and subverts any 'monologic' literary model. The epic form is prototypical of such monologism: 'The epic past is locked into itself and walled-off from all subsequent times'.[55] One cannot interact with this world, only 'accept [it] with reverence'.[56] The novel form emerges in opposition to this model; it features a new view of the individual as unfinalised, ever in search of his essence. Comedy is also crucial to this novelty:

---

[50] Morson and Emerson, *Mikhail Bakhtin: the Creation of a Prosaics*, Stanford University Press, California, 1990, pp.217-18.
[51] *Problems of Dostoyevsky's Poetics* (1929), in Bakhtin, 1994, p.99.
[52] Ibid., p.89.
[53] Ibid., p.101.
[54] Ibid., p.92.
[55] 'Epic and Novel', in Bakhtin, 1986, p.17.
[56] Ibid.

'laughter destroys the epic, [and] any hierarchical...distance'.[57] This role of humour in subversive realism is to occupy much of the rest of Bakhtin's career; his work on Rabelais, and his influential category of 'carnival'. In contrast to Auerbach's thesis in *Mimesis*,[58] for which the Bible is a fusion of high and low styles, Bakhtin generally seems to consign biblical discourse to the epic category. 'Bakhtin tends to treat [the Bible] as official, single-voiced discourse, stressing its public, institutional role in dominantly Christian cultures and periods'.[59]

His essay 'Discourse in the Novel' relegates all poetry to the monologism of the epic: 'In poetry, even discourse about doubts must be cast in a discourse that cannot be doubted... . The language of poetic genres often becomes authoritarian, dogmatic and conservative – sealed off from the influence of extraliterary social dialects... The poet accepts the idea of a unitary and singular language... .'[60] Does every poet do this? As one critic insists, poetry is not necessarily dialogically dumb: 'Bakhtin surely underestimates the degree to which a master of poetic language can use its sonic resources to create the internal dialogue Bakhtin so valued'.[61] In Chapter Five I shall show how this is true of Protestant poetics.

Also in this essay he develops a theory of two ways in which external discourse relates to the individual consciousness. 'Another's discourse...strives to determine the very bases of our ideological interrelations with the world, the very bases of our behavior; it performs here as authoritative discourse, and as internally persuasive discourse'.[62] The former is by definition unquestionable:

> [Authoritative discourse] binds us, quite independently of any power it may have to persuade us internally...it is located in a distanced zone, organically connected with a past that is felt to be hierarchically higher. It is, so to speak, the word of the fathers. It is a prior discourse... . It is not a free appropriation and assimilation of the word itself that authoritative discourse seeks to elicit from us; rather, it demands our unconditional allegiance... . It enters our verbal consciousness as a compact and indivisible mass; one must either totally affirm it or totally reject it. It is indissolubly fused with authority – with political power, an institution, a person – and it stands and falls together with that authority.[63]

On the other hand, external discourse with a claim to authority can be held at a distance, assimilated, 'reaccentuated', appropriated into one's inner world as one voice among others: 'consciousness awakens to independent ideological life precisely in a world of alien discourses surrounding it, and from which it cannot

---

[57] Ibid., p.23.
[58] Eric Auerbach, *Mimesis: The Representation of Reality in Western Literature*, Princeton University Press, New Jersey, 1968.
[59] Reed, W. L., *Dialogues of the Word: The Bible as Literature According to Bakhtin*, Oxford University Press, 1993, p.14.
[60] 'Discourse in the Novel', in Bakhtin, 1986, p.338.
[61] Richter, D. H., 'Dialogism and Poetry', in Palmer, 1990, p.68.
[62] Ibid., p.342.
[63] Ibid., p.343.

initially separate itself... . Our ideological development is just such an intense struggle within us for hegemony among various available verbal and ideological points of view, approaches, directions and values'. [64]

What is obscured is this distinction between 'authorative discourse' and 'internally persuasive discourse' is that authority is instrumental to the latter category as well, if it is through exposure to strong voices that consciousness develops. Yet Bakhtin misleadingly posits an emergent autonomy in which the individual becomes able to control these voices like puppets, having seen through their claims to authority. In reality, interior dialogue is fuelled by the abiding, though conflicting, sense of these voices' *authority*. Bakhtin's insight into the construction of meaning through voices of authority seems to give way to a conventionally liberal model of the autonomous subject. (His essentially negative view of authoritative discourse must be seen in the context of his aversion to Soviet propaganda.)

I suggest that Bakhtin's distinction between the danger of 'authoritative discourse' and the good of dialogical vitality is challenged by the discourse of Christian faith. Because faith is based in the apprehension of the 'authoritative discourse' of the Word (as mediated in scripture and tradition), it would seem to be suspect, to be quintessentially monologic. Yet a unique species of dialogism is entailed in Protestant faith – as much of the rest of my study shall attempt to show. This dialogism, I shall suggest, underlies the 'dialectical' character of Protestant faith. Central to Bakhtin's agenda is his insistence upon the *dialogical* basis of all dialectics: 'Take   a   dialogue   and   remove   the   voices,...remove   the intonations,...carve out abstract concepts and judgements from living words and responses, cram everything into one abstract consciousness – and that's how you get dialectics'. [65]

A form of dialogical openness is created around the apprehension of the 'voice' of the Word, *precisely by virtue of its absolute authority*. For the Word remains alien to fallen humanity, and can only be known in its interaction with other voices. In its apprehension of God's authority, faith is always in agonistic dialogue with the voices of this world – of reason, the flesh and the devil. (As we shall see, Protestant literature is often based in the representation of this rhetorical conflict: Bunyan's *Pilgrim's Progress*, for example, surely anticipates novelistic polyphony in its representation of different 'voice-ideas'.) The argument of faith is ongoing and in a sense open-ended; only eschatologically is it settled. My reading of Protestant tradition will focus on this 'internal dialogism', which I take to be basic to the discourse of faith.

Bakhtin helps to rehabilitate a potentially theological conception of the psyche, and of the world, as constituted by competing voices of authority: 'I hear voices in everything and dialogical relations among them', he once said. [66] His account of self and meaning can thus serve as a useful resource for contemporary

---

[64] Ibid.

[65] Bakhtin, *Notes (1970-1971)*, no. 67, extracts reprinted in Morson, 1986, p.181.

[66] Bakhtin, 'Towards a Methodology for the Human Sciences' (1975), in Bakhtin, 1981, p.169.

theology. The precondition for our apprehension of the Word is our ability to see (or rather to *hear*) the world in terms of voices. For the Word's victory over the powers of this world is perhaps most usefully seen as a *rhetorical* one. What Bakhtin leaves uncharted is the agency of a particular voice of authority, upon which (for faith) all meaning and dialogue hinges: that of the Word. An early instance of this dynamic is the subject of our following chapter.

Chapter 3

Before Protestantism: Augustine

My study is predominantly concerned with the role of authoritative rhetoric in Protestantism. Yet the category's centrality is not the invention of Protestantism. It would be misleading to neglect entirely its role in Christian thought from the preceding centuries. Augustine is our natural point of pre-Protestant reference. Augustine was not a Protestant, but Luther was an Augustinian, and not only in name. He saw Augustine as his primary predecessor, his historical ally.[1] But before discussing Augustine let us briefly consider, in relation to our theme, the tradition he inherits and develops.

Before Augustine

The new faith entered a world of polytheistic tolerance, to which it soon proved intolerable. A crucial factor in what distinguished it, making it both attractive and repellent, was the authoritative rhetoric at its heart. Though it followed Judaism in this, Judaism did not trouble gentiles with its outsized claims. Its claim to universality as well as to absolute certainty and exclusivity was alien to classical religious thought. And this entailed a key difference of tone. 'The Christians…brought the certainty of God and history to questions whose answers eluded the pagan schools… . Among second-century authors, it is the Christians who are the most confident and assured'.[2] This confidence was rooted in the idea of a cosmic victory over Satan: 'While Jewish teachers feared Satan's continuing access as an accuser before God, Christians knew that he had fallen for ever and that his rival kingdom had only a brief while left'.[3]

To educated pagans, Christianity was anti-intellectual in its exaltation of a form of authority over reason. The clearest evidence for this comes from Origen's pagan opponent Celsus in the second century. 'The Christian teachers do not want to give or to receive reasons for what they believe. Their favourite expressions are "Do not ask questions, just believe!" and: "Your faith will save you!"'.[4] He later attacks the illogic of the doctrine of the resurrection of the body: 'And of course they have no reply for this one, and as in most cases where there *is* no reply they

---

[1] 'Our theology and that of St. Augustine, by the grace of God, are making rapid progress in our university' (Luther, Letter to John Lang, 18 May 1517, in *Documents of Modern History*, ed. by E. G. Rupp and B. Drewery, Edward Arnold, London, 1970, p.9).

[2] Lane Fox, Robin, *Pagans and Christians*, Viking, 1986, pp.330-31.

[3] Ibid., p.326.

[4] Celsus, *On the True Doctrine: a Discourse Against the Christians*, trans. by R. J. Hoffmann, Oxford University Press, 1987, p.54.

take cover by saying "Nothing is impossible with God'".[5] One can hardly help sympathising with Celsus' frustration with so bold a creed. We get from his polemic a vivid sense of its rhetorical *primitivity*. For Christians have recourse to verbal superstition: '[They] claim to get some sort of power from pronouncing the names of demons or saying certain incantations, always incorporating the name Jesus and a short story about him in the formula';[6] 'They think that by pronouncing the name of their teacher [i.e., Christ] they are armed against the powers of earth and air'.[7] So primitive a faith should not even be considered alongside true wisdom; they are not in the same league. Celsus' tactic, which is hardly unreasonable, is to associate Christianity with all sorts of other superstition; belief in magic and exorcism, inducement of ecstatic frenzy, cultic brainwashing. But he knows that Christianity is not just another superstitious cult, it is far more sinister. It wants to overtake and exclude intelligent discourse. There is nothing very unusual about what Christians believe, he concludes, 'except that they believe it to the exclusion of more comprehensive truths about God'.[8] His real objection is to the rhetorical aggression faith entails, even internally: different sects of Christians, 'slander each other constantly with the vilest forms of abuse'.[9] Such objections are characteristic of the educated pagan; Galen's case is very similar: 'It is [Moses'] method in his books to write without offering proofs, saying "God commanded, God spake"'.[10]

The early Church Fathers were generally intent upon opposing such charges and claiming the philosophical highground for their faith, often referred to as 'the Christian philosophy'. The thought of Justin, Irenaeus and Clement entailed a tendency to tone down the offence of the rhetoric of divine authority. But this was only one tendency. The North African Tertullian, in the early third century, famously reacted against it, demanding to know what Athens had to do with Jerusalem. The question is itself questionable; Tertullian was highly philosophically literate, and hardly averse to reasoning.[11] Yet he wants a theology free from philosophy's spirit: 'Let them beware who put forward a Stoic, Platonic, dialectical form of Christianity. For us there is no need of curiosity after Christ, no need of inquiry after the Gospel'.[12] Theology's basic error is to err from its own rhetoric of authority, to shy away from its violent particularity, its particular violence. He thus mocks Marcion's nonviolent God, 'who never takes offence, is never angry, never inflicts punishment, who has prepared no fire in hell, no gnashing of teeth in the outer darkness!'[13] Tertullian exhibits a taste for rhetorical

---

[5] Ibid., p.86.

[6] Ibid., p.53.

[7] Ibid., p.118.

[8] Ibid., p.120.

[9] Ibid., p.91.

[10] Galen, *On Hippocrates' Anatomy*, in Robert L. Wilken, *The Christians as the Romans Saw Them*, Yale University Press, New Haven, 1984, p.72.

[11] See Osborne, *Tertullian, the First Theologian of the West*, Cambridge University Press, 1997, p.27.

[12] Tertullian, *De praescriptione haereticorum* (7.11), quoted in Osborne, 1997, p.45.

[13] Tertullian, *Against Marcion* 1.27, in *A New Eusebius*, ed. by J. Stevenson, rev. by W. H.

violence even in the context of piety. As a community, he says, 'we approach God in prayer, massing our forces to surround him. This violence that we do him pleases God'.[14] (As we shall see, this comment is noticed and approved by both Luther and Donne.)

The character of the early church was largely determined by its reaction to two types of people: heretics and martyrs. Both are relevant to our rhetorical theme. The threat of heresy was largely responsible for the dramatic rise of Satan to mythological prominence. To preserve its distinctness from various Gnostic trends, the church had to be obsessively vigilant. Basic to the purpose of Christian teaching was the need to disinfect and inoculate initiates against the demonic power of heresy (this was a central function of baptism). For this reason early Christian writing is polemical in a sense that is alien to classical rhetoric. Civil decorum has no place in battling Satan; and Christian speech begins to understand itself in precisely such terms. As Forsyth says, 'the dialectic of "truth" and "error" came to be viewed as an extension of the central Christian combat myth, of the opposition of light and darkness, God and "the god of this world"'.[15] In the early Christian era, the action that most closely corresponds to divine victory over Satan is thus the rhetorical practice of refuting error and upholding orthodoxy. In Origen's exegesis, the Bible is interpreted at a 'spiritual' level, giving the believer personal involvement in the rhetoric of divine power. The theme of anti-Satanic Christian speech is of course prepared for in Paul: his writing establishes a strong link between the deceiving serpent of Genesis, heresy, and the figure of Satan.

We must also return to the New Testament to understand the rhetorical implications of martyrdom. It is the clearest site of rhetorical possession by the Spirit. The idea is most clearly stated in Matthew: 'When they deliver you up, do not be anxious how you are to speak or what you are to say; for what you are to say will be given to you in that hour; for it is not you who speak, but the Spirit of your Father speaking through you'(10.19-20). By the time of the Diocletian persecution at the end of the third century, martyrdom is essential to Christian self-understanding. It is understood as an extreme form of Christian proclamation; it means *witness*, a form of speech deriving from a court of law. It crystallises the yearning of Christian existence: to signify purely. Ignatius looks forward to his imminent martyrdom as his metamorphosis into 'an intelligible utterance of God' as opposed to remaining 'a mere meaningless cry'.[16] Stories of martyrdoms were the most popular form of Christian literature; they included impassioned speeches attributed to martyrs, in confirmation of Jesus' promise. Martyrs were thought to see visions of heaven and especially of Christ's final victory, and also to hear and speak the Word with especial clarity. Polycarp, for example, hears a voice from

---

C. Frend, SPCK, London, 1987, pp.94-95.

[14] Tertullian, *Apology*, 39.1, in Stevenson, 1987, p.163.

[15] Forsyth, Neil, *The Old Enemy: Satan and the Combat Myth*, Princeton University Press, New Jersey, 1987, p.311.

[16] Ignatius of Antioch, 'Epistle to the Romans', 2, in *Early Christian Writings: the Apostolic Fathers*, ed. by A. Louth, trans. by M. Staniforth, Penguin, Middlesex, 1987, p.85.

heaven, rebukes his judge (a type of Pilate) and 'was overflowing with courage and joy'.[17]

Following the formative influence of heretics and martyrs there enters a third important type: the ascetic. Anthony takes to the wilderness in the early fourth century and starts a craze. 'A key ingredient in the development of monasticism...was the idea of a struggle with the devil (or some monstrous substitute)'.[18] This struggle was rhetorically waged; in the form of auto-exorcistic prayer. A major practitioner was Evagrius of Pontus (346-399), author of *Antirrhetikos, on How to Answer Back*, which 'recorded 487 separate *logismoi*, powerful or obsessive trains of thought, each accompanied with appropriate words of Scripture with which to banish or to welcome the experience'.[19] In its hostility to 'the world', asceticism entails a discourse of aggression: 'There must be something in the idea expressed by Nietzsche in *The Genealogy of Morals* that ascetic behaviour, like the Irish custom of fasting against one's enemies, is always in some fundamental way aggressive'.[20] For figures such as Jerome, the desert cell becomes the site of an alternative discourse defiant of civic values and ecclesiastical worldliness; a discourse in which he could speak freely against his opponents.

This brisk survey has attempted to show how the 'theology of the Word' of the early church is rooted in the various practical situations of witness. Above all, the Christian resource of authoritative rhetoric was essential to the church's ability to define itself against philosophy and heresy.

Augustine's *Confessions*: The Sound of Demons

> As I was...weeping in the bitter agony of my heart, suddenly I heard a voice from the nearby house chanting as if it might be a boy or girl (I do not know which), saying and repeating over and over again 'Pick up and read, pick up and read'. At once my countenance changed, and I began to think intently whether there might be some sort of children's game in which such a chant is used. But I could not remember having heard of one. I checked the flood of tears and stood up. I interpreted it solely as a divine command to me to open the book and read the first chapter I might find.[21]

Who said it and why? Who if anyone uttered the famous cry of 'tolle lege' that, according to his account in Book 8 of *The Confessions*, tipped the balance of Augustine's struggle for faith as he sat in the garden?

---

[17] 'The Martyrdom of Polycarp' 12, in ibid., p.129.

[18] Forsyth, 1987, p.387.

[19] Peter Brown, *The Body and Society: Men, Women and Sexual Renunciation in Early Christianity*, Faber, London, 1988, p.374.

[20] John Bossy, *Christianity in the West 1400-1700*, Oxford University Press, 1985, p.5.

[21] Augustine, *Confessions*, trans. by Chadwick, Oxford University Press, 1991, pp.152-53. Subsequent page references appear in the main text. (Also Latin text: ed. James O'Donnell, Clarendon, Oxford, 1992.)

Next door to Augustine's community of amateur ascetics (let us say) there lives a Roman intellectual named Caius Virilius. He has recently retired from the law-courts, where he made a killing, and is also well known for his sideline of Christian-baiting: you may have heard of his fiery pamphlet *Iterum Leones Rudeant* ('Let the Lions Roar Again'). A historian also, he has retired in order to write his long-awaited work on the religious history of Rome; *The Divine City*. Its aim is to convince any educated citizen of the infinite gulf between the noble grandeur of the Roman spirit and the shallow barbarisms of Christianity and suchlike. It is to be so rigorous a study that he even feels obliged, for the sake of historical accuracy, to dredge through the absurd crudities of Hebraic and Christian 'literature'. It is amusing at first, the claim of their prophets to be possessed by the one true God, who speaks long and muddled polemics through them, which seem to be chiefly concerned with sex and religious worship. But by Jove it gets tedious, far-fetched, infantile. He has recently been feeling so repelled by this reading matter, and so keen to return to the delicate brilliance of the poets, that he has invented rather an unusual scheme. Which is where his son Marcus comes in. He has trained Marcus to call up to his study, on his way home from school each day, 'Time to start reading the Christian books!' The thought that he is doing this research for the sake of his descendants' cultural freedom delivers him from his lethargy and distaste. The cry of inspiration soon became abbreviated to 'Pick it up and read it!'.

Well, maybe not (but who knows any better?). Augustine's account does invite us to reconstruct the scene, to wonder if he is sparked off by a chance intrusion from some entirely disconnected world of activity. Why does he think it *might* be a divine call? It is not only that he is in a state of spiritual tension, of distress at the stalling of his nascent faith. Immediately following the above-quoted passage he explains his interpretation of the cry: 'For I had heard how Antony happened to be present at the gospel reading, and took it as an admonition addressed to himself when the words were read: "Go, sell all you have, give to the poor, and you shall have treasure in heaven; and come, follow me"' (Matt. 19:21). By such an inspired utterance he was immediately 'converted to you' (Ps. 50:15)'(153). Augustine is interpreting his aural world in the light of this story, in imitation of his current spiritual hero. Yet Augustine's situation is very different from that recounted in Athanasius' *Life* of Antony. He does not happen to hear the Scriptures as the direct Word of God but interprets a literal voice as heralding such a scriptural revelation. And it is not even Christ's voice through which God now speaks to him but Paul's admonition: 'Not in riots and drunken parties, not in eroticism and indecencies, not in strife and rivalry, but put on the Lord Jesus Christ and make no provision for the flesh in its lusts (Rom. 13:13-14)'(153). Nevertheless he is converted by this oracular voice as decisively as was Antony; he tells his mother who rejoices at the answering of her long-standing prayer.

The voice that Augustine encounters is multiple. It is the cry of the child (presumably a mundane commonplace) and it is a divine summons. The decision to interpret it as a divine summons is informed by Athanasius' biography of Antony: this literary 'voice' tells him that a biblical text can act as a direct oracle from God. (There is also the precedence of Paul's conversion by celestial voice.)

And so he picks up and reads. In this case it is Paul's voice through which the Word speaks, not (as in Antony's case) that of Christ himself. Thus the sequence emerges: the child's voice, with the voice of Antony's testimony (via Athanasius), leads him to the text, wherein, in the voice of Paul, is the voice of God. There are at least five 'layers' to the voice that Augustine encounters in the garden; it incorporates memory and literature as well as mundane hearing (the child's cry) and bold theology (God speaks to one). This pivotal scene is representative of Augustine's account as a whole: throughout he is converted by the Word of God not as a single agent but as dispersed through different voices: literal, literary and psychological.

The Confessions presents Christian faith in the context of a polyphonic worldview. All meaning, and all psychological motivation, is conceived as subject to the agency of *voices*. These voices are powers, in general negative, demonic powers by which the soul is possessed; these *constitute* the errant soul. Augustine's progression to faith is reliant on a rhetorical and polyphonic model of meaning.[22] Psychomachic psychology, based in the conflict of voices, is for him a crucial bridge between the pagan and Christian thought-worlds.

Immediately prior to the garden scene, Augustine wrestles with the stumbling-block of sex. He presents the struggle as the competition of two rhetorical presences.

> [My old loves] held me back. They tugged at the garment of my flesh and whispered: 'Are you getting rid of us?... . Meanwhile the overwhelming force of habit was saying to me: 'Do you think you can live without them?'
>
> ...From that direction where I had set my face and towards which I was afraid to move, there appeared the dignified and chaste Lady Continence, serene and cheerful without coquetry, enticing me in an honourable manner to come and not to hesitate. To receive and embrace me she stretched out pious hands, filled with numerous good examples for me to follow... . And she smiled on me with a smile of encouragement as if to say: '...Cast yourself upon [God], do not be afraid... . 'Stop your ears to your impure members on earth and mortify them'' (Col. 3:5). This debate in my heart was a struggle of myself against myself.

It is an aural vision, in which the central conflict is vocal. Augustine presents this crucial moment of decision in terms that are both classical and biblical. He is Heracles at the cross-roads, forced to choose between pleasure and virtue, and then he is Odysseus being warned of the destructive power of the Sirens' song against which his (or his crew's) ears must be blocked. This literary motif also figures in late classical philosophy; it is later the basis of Boethius' hymn to philosophy. The biblical model, which is even more closely reflected in this passage, is the scene from Proverbs in which the contradictory rhetorics of Wisdom and Folly call out to the youth in the street, advertising themselves and denouncing each other (like political parties). The rhetoric of sensuality is of course seductive in style as well as content; it whispers and caresses. And, here as

---

[22] 'As an orator, Augustine perceived the world and its fundamental relationships in terms of rhetoric...' (Sarah Spence, *Rhetorics of Reason and Desire: Vergil, Augustine, and the Troubadours*, Cornell, New York, 1988, p.60).

in Proverbs, the rhetoric of Continence is a counter-seduction, charged with alternative erotic power. Augustine implies that he could never have moved from actual sensuality without this *aural erotics* of the Word, this *über*-sexual authority out-doing the rhetoric of worldly seduction. But this aural vision does not actually and finally effect his conversion. It induces a fit of weeping during which 'tolle lege' is heard. Perhaps this model of vocal authority is in itself insufficient, whether because of its pagan connotations, or its femininity. The final and decisive voice is the stronger and stabler textual voice which places Augustine in the manly company of Antony and Paul.

This 'aural erotics' is Augustine's consistent model for the presentation of life, self and faith in *The Confessions*. The world is an arena of voices that claim authority for themselves; all significant phenomena are charged with the power of the voice. False ideas are *false* in a living and dangerous sense, rather than in an abstract empirical one; they are purposefully false, expressions of demonic agency. The world is alive with the sound of demons.

Augustine traces his own formation through external voices. Infancy is marked by impotence, primarily linguistic (as he reminds us elsewhere, 'infant' means speechless);[23] and so by dependence on the authority of elders. Such authority must be obeyed despite its flawed nature; this is also the truth of politics. The flawed authority of his schoolmasters is especially dangerous; it has power to instil wrong desire. The purpose of his education, he complains in a direct address to God, was 'that I should succeed in this world, and should excel in the arts of using my tongue to gain access to human honours and to acquire deceitful riches' (11). Augustine's tone with God here verges on the accusatory: How could you, who are true authority, have let me be subject to such a terribly flawed parody of authority, to such a mis-schooling of desire?

The ideal of worldly success is learned mimetically, including through literature: 'I liked to tickle my ears with false stories which further titillated my desires'(12). With reference to the Psalms he calls these false desires 'fornications': 'and in my fornications I heard all round me the cries "Well done, well done"'(16). Being praised constitutes the major seductive voice of his adolescence. Indeed weakness for praise is a consistent theme of his thought; in Book Ten it is identified as an abiding temptation, and it is one that still troubles him as bishop.[24] It obscures the one consistently positive voice in his life, which he as yet neglects: his mother's. '[W]hose words were they but yours which you were chanting in my ears through my mother, your faithful servant?'(27). Monica is his anti-Siren; though her 'song' is now unheard, she is later credited with effecting her son's salvation through the gentle persistence of her voice, like a recurring theme in a piece of music.

He moves to Carthage to train in rhetoric, 'the fraudulent service of devils'(35). He was on the fringes of a rhetorical brat-pack: 'I lived among them shamelessly ashamed of not being one of the gang', he says, pathetically. They

---

[23] Augustine, *CG* 16.43, p.710.
[24] See Brown, P., *Augustine of Hippo*, Faber, London, 1967, p.206. In *The City of God* love of praise underlies the 'ideology' of Rome (*CG* V, 12, p.15).

called themselves 'The Overturners' (*eversores*). Chadwick's translation 'Wreckers' has an appropriate air of demonic (and Sirenic) menace – for the name is now cited as evidence of demonic agency: 'no truer name could be given them than the Wreckers. Clearly they are themselves wrecked first of all and perverted by evil spirits, who are mocking them and seducing them in the very acts by which they love to mock and deceive others' (38). To desire to deceive, whether as Wrecker or rhetor, is to *be deceived* by the demonic power possessing one.

And now begins his ambiguous relationship with the study of philosophy. It is sparked by Cicero's *Hortensius*, which is credited with positive spiritual influence. (This is unsurprising: Roman philosophy has long had a religious character, even incorporating the rhetoric of devotion. For Seneca, writing in the first century AD, Philosophy is a goddess: 'Her voice is for peace, calling all mankind to live in harmony'.)[25] Reminded of his latent attachment to the name of Christ he tries to read the Bible but is turned off by its stylistic naivety: 'it seemed to me unworthy in comparison with the dignity of Cicero' (40). 'That explains why I fell in with men proud of their slick talk, very earthly-minded and loquacious'(40): the Manichees. To emphasise the seriousness of his error he introduces 'that bold-faced woman', the harlot of Proverbs: 'She seduced me' (43). 'During this same period of nine years...our life was one of being seduced and seducing, being deceived and deceiving' (52). In relation to faith there is no neutrality – only commitment, one way or the other. And commitment means possession, by either demons or the Spirit, and such possession is construed in rhetorical terms.

His various forms of error are read in terms of a theology of the Word: philosophy was an attempt 'to hear your interior melody when I was meditating on the beautiful and the fitting. I wanted to stand still and hear you and rejoice with joy at the voice of the bridegroom (John 3:29)...[but was prevented by] the voices of the error I espoused'(68-69). Pure reception of the Word is prevented by the interference of his own error and pride. The phrase 'interior melody' raises the question of whether Neoplatonic thought is really renounced in Augustine's theology of the Word – a question to which we shall return.

Friendship is identified as another major snare of these years: 'By its adulterous caress, my mind which had "itching ears" (2 Tim. 4:3-4) was corrupted' (60). In recalling its force, Augustine suspends the narrative in self-exhortation: 'Do not be vain, my soul. Do not deafen your heart's ear with the tumult of your vanity. Even you have to listen. The Word himself cries to you to return'(62). The distinction between then and now seems to fall away in his ongoing need for direction through the Word. Within his narrative of spiritual lack, Augustine often supplies for the reader what was missing, in the form of pious laments and prayers. The implication is that the narration of error would be dangerous – for both teller and reader – without the interjection of the converted voice, its supervision of the narrative. Frequently the missing 'truth-content' is expressed in terms of a theology of the Word. This applies to the minimal Christological content: 'He who for us is life itself descended here and endured our death and slew it by the

---

[25] Seneca, *Letters from a Stoic*, Penguin, Middlesex, 1976, XC, p.171.

abundance of his life. In a thunderous voice he called us to return to him... . He did not delay, but ran crying out loud by his words, deeds, death, life, descent, and ascent – calling us to return to him'(84-85). The Incarnation constitutes a voice, a summons. Yet, as he later insists, it is no disembodied piece of rhetoric: 'This your word would have meant little to me if it had been only a spoken precept and had not first been acted out'(182). The Incarnation ensures that God's Word is not *mere* rhetoric. The Gnostic variations on faith have no such guarantee.

Augustine's theology of the rhetorical Word is both moulded by his immersion in the world of classical rhetoric and developed in opposition to it. He is both averse to the human construction of authority (which is what rhetorical practice is) and addicted to strong speech. Is there, he begins to demand, a true rhetoric which is not the toy of human requirements? The problem is sharpened after his disappointment with the Manichee bishop Faustus, who is all talk, no substance. His growing awareness of the distinction is attributed to God: 'Already I had learnt from you that nothing is true merely because it is eloquently said, nor false because the signs coming from the lips make sounds deficient in a sense of style... . Wisdom or foolishness are like food that is nourishing or useless... . Food of either kind can be served in either town or country ware'(78). He moves to Milan, newly hungry and newly wary.

Although truth is distinct from rhetorical packaging, the eloquence of Ambrose, bishop of Milan, is of a different order. Augustine is at first moved only by professional admiration for a master speaker: 'My ears were only for his rhetorical technique; this empty concern was all that remained with me after I had lost any hope that a way to you might lie open for man. Nevertheless together with the words which I was enjoying, the subject matter, in which I was unconcerned, came to make an entry into my mind. I could not separate them'(88). He has just learned, as he thinks, to separate rhetoric from truth, and retreats into a merely aesthetic attitude. But the Word comes to him by means of his aesthetic appreciation of Ambrose. Though it is not bound to rhetorical means, the Word remains free to make use of them. Ambrose awakens Augustine, through rhetoric, to what is beyond mere rhetoric. He now entertains the possibility of the truth of Catholic faith and enrols as a catachumen.

His mother joins him in Milan, and he finally ends his rebellion against her expectations. Like a modern teenager he had long been embarrassed by her piety, her blushworthy 'womanish advice'(27). And to the young aesthete her simplicity corresponds to that of the scriptures, which he considers beneath him. Yet, due to the force of maternal influence, the Christian 'style' is in his blood. His philosophical study uncovers a latent 'prejudice' in favour of Christ's name, which 'my infant heart had piously drunk in with my mother's milk, and at a deep level I retained the memory. Any book which lacked this name, however well written or polished or true, could not entirely grip me'(40). Monica's role is Christological, even incarnational; she proclaims Christ as naturally and physically as she lactates. It is her *bodily* signification of the Word that ultimately refutes the alternative creeds. She thus relates to the incarnation as well as to the 'mother' Church. (In a sense, then, 'Mum's the Word'.)

He looks back on the long ten years of Manichaean error as a vain attempt to evade the style of Catholic truth. Much of its appeal lay in its esoteric subtlety and its undogmatic open-endedness (it rather resembles a lot of modern 'theory'). Brown suggests that it 'had enabled the young Augustine to disown, for a time, and at a heavy cost,...the hard, "paternal" qualities associated with the omnipotent Father of Catholic belief'.[26] Rather in the manner of Kierkegaard perhaps, Augustine's spiritual development is marked by an almost schizophrenic attitude to authority. He can only rebel from a seemingly rigid and crude account of divine authority, yet is drawn back to it. He develops a positive conception of the role of authority in Catholic faith.

> I thought it more modest and not in the least misleading to be told by the Church to believe what could not be demonstrated...rather than from the Manichees to have a rash promise of knowledge with mockery of mere belief, and then afterwards to be ordered to believe many fabulous and absurd myths impossible to prove true (95).

His conversion entails his preference for a truth-tradition which *openly* grounds itself in its authority rather than pretending to reasonability. The weakness of human reasoning necessitates trust in 'the authority of the sacred writings'. His conversion most basically consists in his 'falling for' (in the sense of rapture rather than delusion) the style of authoritative biblical rhetoric that he has long attempted to evade. Faith consists in the acceptance of this distinctive rhetoric of authority which he has for so long struggled against. This acceptance is performed in the strange new style of the book, a style not of rational control but of prayerful address, of yearning doxology.[27] Also crucial to his conversion is the habit he learns from Ambrose of interpreting scripture according to the needs of individual faith. Scripture becomes a rhetorical arsenal, with authoritative verbal weapons to counter all variety of doubt – 'Your words stuck fast in my heart and on all sides I was defended by you'(133). His incessant quotation of scripture serves as a running commentary on his life. Or rather it is the other way round: his life becomes a commentary on and exposition of the power and relevance of the Word.

Augustine's early theology of the Word is most clearly illustrated by the final 'vision' he shares with his mother, just prior to her death. They imagine the possibility of 'the tumult of the flesh' falling silent, and of all created things proclaiming their creator through an absolute silence: 'then he alone would speak not through them but through himself. We would hear his word, not through the tongue of the flesh, nor through the voice of an angel, nor through the sound of thunder, nor through the obscurity of a symbolic utterance. Him who in these things we love we would hear in person without their mediation'(171-72). This

---

[26] Brown, 1967, p.53.

[27] Fenn considers that Augustine 'attempts to accomplish through language what might otherwise be achieved through public ritual' (Fenn, R., 'Augustine: Death Anxiety and the Power and Limits of Language' in Capps and Dittes, 1990, p.318). 'It is as if Augustine were using words as some natives use sound: to ward off disaster, to dispel as well as to conjure, and to distract himself from mourning and even melancholy by incessant embroidering in his speech' (ibid., p.324).

'aural vision' has distinct Neoplatonic overtones, in its yearning to surpass the material. In the first stage of his theology his conception of the Word is more philosophical: his 'adoption of [Neoplatonic] precepts often obscured his view of the full significance of God's Word as proclamation'.[28] Yet, as we shall now see in relation to his grand exposition of Christianity's difference, his trajectory is *away* from such thought, towards a fully biblical view of the Word, and so to a more fully rhetorical conception of revelation and salvation.

The City of God: Paganism Outspoken

The City of God [29]expounds Christian faith in the context of pagan charges that it is responsible for the collapse of the Roman empire (in 410, just prior to the time of writing, Rome was sacked by the Goths). At the end of Book One he declares the theological significance of his counter-polemic: 'and therefore we must not fail in our duty, so that, when we have refuted their impious attacks – insofar as God gives us strength – we may establish [*adseramus*] the City of God, and true religion, and the true worship of God' (1.36, p.47). This rhetorical task participates in the City of God's establishment, or assertion. He is not just writing *about* the City of God; he is writing it into being, against its opponents.[30] His writing participates in its necessarily oppositional, agonistic nature. The task is to answer the charges hurled at Christian faith and to turn defence into attack. It is the classical religious heritage as a whole that must be discredited. (Though there are precedents for such a historical apologetic, the new historical situation enables a wider scope and a bolder thesis.)

Though his target is wide, I suggest that Augustine pursues a particular line of attack. Pagan religion is rhetorically deficient. It says nothing worthwhile and plenty that's not. First it is charged with lacking moral purpose; with failing to 'speak out' on moral issues, as a modern pundit might say. He anticipates the rejoinder that pagan religion is morally neutral, allowing for individual choice.

> Nevertheless, it was the responsibility of the gods, as counsellors, not to conceal the instructions for a good life from the people who worshipped them. They should have presented and proclaimed them plainly; they should have confronted and convicted sinners by their prophets, threatening punishments to evildoers and promising rewards to those of upright life. Yet the temples of these gods never rang with any such clearly and emphatically uttered exhortations (2.4, p.51).

---

[28] A. D. R. Polman, *The Word of God According to Augustine*, W. B. Eerdmans, New York, 1961, p.32.

[29] Augustine, *Concerning the City of God against the Pagans*, trans. by H. Bettenson, intro. by J. O'Meara, Penguin, Middlesex, 1984. (Also: *De Civitate Dei*, ed. J. E. C. Welldon, SPCK, London, 1924.)

[30] Again, language seems to inherit the power of ritual. Fenn argues that this dynamic arises from a loss of belief in the power of baptism to inoculate believers from the world: 'The task of division and exhortation had devolved upon language alone' (Fenn, R., in Capps and Dittes, 1990, p.320).

Authoritative moral utterance is the job-description of supernatural power; its neglect is the greatest imaginable deficiency in divinity.[31] Instead of 'speaking out', the gods are involved in the promotion of immorality: primarily through their dramatic and poetic representation. Whether or not such is accurate, the gods clearly allow themselves to be represented as lustful, vengeful and so on. The result is to encourage 'the most depraved desires in human hearts by giving them a kind of divine authority' (2.14, p.64).

> Would that they had merely refrained from counselling chastity and restraint, without demanding from the people acts of depravity and shame, by means of which to establish a pernicious authority through a false claim to divine power! I challenge them then to read our Scriptures, and to find...those uniquely impressive warnings against greed and indulgence, given...in a tone resembling not the chatter of philosophical debates, but the thunder of oracles from the cloud of God (2.19, p.70).

Here is the supreme difference, that recurs throughout his thesis. Christianity associates divinity with *authoritative moral speech*, uniquely present in scripture. Paganism leaves moral discourse to the philosophers, which is like putting children in charge of government: absurdly irresponsible. Its gods are either morally dumb or tacitly promoting immorality.

A modern reader might be surprised that Augustine seems to credit the pagan gods with reality. Why not just deny their existence and put the blame on human sin? Because he wants to mythologise sin; he wants the reader to associate pagan divinity with demonic agency. Behind these false myths lie real forces vanquished in Christ. If the god-myths are just nonsense, then philosophical scepticism becomes warranted, and the reality of Christian divinity becomes open to question. He thus returns again and again to the theme of Christ's victory over the pagan-demonic. This is also represented as a purge and an exorcism.[32] Part of the exorcism is surely administered on himself. At the end of Book Four, for example, he favourably compares the simplicity of Jewish monotheism with pagan polytheism, and refers to the Exodus story: 'Without the invocation of Neptune the sea divided...'(4.34, p.177). Surely there remains part of him that recalls thrilling to epic narrative, and lamenting the aesthetic deficiency of the Bible. Elsewhere he discusses Janus, the two-faced door-god. As so often, he seems both fascinated and appalled by the sheer complexity of the pagan mythological structure. He curtly remembers himself with a clever contrast: 'And yet no soul can escape from futility by any of those numerous doors except the soul that has heard the Truth saying, "I am the door"'(7.8, p.265). Christianity stands out in its capacity for effective, authoritative speech. It declares its own difference. As in prophetic mockery of idolatry, the many gods are discredited by their *dumbness* (the slang word usefully suggests both silence and stupidity).

Augustine is explicitly concerned with historiographical rhetoric. In confronting and deconstructing Roman history, he knows that he is up against the high rhetoric of the historians. 'To help us form our judgement let us refuse to be

---

[31] See also 2.6, p.54.
[32] 2.29, p.87; 10.22, p.402.

fooled by empty bombast, to let the edge of our critical faculties be blunted by high-sounding words like "peoples", "realms", "provinces"'(4.3, p.138). The conventional view of the Roman past must be divested of its rhetorical pathos, exposed as the ideology of large-scale armed robbery (4.4, p.139). His historical approach is a sort of demonological materialism. 'Nobility' and 'civility' are ideological covers for lust, greed and violence (Marx would so far agree); and underlying these drives are demons. These demons continue to inspire their historian apologists; just as the Spirit inspires the Christian historian, his opponents are 'possessed by a raging madness of blasphemy' (6, Preface, p.225).

True religion is both liberating and enlightening. It frees us from demonic possession and enables us to know the truth about past delusion. True religion entails 'the power to prove that the gods of the nations are unclean demons' (7.33, p.294); the Christian 'must not let himself be frightened by the superstitions with which [the demons] are worshipped; let him acknowledge the true religion, by which the demons are unmasked and overcome'(7.35, p.297). Here is a theological rhetoric of freedom, confidence and enlightenment reminiscent of Kant's *Sapere Aude* and Barth's entire theology.[33] And, for Augustine as for Barth, the style is essential to the argument. To be persuasive, this discourse must be a performance of these virtues, of which confidence is not the least.[34] (We shall return to confidence as a rhetorical strategy in relation to Luther and Barth.) Furthermore this style must convey its theoretical basis: the authority of God's Word. The reader must feel that she is in the presence of the actual routing of the demons and their deceiving apologists. The force of Augustine's argument participates in the historically active Word.

In Part Two he establishes that the City of God is founded on the authority of scripture (11.1, p.429), which is in turn instituted by Christ (11.3, p.431). Philosophy, by contrast, has no overriding author. Though Athens bred all sorts of brilliant ideas, these contradicted each other, and no sort of authority emerged 'to adjudicate among all those diverse views, and to have some of them approved and accepted, others rejected and repudiated'(18.41, p.818). Philosophy tends towards relativism and confusion. Because of the co-existence of true and false ideas, 'there is every reason for giving that city the symbolic name of Babylon. For "Babylon" means "confusion"'(ibid.). In contrast, the Jews received 'the utterances of God' (ibid.). The Bible is distinguished by the unity of its authority. Even the translation of the Hebrew scriptures into Greek, the Septuagint, is overseen by 'the very same Spirit that was in the prophets when they uttered their messages'(18.43, p.821).

The unitive authority behind faith provides it with *certainty*, in contrast to philosophical doubt, the chief characteristic of the New Academy: 'The City of God roundly condemns such doubt as being madness'(19.18, p.879). Certainty is associated with sanity and health. And there is an *aesthetic* element to this

---

[33] '[I]t is no accident that Barth's two greatest forerunners as theologians of freedom are Augustine and Luther... . 'Yes' was the overwhelming content of their gospel...' (Gorringe, 1999, p.279).

[34] He explains that biblical miracles were not achieved by magic spells but 'by simple faith and devout confidence' (10.9, p.383).

preference: instead of sterile doubt and tedious pedantry we are offered the drama of divine utterance. He thus dispenses with Porphyry's lengthy defence of polytheism, showing how simply the issue is settled: '[God] forbids this in a voice of thunder in his Law, which he gave to his Hebrew people, when he said, in words heavy with menace, "Anyone who sacrifices to other gods will be extirpated"' (19.23, p.888). Instead of 'rational' analysis of polytheism as an anthropological issue, we have an actual event of strong speech, in this case a divine threat. Augustine's reference to the divine judgement should be understood in a strong sense – as its repetition. This dramatic opposition between philosophical musing and divine utterance is his repeated tactic. He uses it repeatedly against philosophers, throwing scripture at their doubt.[35] Their arguments are *referred* to God, who has already refuted or dismissed them, or does so in an eternal sense: this triumph is re-performed in his own discourse.

The tone of 'mere assertion' becomes more marked towards the end of the book, as if Augustine has worked up his proclamatory confidence to such an extent that he is now tempted to overdo it. It emerges in his exegetical method, whereby all of the Old Testament patently signifies Christ. A hint of triumphalist intimidation surfaces elsewhere towards the conclusion. To expect miracles, for instance, is declared mere folly: 'Anyone who still looks for portents, to make him believe, is himself the greatest portent, in refusing to believe when all the world believes' (22.8, p.1033). *All* the world? Even if this were so, would it be grounds for believing? (To Kierkegaard, the seeming belief of everyone is the biggest barrier to faith.) In a similar vein, he states his opinion that no one who hears scriptural truths 'can fail to yield his assent to them', even if, 'with an obstinacy closely akin to madness [he denies this]' (20.1, p.895). He thus casts doubt on the sincerity of his opponents; religious error can never be in good faith. To modern ears, this is an offensive and rather desperate theological tactic, but it should be seen in the context of his overall strategy: to construct a rhetoric of confidence in divine authority. This entails heavy recourse to the classical rhetorical trope of hyperbole.

Before leaving Augustine we must take note of his thoughts on rhetoric in *On Christian Doctrine*. In Book Four he deals explicitly with rhetoric, at once distancing himself from what he learned in the pagan schools. Despite its negative connotations, rhetoric cannot be ignored: 'Since rhetoric is used to give conviction to both truth and falsehood, who could dare maintain that truth, which depends on us for its defence, should stand unarmed in the fight against falsehood?'[36] Arming the truth rhetorically is thus a basic concern of theology. If faith abandoned rhetoric, error alone would be attractive and 'we would expound the truth so as to bore our listeners, cloud their understanding and stifle their desire to believe'.[37] It cannot be left to the opposition alone to 'issue passionate exhortations'.[38] Rhetorical skill must be 'acquired by good and zealous Christians to fight for the

---

[35] *CG* 19.4, p.852; 22.4, p.1026.

[36] Augustine, *De Doctrina Christiana*, ed. and trans. by R. P. H. Green, Clarendon, Oxford 1995, IV.p.197.

[37] Ibid.

[38] Ibid., p.199.

truth';[39] it is indispensable to 'the defender of true faith and vanquisher of error'.[40] The Christian teacher must be able to convey religious passion, in the form of 'entreaties, rebukes, rousing speeches, solemn admonitions, and all the other things which have the power to excite human emotions'.[41]

Yet Christian passionate speech must not be assimilated into the classical framework of oratorical technique. The Christian teacher must learn from scripture a special sort of eloquence. 'There is a kind of eloquence appropriate to writers who enjoy the highest authority and a full measure of divine inspiration.... . [T]he humbler [the style] seems, the more thoroughly it transcends that of others not in grandiloquence but in substance'.[42] The role of this 'special' plain style is illustrated in relation to Paul and then the prophets. In Amos he notes 'the invective, crashing with an explosive roar upon sleepy senses to awaken them'.[43] He soon turns to Jeremiah: 'What eloquence – all the more terrifying for its directness, and all the more compelling for its steadfastness! It is indeed the "axe which shatters rocks"'.[44]

Despite its use of the plain style, Christian speech belongs to the 'grand style' in that it seeks to move and to change minds. Yet it is a distinctive instance of this, for it must convey the intrinsic, supra-rhetorical authority of its subject matter. A sort of paradox emerges. An authority (e.g. an emperor) does not need rhetoric, for he commands rather than persuades. Christian speech must signify, rhetorically, an authority which is above reliance on human rhetoric. Augustine does not quite address this contradiction, but he makes it clear that Christian rhetoric does not quite 'fit'. The classical division of styles is according to subject matter. But the Church's preaching is always concerned with eternal life, even when it focuses on minute particulars. In support of this he notes that Jesus gets suddenly passionate over small matters; 'he show[s] his inner feelings with such frequent and violent changes in his voice'.[45] Again, part of Christianity's distinctiveness lies in its seemingly excessive recourse to rhetorical violence. Much of Augustine's purpose in this work is to confront this issue, and to apply rigorous critical thinking to it. Earlier in the work he reflects on the power of metaphor; on the fact that 'somehow it gives me more pleasure to contemplate holy men, when I see them as the teeth of the church, tearing men away from their errors and transferring them to its body, breaking down their rawness by biting and chewing'.[46] For Augustine the performance of the Christian rhetoric of authority, even at its most violent, does not preclude the possibility of its critical analysis. Similarly, belief that Christian speech is governed by the Holy Spirit does not detract from the need to study it, learn it. He cites the promise in Matthew 10:19 that the Spirit will speak in those who face martyrdom, and asks: 'why should he

---

[39] Ibid.
[40] Ibid., p.201.
[41] Ibid., p.203.
[42] Ibid., p.207.
[43] Ibid., p.217.
[44] Ibid., p.233.
[45] Ibid., p.243.
[46] Ibid., p.63.

not also speak in those who deliver Christ to their pupils?'.[47] Christian teaching-speech is a function of Christian proclamation, whose true agent is the Word. The problem is that Augustine is engaged in *teaching* Christian teaching-speech. This could seem rather cynical; to teach the rhetorical style which gives the impression of God speaking. What it signifies is an increasing self-consciousness in Christian rhetoric. A certain sort of artifice, or technique is required. Christian speech is a matter of human effort and ingenuity *participating in* God's Word, in the form of its literary tradition. We have to learn to speak in such a way as to mediate the authority of prophet and apostle, which entails imitation of them. And the Spirit must be understood to be also present in this process of literary influence.

More could be said of Augustine's theology in relation to our theme, of course, but we must press on to its Reformation rediscovery. To summarise Augustine's anticipation of Protestant concerns: he identifies Christian truth with the authority of the Word of God, known in its *agon* with other voices, and his theological discourse participates in this rhetorical victory. This entails an association of divine power with language, to an extent that is unprecedented.[48] This rhetorical mediation of revelation is theology's alternative basis to philosophy, and the heresies it spawns, particularly Pelagianism of course. His assertion of the Fall against the Pelagians entails a theology based in its rhetorical performance of divine authority – we shall see this in more detail in relation to Luther. Also, I suggest, Augustine sows the seeds of rhetorical self-criticism; partly in that he develops the dialogical resources of the tradition, incorporating classical psychomachy into biblical midrash, and partly in his close analysis of the practice of Christian speech. In Luther, Kierkegaard and especially in Barth we will see the development and the critical refinement of these themes.

Perhaps these factors do little to mitigate the evidence of his authoritarianism, his notorious conflation of ecclesial with worldly power. Yet it can at least be shown that Augustine is conscious of the need to distinguish the power of the Word from that of its human mediators. 'If threats are made', he said, 'let them be made from the Scriptures, threatening future retribution, that it should not be ourselves who are feared in our personal power, but God himself in our words'.[49]

---

[47] Ibid., p.237.
[48] '[A]s with the later Reformation, the Augustinian reform begins in an attempt to invest language with the powers formally [*sic.* ?] ascribed to ritual itself' (Richard Fenn, in Capps and Dittes, 1990, p.318).
[49] Augustine, Epistle 22.5, in Lane Fox, 1986, p.544.

PART TWO: PROTESTANTISM

The Reformation is a revolution in how divine authority is signified. Before, it is signified through the authority of the Church, primarily through the rite of the Mass. After, it is signified through scripture – or more precisely through a certain reading of scripture, and through scripturally inspired Christian proclamation, and the church is re-conceived as the servant of such signification (sacramentalism is similarly reconceived). The verbal-rhetorical becomes the explicit locus of religious authority. Protestantism thus raises the stakes of authoritative rhetoric, of discourse as divinely significant. This theological investment of rhetoric affects and infects modernity in a way that cannot be overstated. Authority in its highest (religious, salvific) sense becomes attached to the verbal-rhetorical as never before.

But this development brings acute theological problems. Most centrally: how is this proclaimed Word to be distinguished from the human rhetoric that proclaims it, from any ideological use made of it? On one level the solution is simply Christological. In that it exists to refer to Christic practice, this rhetorical idiom contains an inner mechanism of its own judgement and limitation. This rhetorical idiom is rooted in a narrative of the rejection of violence. But in practice the issue is rather less simple. How can this discourse maintain any degree of authenticity, when its basis contradicts human nature so radically? For its Christic basis would seem to prevent its possibility as a human discourse, to indict it of betrayal at every step. For no human rhetoric of authority is entirely free of hubris, even of violence. Protestantism's solution is to develop a *dialectical* rhetoric of authority, a discourse which foregrounds the gulf between divine and human possibility. It must perform its awareness that divine authority eludes human expression; it must stage a conflict between God's grace and the finitude of its own rhetorical endeavour. In what follows I shall show how Protestant thought contains a self-critical dynamic within its own rhetoric of authority, a capacity for remembering that, despite its subject-matter, it remains a (very unusual) form of human rhetoric, 'on this side' of the eschatological divide.

Further problems relate to the story of Protestantism's relationship with modern secular thought. For here the Protestant investment in rhetorical authority becomes intensely dangerous. It begins to lose its reference to Christ, which is what legitimates and judges it. In Christian terms, therefore, it loses its authority, it becomes a parody of prophetic speech. It becomes appropriated by secular thought, which has acquired a distinct taste for it. Protestantism has created a monster, now beyond its control. (It is monstrous in the literal sense: its strangeness and danger is a negative manifestation of the divine.) Both fascism and communism are based in parodies of prophetic rhetoric. I will briefly discuss Romantic thought's implication in this process.

Alongside this process of secular abstraction from Christian particularity, Protestant theology commits its own fault. It shies away from its own peculiar idiom of authority, based in the rhetoric of divine sovereignty and human limitation. It prefers to give an account of authority in terms of reason, humanism, Enlightenment. The Christian rhetorical heritage of strictly biblical reference is largely ceded to charismatic and lunatic fringes within the church. Within theology there is some resistance, of course. A counter-tradition attempts to reclaim the rhetorical inheritance. Kierkegaard and Barth are two of the major figures. I want to show how they remind Protestant theology of its rhetorical calling, and in the process develop the dialectical depth of the idiom.

This brief sketch might be charged with evading the political complicity of the Reformation. Is it not guilty from the first of lending pseudo-religious authority to power-politics? Is its emergence not implicated in the aggrandisement of the early modern state? Frankly yes. It can only emerge, and separate from Rome, by immediately compromising itself, by offering a new sort of authority to Protestant princes in exchange for their protection. This is the tragedy which ails it for centuries, which is even at the root of its present weakness in the West. If Protestantism is politically tainted from the start, is it not then entirely regrettable? No, because it enables Christianity's critical development, its gradual separation from political interest.

The Church exists to communicate divine authority in Jesus Christ. It fails while it is implicated in political authority; while its rhetoric of authority is allowed any political reference. (Of course it will speak about politics, yet its speech must not serve any political power.) The medieval church, in various ways and over centuries, had become entwined with political power; it could only ever achieve semi-detachment. After the Reformation, the Protestant church seems to be merely the mirror image of this. Its involvement in the power of the state seems if anything worse. But now a crucial inner shift has occurred; a nonpolitical rhetoric of Christian authority has become at least a theoretical possibility. The Reformation establishes the theological legitimacy of opposing prophetic rhetoric to both political and ecclesiastical power. Because of its prophetic basis (which means its desire to see authority only in the rhetoric of 'God'), Protestantism cannot be contained, or comfortably harnessed to political power. Its inner logic is to *dissent* from any confusion between divine and worldly authority – thus the endless splintering-off of new and 'purer' Protestant churches. This process of dissent is ambiguous and complex. Yet within this process unfolds the genuine logic of Protestantism: the (arduous, fraught) demand for a rhetoric of authority with *pure* reference to God.

In this Part I am charting certain moments within this account of religious modernity. I devote much attention to the dangerous influence of Protestant rhetoric on modern secular thought, and more particularly to the strange relationship between Protestant rhetoric and modern literature. I am hereby constructing a sort of negative apologetic. Perhaps the best argument for a rhetorical theology of the Word is to discredit the competition. It can show that all other rhetorics of authority fail to signify any alternative good, it can deconstruct and discredit them, showing how instead they tend towards the promotion of authoritarian violence. An important part of my argument is that Christianity emerges from modernity as the only kosher rhetoric of authority, the sole nonviolent idiom of strong speech, the uniquely peaceful account of Truth.

It emerges that I am arguing on two fronts at once. Firstly I want to defend the Protestant rhetoric of authority from charges that it is intrinsically authoritarian (an exercise begun in Chapter Two). I do so by arguing for its self-critical capacity, which begins in Luther's dialogism and culminates in Barth's dialectical theology. Also I want to turn defence into attack, by showing that the truly dangerous modern forms of authoritative rhetoric emerge from the secularisation of Protestant rhetoric and not from the thing itself. The thing itself contains a powerful cautionary principle: it exists to advertise the nonviolent practice of Christ.

Chapter 4

'Non vi sed verbo': Luther and the Rhetorical Militancy of Faith

'Melanchthon is a better logician than me, he argues better.
My superiority lies rather in the rhetorical sphere.' (Luther, *Table Talk*, p.24)

It is Luther who most obviously places 'authoritative rhetoric' on the agenda of Protestant theology. Through Luther a forceful mode of speech, a forthright and militant style, becomes fundamental to Protestant discourse. In opposition to the conventions of civilised discourse, it has at its heart a violent directness which derives from the need to convey the power of the Word in its very concrete battle against the devil. Also, in contrast to the dominant humanist ideal, it is a literary style which returns to the oral origins of all discourse: it seeks to communicate the speaking voice of preaching and prayer.[1] Ultimately, indeed, it seeks to communicate the speaking voice of the Word of God. To 'communicate' in this context means to reconstruct, to revitalise the 'voice' of the biblical text. The Protestant presupposition is that the Word speaks to us with authority, and the communication of this voice of authority is the new criterion of theology. This presupposition seems to be influenced by the humanist revival of rhetoric.

Prior to the Reformation, humanism engenders a new familiarity with all human authors: even the greatest of the classics and the most esteemed of the Fathers are, for Erasmus, subject to criticism; we who write now are on a level with them. To some extent this even applies to the Bible; it begins to be seen as a human, historical document, and secular humanism will in turn deny the biblical authors privileged status over other ancients. Luther learns from humanism the confidence with which to interpret the Bible anew, and thus to refute patristic 'authority' where he deems it erroneous. Yet in Luther this new textual confidence extends to the Bible in a new way, unknown to Erasmus: it takes the form of imitation. In faith we are entitled, indeed we are obliged, to imitate the rhetoric of prophet, psalmist and apostle. Though the Bible is directly inspired in a way which our speech is not, its speech-forms are not alien to us, like exhibits behind glass in a museum. Instead the biblical speech-forms must live on in our own speech; their repetition is the basis of Christian faith. It is biblical rhetoric, rather than the philosophical rhetoric of the schoolmen, that is prototypical for Protestant discourse. Theology must be bold enough to speak of God as the Bible does; even to take on the authoritative tone of biblical proclamation. The Reformation does

---

[1] See R. W. Scribner, 'Oral Culture and the Transmission of Reformation Ideas', in Robinson-Hammerstein ed., 1989, p.84; Sparn, R., 'Preaching and the Course of the Reformation', in ibid., pp.177-78.

not passively accept the authority of scripture as a given: its authority must be known through its reperformance. In this chapter I am for the most part exploring this dynamic in relation to two of Luther's most central texts: *The Bondage of the Will* and the *Galatians* commentary.

Yet, as will soon emerge, there is another dynamic built into this one of proclamatory triumphalism. The claim to hear and speak God's Word is full of dangers – as Luther was only too aware in his battles with the radicals. The Reformation discovery of the power of the Word is not sustainable without a critical, regulative principle at its heart. I shall suggest that this emerges in Luther's *dialogical* conception of faith.

Beginnings

Though a general introduction to the Reformation is unwanted, the scene must briefly be set from the perspective of my theme.

Partly due to the efforts of Augustine, the Christian rhetoric of authority has long lived within the walls of the Roman Church; protected, caged. It is assimilated into a complex matrix of sign and symbol, image and ritual, devotional practice and doctrine, Church and state. Protestantism is the shattering of this matrix. From the beginning it has the character of an almighty and violent risk. The essential task of Protestant theology is to justify this risk, which of course entails its perpetuation.

For centuries before Luther there are bursts of opposition to Rome. Such opposition takes the form of an attempted redefinition of religious authority by means of the construction of an alternative rhetoric of authority. The Bible is obviously the source for such attempts; it is the Trojan horse doomed to undo Roman hegemony. Its major pre-Reformation medium is monasticism, which had always entailed a protest against a powerful Church. For here Christ's poverty and nonviolence were remembered. And monasteries were centres of learning: it is little surprise that the Reformation was sparked by a monk. The Church had kept the orders under close control since the protest of the Fransiscans in the fourteenth century. In its power to assimilate potential opposition the Church seemed unassailable. Also of course in its longstanding deal with temporal power, which rendered religious radicalism a political threat also. Princes were easily reminded that it was in their interest to defend the Roman faith. The relationship of *regnum* and *sacerdotium* was hardly a honeymoon, but Christian princes were loath to exchange the devil they knew for another. In the late fourteenth century in England Wycliffe preached an early form of Protestantism, attacking the Mass, asserting the priesthood of all believers. His movement was associated with the Peasants' Revolt of 1381 and was suppressed with it. Hus soon followed his lead in Bohemia, and was burned as a heretic: recently enough to give Luther pause for thought. The failure of these movements was rooted in their relationship to politics. As soon as they were identified with the cause of the rebellious poor they were crushed with ease by the powers that were.

Shortly before the rise of Luther some important new factors had emerged. Foremost among them is humanism, the rediscovery of classical learning. Erasmus, the international champion of this movement, typified its relation to religion. The Church was called to modernise itself according to the dictates of reason, humanity and the true gospel, which was newly accessible through the biblical texts. All of which dictates were held to be in perfect accord, essentially one. The 'philosophy of Christ' was borne out by classical wisdom and by Common Sense (the latter was a powerful new idea, or rhetorical strategy). Religious innovation took other, related forms. With the help of printing, an emerging class of pious literates effected a shift away from the strictly ecclesiastical locus of faith – most notably the Dutch-based *Devotio Moderna* movement. The new piety had roots in mystical writing, which had surfaced for centuries, with its implicit devaluation of ecclesiastical business.

In Germany, humanism had strong links with an emergent nationalism. The informed anticlericalism of Hutten and others soon helped to empower Luther's stand. But German humanism was not in itself capable of effecting change. Like all humanism it was a minority phenomenon, lacking demagogic power. Its chief concern was political order, the health of the body politic (one of its favourite images). Enlightenment should serve this end rather than involve itself in the stirring up of vulgar passions. There were other factors. Popular political radicalism lurked in the wings, soon to earn Luther's disgusted rebuke. Chiliastic belief in the imminence of the New Age of the Spirit had been on the rise for centuries, ever since Joachim of Fiore's prophetic exegesis. Such belief informs not only the utopian radicals but Luther's own conviction that the Last Days had begun.[2]

Before our close reading of Luther's rhetorical practice, his theological beginnings must be briefly recounted. His rise is startlingly sudden. He becomes known through a minor public controversy, what seems a local storm bound to blow over like the rest. But suddenly the stakes are very high. It is hard to resist romantic-sounding stuff about the power of his voice, his stubborn vision.[3] He has been a zealous Augustinian monk since 1505; and becomes a biblical scholar, a practitioner of post-Erasmian exegesis. He becomes sharply dissatisfied with scholastic theology, the legacy of Aquinas; he is particularly upset about the ubiquitous study of Aristotle. This dissatisfaction is largely rooted in nominalism, a critical movement with hints of empiricism, and even deconstruction. He might be called a radical nominalist, or perhaps a post-nominalist. Suspicious of all intellectual authorities, he exalts scripture as a surer sort of authority altogether. His breakthrough (whether gradual or sudden) involved a new and positive understanding of 'the righteousness of God', which is the power of his grace, as opposed to his mere power to terrify. In 1517 comes the public controversy, the Ninety-Five Theses. He objects to the Church's method of fund-raising. The selling of indulgences was rather like the National Lottery: a voluntary tax as

---

[2] Luther was particularly influenced by Bernard of Clairvaux's warning that the Church would be taken over by Antichrist (see Oberman, 1989, p.68).

[3] Yet it is 'the task of the historian to oppose stubbornly and with all his might the poet's adoration of Luther as a genius' (ibid., p.82).

effective as it was ideologically dubious.[4] Though some of Luther's objections reflected popular anticlerical feeling, his motive was strictly theological, or rather pastoral. The selling of indulgences gave the common people a skewed idea of what Christianity was about. It directly obscured his new theological obsession: God's free grace as the basis of faith. To Luther's surprise the theses, intended only to provoke a local discussion, became widely disseminated. Soon the pope sent for him. The Elector Frederick, his local ruler, scented a popular cause and managed to get him a hearing in Germany instead. The first round happened at Leipzig in 1519, and a fuller bout at the Imperial Diet at Worms in 1521. Between the two, in 1520, he wrote his first wave of polemic treatises.[5] It would hardly have surprised any reader of these that he did not back down.

Most importantly, he attacked the entire sacramental system in *The Babylonian Captivity of the Church*. It had to be radically downsized, reinvented according to the true source of religious authority: the Word of God, rooted in scripture. And so the positive theme of Luther's writing emerges: proclamation of the Word. Christianity is declared to be a proclamatory religion. The supernatural power of its rhetoric is what grounds it and so justifies the existence of the Church: 'The function of the priest is to preach; if he does not preach, he is no more a priest than the picture of a man is a man'.[6] And this alone is the locus of the supernatural. Consequently, the Mass is a supernatural event only by virtue of its reperformance of Christ's *words*: 'This is my body/blood'. 'Though philosophy cannot grasp it, yet faith can. The authority of the word of God goes beyond the capacity of our mind'.[7] Salvation is not attained by any human means but by the promises of God; 'All things depend on His authoritative word, and are upheld and maintained by it'.[8] Unless it can be shown to serve the authority of the Word, ecclesiastical power is an illegitimate and even demonic form of human power. In contrast, as we shall see, Luther's own writing claims to participate in the authority of the Word.

As already hinted in my general introduction to Protestantism, grave dangers lurk. This new rhetoric of authority which claims to serve the Word of God is immediately implicated in human power structures. Luther implicitly offers it up as a political resource. His *Appeal to the Ruling Class* (1520) calls for political leaders to deliver their people from Roman bondage by any means necessary, thus offering them a new image of religious heroism. Yet herein lies his novelty and his success. He is determined to remain on the right side (or the right wing) of temporal power; and so to avoid the political pitfall of previous religious radicalism. Instead he offers the princes a better deal than they had under the old religious order; he offers them a new model of power and helps them into the driving seat. When in 1525 he denounced the Peasants' Revolt he taught them the

---

[4] See Hobson, T. W., 'Another Dome, Another Scam: Martin Luther and the National Lottery', *Modern Believing*, Sheffield, April 2001, pp.35-39.
[5] On the polemic genre see Matheson, P., *The Rhetoric of the Reformation*, T & T Clark, Edinburgh, 1998, *passim*.
[6] Luther, 'Pagan Servitude of the Church' vi, in Dillenberger ed., *Martin Luther, Selections from his Writings*, Doubleday, New York, 1961, p.348.
[7] Ibid., p.270.
[8] Ibid., p.274.

political use of theological polemic. The lesson is later repeated in relation to the radicals, then the Jews.

This brief account of his early career may be concluded with his marriage, in 1525, to Katherine, an ex-nun. He did this, he said, 'in defiance of [the devil]'.[9] With Luther, everything is a statement, a parable of the fierce affirmation.

The Bondage of the Will: **Faith as Assertion**

The Bondage of the Will (1525) is one of the key texts of the Lutheran Reformation.[10] Along with his *Little Catechism*, Luther himself considered it the best of his works.[11] And it is the text in which Luther's rhetorical reinvention of theological discourse is most clearly effected. The overt theological issue is very simple, capable of being covered in a few pages rather than a few hundred: the human will is not free but entirely dependent on the sovereign grace of God. The corresponding doctrines of the Fall and of God's sovereignty are restated at tireless length. Erasmus' diatribe against Luther of the previous year is accused of ignoring these doctrines, or of only paying them lip-service. Yet I suggest that the wider theological issue at stake (to which the doctrinal issue remains central) concerns the nature of theological discourse. The book is very largely a polemic against the stylistic inadequacy of Erasmian theology, whose conformity to humanist discourse disqualifies it as Christian theology. Its rhetorical allegiance is with Cicero rather than Christ, and such a *stylistic* failure is the greatest possible *theological* failure also. (In spite of his present 'tactic', Luther was not entirely averse to classical study: 'Without knowledge of the humanistic sciences, pure theology can by no means exist... . Through the study of poets and rhetoric people are wonderfully equipped for grasping the sacred truths and handling them successfully'.)[12]

The relationship between the two men began more positively. As we have noted, Luther was indebted to Erasmus' textual groundwork. And Erasmus was at first an admirer of the young monk; he dedicated his 1520 work *Axiomata* to him. Yet it soon seemed that the unity of the Church needed defending against this force he had helped to unleash. In 1524 he complied with the Church's request to write an attack on Luther, *The Freedom of the Will*, and Luther never forgave him for his betrayal of the cause.

Luther begins with an admission of rhetorical inferiority, which is itself a rhetorical device, of course. Yet he declares himself unafraid: 'For "though I am rude in speech, yet" – by the grace of God – "I am not rude in understanding"(cf. 2 Cor. 11:6); with Paul, I dare to claim that I have understanding, and that you have not – though I freely grant, as I must, that you have eloquence and that I have

---

[9] Luther, *WABr* 3.482, pp.81-83; 4 (5?) May 1525, in Oberman, 1989, p.278.
[10] Luther, *The Bondage of the Will*, trans. by J. I. Packer and O. R. Johnston, James Clarke, London, 1957. Page references will appear in the text.
[11] Luther, Letter to Capito, July 9th, 1537, in Packer and Johnston, *Introduction to* The Bondage of the Will, p.40.
[12] Luther, Letter to Eobanus Hesse, 29 March 1532, in Luther, *Letters II*, p.34.

not'(63). The famous eloquence and learning of Erasmus is thus used against him: in the particular arena of Christian discourse, such is irrelevant, even a hindrance. The citation of Paul establishes the true rules of Christian discourse – one of which is that true understanding transcends learning and eloquence. (The act of appealing to Paul's authority is itself a demonstration of the particular logic of Christian discourse, of course.) It is strictly by these rules that Luther will engage with Erasmus: the neutral terms of humanist discourse are explicitly renounced from the first.

The following chapter, 'Review of Erasmus' Preface', begins with a sub-section entitled 'Of the necessity of assertions in Christianity'. This is the most important part of the book for my purposes: it is explicitly concerned with the positive rhetorical basis of theology. In his own Preface Erasmus had professed a distaste for assertions and a preference for the Sceptics' position wherever the authority of Scripture and the Church permits it. As Boyle explains in her study of the dispute, Erasmus' entire discourse consciously evokes the conciliatory spirit of sceptical inquiry in opposition to the emergent dogmatism and violence of theological disagreement. In contrast to the modern sense of the term, a *diatribe* is a classical form of disputation of a gently pedagogical nature, associated with Epictetus. In his use of this genre, 'Erasmus revived the posture of modified Skepticism', thus rejecting the dogmatism of Stoicism.[13] In defiance of his ecclesiastical brief, he abjures epideictic rhetoric, which praises or blames, in favour of deliberative, which attempts to weigh an issue fairly. In so doing he is attempting to alter the climate of theological dispute so as to reconcile Luther with the Church. Luther, of course, refuses to accept this intellectual style.

> To take no pleasure in assertions is not the mark of a Christian heart; indeed, one must delight in assertions to be a Christian at all. (Now, lest we be misled by words, let me say here that by 'assertion' I mean staunchly holding your ground, stating your position, confessing it, defending it and persevering in it unvanquished.... And I am talking about the assertion of what has been delivered to us from above in the Sacred Scriptures. Outside that field, we do not need Erasmus or any other teacher to tell us that over matters which are doubtful, or unprofitable and unnecessary, assertions and contentions are not merely stupid, but positively impious; Paul condemns them often enough!... .)
>
> Away, now, with Sceptics and Academics from the company of us Christians; let us have men who will assert, men twice as inflexible as very Stoics! Take the Apostle Paul – how often does he call for that 'full assurance' which is, simply, an assertion of conscience, of the highest degree of certainty and conviction...And what need is there of a multitude of proofs? Nothing is more familiar or characteristic among Christians than assertion. Take away assertions, and you take away Christianity. Why, the Holy Spirit is given to Christians from heaven in order that He may glorify Christ and in them confess Him even unto death – and is this not assertion, to die for what you confess and assert? Again, the Spirit asserts to such purpose that He breaks in upon the whole world and convinces it of sin (cf. John 16.8), as if challenging it to battle (66-67).

---

[13] M. O. Boyle, *Rhetoric and Reform: Erasmus' Civil Dispute with Luther*, Harvard University Press, Mass., 1983, p.17.

'Assertion' is a violent mode of speech, though it here seems more defensive than aggressive. A 'position' is occupied in both argument and battle: Christians must occupy a fixed position as if their lives depended on it – indeed, in martyrdom, they value this position above their lives. Luther is careful not to defend 'assertion' as a general principle. Faith is a special case, in which what is objectively uncertain must be spoken of with militant certainty. This rhetorical mode is not merely a matter of 'style' in any peripheral sense of the term: it is in this rhetorical 'style', Luther explicitly states, that Christian faith most essentially consists. In Luther's discourse 'the assertive rather than the persuasive denotation of *logos* is established as the root of theology'.[14] His assertiveness 'counters the persuasion which classically defines rhetoric... It is rhetoric against rhetoric'.[15] Furthermore, this Christian 'style' is the locus of inspiration, of participation in the Spirit, who 'glorif[ies] Christ' through us. Luther thus makes pneumatological claims for his own rhetoric. He concludes this section by declaring: 'The Holy Spirit is no Sceptic, and the things He has written in our hearts are not doubts or opinions, but assertions – surer and more certain than sense and life itself'(70). Despite the seriousness, it is worth noting that there is in this passage an element of performance, even of theatricality. The exclamation beginning 'Away, now, with Sceptics' is a rallying cry, a piece of epic imposture. He is defiantly showing off; demonstrating his greater rhetorical *freedom*.

For admitting his sympathies with scepticism, Erasmus is chided for his *'undogmatic temper'*(67): the deprecation of assertions implies the dial of 'all religion and piety in one breath'. He is a mere theologaster, whose true allegiance is with sceptical philosophers: 'You ooze Lucian from every pore; you swill Epicurus by the gallon' (74) – significantly, these images suggest possession, intoxication; anti-inspiration. This results in a boring, bloodless theology: 'This is why rhetoricians require passion in one who pleads a case. Much more does theology require passion, to make a man vigorous, and keen, and earnest, and prudent, and energetic!' (146). Theology ought to *outdo* all other rhetoric; to demonstrate in public its greater passionate seriousness. For Luther as for Augustine, passion must coexist with intellectual rigour: in contrast to his opponent, he says, his task 'is to *assert*, with precision, consistency and warmth, and give solid, skilful, substantial proof for my teaching'(219).

Erasmus' Preface is accused of valuing ecclesiastical peace over religious truth. Like the prophets, Luther denounces the emptiness of any 'peace' not founded on God's command. He concedes that his doctrine will lead to worldly strife, and (at first) claims to relish this prospect no more than Erasmus:

> Do you think that because your heart trembles at these upheavals you are the only one who has a heart? I am not made of stone either; I am no child of Marpesian crags. But (since it must be one or the other) I would rather be joyful in God's grace and bear the brunt of this temporal uproar for the sake of the Word of God – which demands to be asserted with invincible and unshakeable zeal – rather that, I say, than to be ground to powder under the wrath of God by the unbearable torments of

---

[14] Ibid., p.88.
[15] Ibid., p.90.

the uproar that shall be everlasting! (90-91).

Religious truth constitutes a greater power, a superior violence to anything in the world. Its *demand to be asserted* is more to be feared than the threat of worldly violence. Because conflict between the Word and the world is inevitable, Christians must learn to rejoice in it: thus does Luther rejoice at the present upheavals, 'knowing for sure that the Pope's kingdom and all its allies will fall; for the Word of God is now in full cry, and these are its principal target'(92). The Word of God is a *war-cry*; a form of violence is of its essence.[16] One of the central insistences of the book is that whoever does not serve this righteous violence is necessarily in the service of the violence of Satan. For God and Satan are at war.

> Christians know that...Christ's kingdom continually resists and wars against that of Satan... . The knowledge and confession of these two kingdoms...would suffice by itself to confute the doctrine of 'free-will', seeing that we are compelled to serve in Satan's kingdom if we are not plucked from it by divine power. The common man, I repeat, knows this, and confesses it plainly enough by his proverbs, prayers, efforts and entire life (312).

This is the 'two kingdoms' doctrine that really underlies Luther's theology: 'Luther cannot be understood unless he is seen located between God and the Devil, who have been involved in a struggle – not a *metaphysical* but a *real* battle – ever since the beginning of the world – a battle which now "in these last days" is reaching a horrible climax'.[17] His final point in the above is that 'primary' Christian speech takes for granted what scholastic discourse obscures: the rhetorical violence entailed in faith. Luther breaks down the barrier between theological discourse and the primary Christian speech of liturgy, prayer and preaching, all of which not only acknowledge but *participate in* the 'power-struggle'. For Luther, faith is literally *inconceivable* without this imagery of power-struggle which he finds in the Bible. Especially towards the end of the book, the doctrinal dispute is explicitly presented as a particular instance of the larger, cosmic conflict. There is no absolute divide between Christ's battle with Satan and Luther's battle with Erasmus' error, for the source of all erroneous thinking is certainly demonic – just as true theological speech directly corresponds to the agency of the Word. Consequently, Erasmus' arguments are weak and doomed; in a mock-epic touch he likens them to a batallion of flies: 'Such are the man-made dreams of the Diatribe as they oppose the armies of the Word of God!' (175).

The divine power against which Erasmus vainly contends is exercised by Luther himself. We are told that the next chapter will deal with the Diatribe's 'attempts to refute my arguments... . Here you will see what the smoke of man can do against the thunder and lightning of God!'(189). It is in the form of scripture

---

[16] Elsewhere, the Gospel takes the form of a victory-cry: 'The Gospel is a good report which one sings and tells with rejoicing, like the report of David overcoming Goliath' (Luther, 'Preface to the New Testament', *Works VI* 439.42, in Kerr, 1966, p.8).

[17] Oberman, 1994, p.57.

that Luther has the arsenal of God at his disposal. John 1.12 is 'a thunderbolt...against "free-will"'(187-88), and his 'Achillean weapon' is 'the statement in John 15: "Without me you can do nothing"'(259). Though its origin is always divine, the locus of this power is constantly shifting between the Spirit as ventriloquist, scripture as arsenal, and Luther himself as warrior-rhetorician.

In his penultimate chapter, Luther cites Romans 3:10-12, which alludes to Psalm 14:2-3: 'no man is righteous...': 'Paul's words...are awful thunderclaps and piercing thunderbolts; they are in truth what Jeremiah calls "the hammer that breaketh the rock in pieces"(23:29)'(282). Though Paul of course follows the prophets and invokes their authority for his own teaching, Luther here reverses, or at least confuses, the sequence. The prophets are used as commentators on the authority of Pauline rhetoric. Through this levelling, or scrambling, of the palimpsest of textual authority, Luther suggests the comparable authority of his *own* discourse, which, like Paul's, invokes the prior authority of scripture. (In Chapter 8 we shall observe the same dynamic at work in Barth's *Romans*.) In Luther's presentation of them, Paul's own words are often depersonalised, the property of anyone who faithfully invokes them. The ultimate agency of the Word abolishes any absolute hierarchical distinction between human authors who testify to it; the power of these words depends upon their distance from any human authorship. They must be presented as ventriloquised through Luther, as through Paul.

Luther's relentless tactic is one of identification with biblical, and thus divine, authority. And the key means by which he creates an impression of affinity with both the scriptural authors and the divine Author himself is through emphasising the particular *rhetorical violence* common to each. We shall now pursue this theme in relation to his *Galatians* commentary.

The *Galatians* Commentary: Faith and Violence

Luther is clear from the first that the discourse of his commentary is implicated in a form of violence. He explains in the Preface that his words are explicitly aimed at Satan, in his role of perverter of true doctrine. The intention of 'this extremely verbose Commentary...[is] to stir up my brethren in Christ against the wiles and malice of Satan' and to announce that 'a dreadful day of destruction' awaits him (17-18).[18] The violence referred to is both that of a human resistance movement and that of an eschatological victory.

Throughout the commentary it repeatedly emerges that it is *Christus Victor* who must be preached against the devil. Such preaching *re-presents* his victory, makes it present again: 'By the preaching of this doctrine, the devil is overthrown, his kingdom is destroyed, the law, sin and death...are wrested out of his hands: briefly, his prisoners are translated out of the kingdom of darkness and into the kingdom of light and liberty'(29). Our testimony has eschatological force; by it we

---

[18] Luther, *Commentary on the Epistle to the Galatians* (1535). References to quotations will follow in the main text.

'triumph against all the gates of hell'(35). What Christ has done, true Christian speech does too. Put differently, Christ himself vanquishes the devil in the form of Christian testimony that he does so. A theology of ventriloquism is established whereby our speech is the medium for the speech-*act* of the Word.

In its participatory reference to *Christus Victor*, the rhetoric of Christian testimony constitutes a form of violence. As in *The Bondage of the Will*, Luther repeatedly defends Paul's rhetorical violence in terms of pneumatological possession: 'He hath nothing in his mouth but Christ; and therefore in every word there is a fervency of spirit and life. And mark how well and to the purpose he speaketh... . These words are very thunderclaps from heaven against all kinds of unrighteousness...'(46-47). Of a later text it is said: 'And here with this thunderclap falleth down all the orders of monks and friars' (185) – the suggestion here is that this power is also (or especially) realised in Luther himself, whose own polemic has this particular target. His hermeneutic is one of anachronistic, or supra-chronistic, inclusion: the Spirit is not bound by the historicity of this text.

The task of identification with the Pauline voice is required of all Christian witnesses: 'Against [the devil and his ministers] we ought, by the example of the Apostle, to be impatient, proud, sharp and bitter, detesting and condemning their false jugglings and deceits with as much rigour and severity as may be'(58). We can also learn such speech from Christ himself, who 'rebuketh the Pharisees, calling them serpents, the generation of vipers, the children of the devil. But these are rebukings of the Holy Ghost'(187). In relation to the Gospel, normal rules of discourse are suspended; we are forbidden to be 'politic', tactful, respectful of worldly status: 'For we must diligently mark this distinction, that in matters of divinity we must speak far otherwise than in matters of policy'(105-06).

Despite the emphasis on rhetorical violence, Luther is able to remember that this discourse exists for the sake of nonviolent praxis. He thus explains that 'as concerning faith we ought to be invincible, and more hard, if it might be, than the adamant stone; but as concerning charity, we ought to be soft, and more flexible than the reed or leaf that is shaken with the wind...'(111). Without its basis in Christic nonviolence (which Luther is surely guilty of under-emphasising), the rhetorical violence of faith would be the ideology of a form of fascism, a resource for the celebration of actual human strength. 'In principle, at least, Luther eschewed physical violence, though his close alliance with the Saxon court qualifies this. It is ironic, indeed, that it is precisely his outrage at what he sees as the physical violence of Müntzer and the Papacy, for example, which provokes his most outrageous verbal violence'.[19] It is ultimately the cross that ensures a separation between actual and rhetorical violence. (We have already admitted that Luther fails in keeping these realms separate; he allows Christian rhetoric to find political reference. Yet this failure does not discredit the idea of a distinction between worldly and eschatological power. As well as learning from them, faith must learn a sort of indifference to Christianity's historical failures, must refuse to be defined by them.)

---

[19] Peter Matheson, *Rhetoric of the Reformation*, T & T Clark, Edinburgh, 1998, p.12.

Why is there this repeated and protracted emphasis throughout Luther's works on the legitimacy and even virtue of rhetorical violence?[20] On one level, of course, it is in Luther's interest to justify his own rebellion against Rome through identification with the strongest biblical voices. Yet it goes theologically deeper than this; such rhetoric becomes theologically foundational. In its critique of the sacramental system, Luther's theology is largely negative: the old means of mediation is discredited. Faith, of course, is declared to be an unprecedentedly direct link with the divine event of redemption: yet the logic of this new affinity is by no means obvious. The 'God-man-distinction' (so powerfully expounded in *The Bondage of the Will*) would seem to render any such affinity illusory, or hopelessly limited. I suggest that, for Luther, the central correspondence between us and Christ is this: in faith we participate in the anti-demonic violence of the Word himself. It is thus that we participate in the Trinity; we figure in a pneumatology of the *militant* Word. When, in Luther's work, a strong affinity is suggested between the agency of Christ and the agency of the Christian, it is generally in the context of violence. The Word is above all incarnate in Christian rhetoric of divine victory over the devil. We shall conclude with a final, and rather startling instance of this from the Galatians commentary.

For Luther, the faithful are assaulted by endless demonic assaults which take rhetorical form: the devil and his crew accuse and condemn us. At one point the superior 'voice' of the Word is represented as turning this accusatory violence against Satan. Thus Paul's assertion in chapter three that he is 'dead to the law' constitutes a counter-violent rebuke to his tormentor. Against the power of death Christ becomes aggressor, even *crucifier*: 'Christ...destroyeth my death in his body, and by this means spoileth hell, judgeth and crucifieth the devil, and throweth him down into hell' (162). The violence of the cross is reversed, and the Christian is implicated in this counter-violence: merely to acknowledge Christ's triumph 'is to dash out the teeth of the law, to wrest his sting and all his weapons from him, and to spoil him of all his force' (163). (The dental image is particularly potent: it depicts extreme yet defensive violence, and serves to deprive the Law of the power of *speech*.) The devil is then threatened with the name of Christ: 'Indeed thou art my tormentor, but I have another tormentor, even Christ, which shall torment thee to death.... *Likewise if the devil scourge me, I have a stronger devil, which shall in turn scourge him and overcome him*'(165-66). Christ's victory, which is the basis of our faith, entails his ability to 'out-Satan' Satan. The speech-act of the Word beats Satan at his own, violent game. In these passages there is a relentless rhetoric of reversal and of out-bidding. The devil's aggression becomes ironic, for, in a piece of cosmic ju-jitsu, it is redirected against him. The repetition and reversal suggest the text's indulgent glorification of this counter-violence; its performance of Satan's ritual humiliation.

---

[20] This violence is prominent in Luther's account of preaching, e.g.: 'a preacher...must have teeth in his mouth and be able to bite and fight' (*Table Talk*, p.203); and in his account of prayer: 'Prayer is a strong wall and fortress of the church, a godly Christian's weapon' (ibid., p.173).

Luther's theology is based around the image of the victorious Word, where 'Word' refers both to Christ and to our recounting of him. Christ is thus present in the supreme 'sacrament' of Christian testimony – and more particularly in the combative assertiveness of Christian rhetoric. The key 'point of contact' between him and us is the rhetorical image of the Word's defeat of Satan, which is both *his* final victory and the ongoing endeavour of *our* faith. Of course redemption can be understood in other 'images', such as those of reconciliation, healing and peace. But the strength of Luther's theology is to focus upon the image which most powerfully links the divine event of redemption to the rhetorical event of our faith.

Language and Sacrament

I have proposed that Luther's theology of the Word conceives of faith as rhetorical participation in the Christ event: the latter is made 'really present' by rhetorical means, 'incarnated' in our proclamation. We must now briefly ask how this relates to medieval sacramentalism and to linguistic and semantic theory.

Humanism's revival of rhetoric forms a crucial part of the background to Luther's theology of the Word. 'For the Renaissance...questions of faith and rhetoric are nearly allied. Faith rests on the unseen, on a promise, whose truth seems contradicted by the empirical evidence... . Renaissance rhetoric seeks to make spiritual reality visible'.[21] According to another critic, the Renaissance establishes a 'rhetorical-anthropological horizon [which] determines Luther's very theology'.[22]

This early modern rhetorical turn constitutes a challenge to the dualistic metaphysics of signification. Ever since Plato, words were held to signify pre-existing reality: since the Church Fathers their miraculous power to do so was guaranteed by God. This dualistic conception remains dominant into modern times; it abides into the rational Enlightenment. Yet an alternative conception emerges in the Renaissance and significantly affects Luther's theology. (Nominalism had already mounted half a challenge in its denial of 'realist' essences, yet it is not until humanism that the old view is fully challenged.) 'Meaning and words belong together as a matter of course in rhetorical activity, which in fact uses words precisely to attain understanding and new insight... . Luther does not distinguish between the subject itself and the word as a derived designation for it, so that the word merely 'signifies' that which is spoken about. The fact that subject and language belong together is an obvious presupposition of rhetorical activity'.[23]

Lorenzo Valla anticipates the revolution associated with Saussure and Wittgenstein: he locates the ability of words to mean in their *use*. This insight is

---

[21] D. K. Shuger, *Sacred Rhetoric: the Christian Grand Style in the English Renaissance*, Princeton University Press, New Jersey, 1988, p.22.

[22] Lindhardt, J., *Martin Luther: Knowledge and Mediation in the Renaissance*, Edwin Meller, Lewiston, 1986, p.76.

[23] Ibid., p.90.

also implicit in the work of Erasmus: his study and translation of historical texts has hermeneutical repercussions. Growing interest in classical rhetoric also affects 'the humanist conception of language as the inevitable medium and mediator of all human experience'.[24] Rhetoric affects Erasmus' conception of how scripture works, how it enables faith. His is 'a "literary" kind of exegesis which seeks to engage the emotions of the reader': it is based in a new conception of '*sermonis vim*', of 'the power of language to constitute experience in and for the reader'.[25]

Luther develops this new view of language with more drastic theological consequences. Through him, the new hermeneutic 'was to invade the very stronghold of magical reference, of truth as the correspondence between utterance and fact finally guaranteed by God'.[26] The Word's semantic power was strictly controlled by the Church's 'four-fold' method of exegesis. Luther's insistence upon the literal sense alone is based in his conception of the Word as an immediately effective and affective power over the reader. Because the Word directly communicates the divine promise to us, it overturns the old idea of words as mere signs of reality. In the new conception, words have actual power; they are creative of a new reality: 'The potent efficaciousness of the Word as [Luther] experienced it furnished him, after 1517, with the hermeneutic unification of words and meanings that was an equally potent polemical weapon against traditional dualisms'.[27]

This new conception of verbal creative power stands in contrast to medieval sacramentalism, which may be seen as a validation of semantic dualism. In the transubstantiation, the sign becomes the thing, the bread the body: this magical occurrence presupposes the dualist separation of sign and thing signified. Luther makes language the exclusive focus of sacramentalism and in the process reinvents it: 'The words and narratives of the Gospel are a kind of sacraments: that is, sacred signs by which God effects in believers what the narratives signify'.[28] For Luther, faith has more than signs; it has the thing itself. The event of the Word entails the abolition of any distinction between sign and reality. The reality of our redemption is not signified by words but *effected* by words: God's promises, knowable directly, are the very substance of faith, the content of revelation. Scripture contains God's 'performative' speech, which cannot be secondary to any nonlinguistic reality. In Christian discourse language exists (or happens) in a stronger sense than the referential system can accommodate.

Luther's emphasis upon the verbal nature of revelation strips the eucharist of its privileged status as *the* sacramental moment. By its nature the Roman mass testifies to institutional authority: God's presence is located in the Church, whose priests are the exclusive performers of the ritual representation. If, instead, the ultimate mode of God's presence is *language*, institutional authority loses its significance, its signifying power. Luther's position on the Eucharist is designed to

---

[24] Waswo, R., *Language and Meaning in the Renaissance*, Princeton University Press, New Jersey, 1987, p.218.
[25] Ibid., p.230.
[26] Ibid., p.210.
[27] Ibid., p.241.
[28] Luther, quoted in Gerrish, 1982, p.75.

advertise his refiguring of sacramentalism. It should be understood in defiant, almost arrogant terms. The old rite must be seen to be *subordinated* to the Word's performative power to declare that this is the body of Christ (or to declare whatever it likes). The impressive charade of the Church can now be done *for real*. It is demystified in favour of the true mystery of the Word's agency. There is perhaps a useful analogy in a scientist who continues to perform a 'trick' that was once presented as magic, in order to show that his form of power outdoes the magician's. The seeming magic of the old rite must be exorcised by its reperformance on wholly new terms.[29] By contrast, the Zwinglian and Calvinist position that bread merely signifies body is a surrender of pathos. The claim of transubstantiation must be outdone by the new pathos of the creative Word. It may be objected that Luther's linguistic emphasis is insufficiently incarnationalist: what replaces the Church's em*body*ment of Christ? Christ's most concrete manifestation is in the textual performance of proclamation: the speaker may even be understood as a Christic reincarnation.[30]

For Luther then, Christian rhetoric is sacramental in a wholly new sense which precludes the metaphysical dualism separating language and reality. If our language does not refer to pre-existing reality, must it then create reality? Does this not raise the spectre of postmodern relativism, endless indeterminacy, even Nietzschean perspectivism? This conundrum can only be solved by reference to the Christian narrative, wherein God takes the form of human weakness – including the weakness of a form of rhetoric. As the Word, Christ takes the form of the rhetoric that testifies to him. We are saved from the nihilistic freeplay of signs by the story which equates divine purpose with the privileging of certain particular signs, of a certain rhetorical idiom. There is thus a third account of meaning, particular to faith. We need neither accept referential dualism nor 'relational' scepticism. There is also the story of God becoming sign – of his self-revelation in and as human language.

Luther instigates the constructivist logic of Protestant rhetoric. The representation of the drama of the Word is not representation in any weak sense but re-creative of the actual event of the Word (this must also be understood as a theology of participation). In Luther's theology we have seen that rhetorical violence is crucial to this 'rhetorical participation'. This textual mode has to replace the institutional authority of the Church. In place of a mighty institution there is only a rhetorical idiom that is weak, embattled, homeless, 'utopian' in the literal sense. Such rhetoric is necessarily polemical, aggressive, scandalous. What

---

[29] There is a further analogy in the Elizabethan theatre's demystification of the ceremonial theatre of Rome. See Greenblatt, 'Shakespeare and the Exorcists', in Greenblatt, S., *Shakesperean Negotiations: the Circulation of Social Energy in Renaissance England*, Clarendon, Oxford, 1988, *passim*.

[30] This relates to Certeau's thesis in *The Mystic Fable*. He reads seventeenth-century mysticism as a quest for 'the bodied word', which is no longer to be found in the politicised Church. The old desire for the bodily presence of Christ must now be accommodated in rhetoric alone. And such discourse seeks to be concretely, tangibly other (Michel de Certeau, *The Mystic Fable vol 1; the Sixteenth and Seventeenth Centuries*, trans. by M. B. Smith, Chicago University Press, 1992, *passim*).

remains to explore is how Luther tackles the problem at the root of theological rhetoric: how can human words represent the Word of God?

The Dialogic Form of Luther's Theology of the Word

> Luther's thought is at once dialectical, involving two points of view, and dialogical, involving two arguers. Luther's entire theology is a 'dialogical theology' – dialoguing with the heretics, with the papists, with Erasmus, with the biblical writers, and with himself. The Christian life is for Luther precisely this life of discussion, or inner dialogue.[31]

Luther's theological method in *The Bondage of the Will* and the *Galatians Commentary* consists in the rhetorical mediation of the Word's authority. It is the Word who has already refuted all error and opposition: theology, and indeed faith, *re-cites* its victory. It can now be shown that this dynamic takes a distinctly *dialogic* form (in the sense of dialogism outlined in Chapter Two). Faith apprehends, and reasserts, the Word's authority in a situation of rhetorical conflict: the Word cannot, in this world, be known otherwise than in its polemical opposition to other 'voices', which constitute demonic forces.

In *The Bondage of the Will*, human reason is one such 'voice' to be defied. At one point reason is personified as a distorter of scripture; she 'explains and pulls the Scriptures of God whichever way she likes'. But Luther is unafraid of her: 'I shall enter this dispute readily and with confidence, for I know that all her gabblings are stupid and absurd...'(152). The role of confidence is crucial in these confrontations; for Luther confidence is a militant resource, a gift of the Spirit.[32] Soon he addresses 'her' directly as 'mistress Reason'(154) – he also addresses Erasmus' work as 'mistress Diatribe'(160). Further on he insists that the doctrine of divine foreknowledge is necessarily beyond our full comprehension.

> But here Reason, in her knowing and talkative way, will say: 'This is a nice way out that you have invented – that, whenever we are hard pressed by force of arguments, we run back to that dreadful will of Majesty, and reduce our adversary to silence...'. I reply: This is not my invention, but a command grounded on the Divine Scriptures... (176-77).

The assertion of the intrinsic authority of the divine command is faith's proper response to the objection of Reason. Here is the 'assertive style' of faith in action: because of the opposition of worldly 'voices', faith cannot be otherwise.

---

[31] E. B. Koenker, 'Man: *Simul Justus et Peccator*', in H. O. Kadai ed., *Accents in Luther's Theology: Essays in Commemoration of the 450th Anniversary of the Reformation*, Concordia, St. Louis, 1967, p.101.

[32] And for Barth, who quotes him: 'Faith is nothing else but a steady, undoubting, unwavering, sure confidence' (Karl Barth, *The Holy Ghost and the Christian Life*, trans. by R. Birch Hoyle from lectures delivered at Elberfeld on October 9th, 1929, Muller Press, London, 1938, p.49).

Contradicted, it must answer back; embattled, it must learn to fight. Elsewhere the encounters are more violent: 'Do not follow [Reason's] beautiful cogitations. Throw dirt in her face and make her ugly... . Reason should be drowned in baptism'.[33]

Throughout his works, Luther makes personifications, or 'characters', of all sorts of abstractions to which he is opposed, and he usually addresses them with a rather startling degree of rudeness. In keeping with the Western tradition of personification, they tend to be female.[34] Personification, or 'prosopopeia', is 'the translation of any nonhuman quantity into a sentient human capable of thought and language, possessing *voice* and *face*'.[35] It is a rhetorical or literary trope, and not to be confused with the animist *belief* that an inanimate force has a personality. Yet the distinction is problematic in relation to Luther: is the devil an actual personal force or a mere rhetorical figure?

The violence that accompanies Luther's personification is largely an inheritance from Prudentius, whose *Psychomachia* is the major source of the Christian allegorical tradition. Its representation of single-combat between various Virtues and Vices is strangely violent, containing 'grisly descriptions of bloody decapitation, dismemberment, and the mutilation of faces', in the classical epic tradition.[36] The destruction of the enemy's mouth is especially significant, as its capacity for speech is destroyed (we have already met this in relation to the Psalms). We shall presently see an example of this from Luther.

For Luther it is very often a matter of rebuking a servant who has forgotten her place, or developed ideas above her station: 'Let philosophy remain within her bounds, as God has appointed, and let us make use of her as of a character in a comedy, but to mix her up with divinity is not to be endured'.[37] (This example reminds us of the theatrical nature of Luther's theology, the fondness for role-playing and doing voices.) His Galatians commentary distinguishes between gospel and law, insisting upon the latter's subordination:

> But if it shall presume to creep into thy conscience, and there seek to reign,... say thou: O law...keep thyself within thy bounds...for I am baptised, and by the Gospel am called...to the kingdom of Christ... . [M]y conscience...is the seat and temple of Christ the Son of God... . [H]e shall keep my conscience joyful and quiet in the sound and pure doctrine of the Gospel. [38]

This inclusion of a confession of faith within the rebuke is typical, and significant. It is often found in relation to Luther's main object of scornful rebuke, who is of course the devil himself. Oberman observes that 'professions of faith and scorn for

---

[33] Luther, *Sermons 1*, *Works* vol. 51, Jan 17 1546, ed. and trans. by Doberstein, J. W., Fortress, Philadelphia, 1959, p.45.
[34] See Paxson J., *The Poetics of Personification*, Cambridge University Press, 1994, p.173.
[35] Ibid., p.42.
[36] Ibid., p.66.
[37] Luther, *Table Talk*, trans. by W. Hazlitt, Harper Collins, London, 1995, p.26.
[38] *Commentary on the Epistle to the Galatians*, James Clarke, 1956, p.28.   Elsewhere law is explicitly feminised: 'Madam Law, your reign is over!' (*Table Talk*, p.150).

the Devil are the proper weapons to be used against hell'[39]; 'the Reformation symbol of Christ's presence is not the halo of the saint but the hatred of the Devil'.[40] (Elsewhere, Oberman highlights the role of crude and scatological language in this dynamic: 'All true Christians...are called upon to combat the God-awful, filthy adversary, using his own weapons and his own strategy: "Get lost Satan, eat your own shit!"';[41] 'The very ferocity of Luther's language, his high pitch, has the double purpose of unmasking the devil and shouting to God...so loud that he will intervene to skin the devil and expose him for all to see'.)[42]

In the Galatians commentary Satan is addressed with mock respect and then counter-threatened: 'Sir Devil, I fear not thy threatenings and terrors, for there is one whose name is Jesus Christ, in whom I believe; he hath abolished the law, condemned sin, vanquished death, and destroyed hell... . This faith the devil cannot overcome, but is overcome of it'.[43] Through confessing his faith the believer defends himself, as with the sign of the cross, and lays claim to the only power which Satan fears: 'I say to Satan: Like as thou camest to confusion by Christ and St. Paul, even so, Mr. Devil, shall it go with thee, if thou meddlest with me'.[44] On the very same page he takes a similarly threatening tone with death: 'Thus when I feel the terror of death I say: Thou hast nothing to do with me, O death; for I have another death which killeth thee my death'. To have faith means, perhaps above all, to exercise this power in the battle against Satan and his avatars.

The focus, or object, of the rhetorical battle is our attitude to scripture, and the Word it mediates. The common aim of the demonic voices is to discredit the promises of God, to rob us of our assurance. Against them faith must stubbornly assert its trust in the Word. In doing so it renders the devil harmless and 'vexes' him, an activity which faith positively enjoys: 'We cannot vex the devil more than by teaching, preaching, singing, and talking of Jesus'.[45]

Such 'heroic' defiance is not humanly possible however; only as channels of the Word can we endure: 'Whoever, without the word of grace and prayer, disputes with the devil touching sin and law, will lose. [For he is] a crafty rhetorician'.[46] Our chief weapon in this rhetorical duelling, or 'fliting', with Satan is scripture, of course. The very purpose of Luther's exhaustive commentaries (as of his sermons and all his theology) is to mediate the arsenal of scripture; they are anti-demonic manuals for the embattled believer: 'Let us therefore arm ourselves with these and such like sentences of the holy Scripture, that we may be able to

---

[39] Oberman, 1982, p.159.

[40] Ibid., p.155.

[41] Oberman, *The Impact of the Reformation*, T & T Clark, Edinburgh, 1994, p.61.

[42] Ibid., p.63.

[43] Luther, *Galatians*, p.164.

[44] Luther, *Table Talk*, trans. by W. Hazlitt, Harper Collins, London, 1995, p.300.

[45] Ibid., p.90.

[46] Ibid., p.299.

answer the devil...';[47] 'You must rest on a strong and clear text of Scripture if you would stand the test. [Otherwise] the devil will pluck you like a parched leaf'.[48]

This form of 'dialogism' is rooted in the rhetorical violence we have already considered; it participates in the victorious power of the Word. Faith is not merely passive acceptance of Christ's victory but *rhetorical participation* in the ongoing violence of that victory. This dialogical violence can also be seen as a form of *exorcism*: the devil is expelled by the 'magically' powerful invocation of the Word. In Luther this takes a strictly rhetorical form: the voices that tempt us away from faith can be contradicted by the divinely powerful 'voice' of the Word, mediated both in scripture and in our own recitation of it. In contrast to medieval magic, no esoteric obscurity or special shamanic power is required: every Christian must be his own exorcist, personally capable of channeling the Word's power. To have faith is to know the Word as the power which controls demons. 'At its centre the idea of *fides ex auditu* was an appropriation of the Biblical image of "the speaking of the name" as the means by which the power of demons was broken and the lordship of the Creator restored'.[49] Also, of course, it differs from other exorcism in its constant reference to a single, transcendent and eschatological event of exorcism which is rhetorically appropriated. The event of redemption is re-staged in the rhetorical violence of these dialogical encounters.

The violence of these dialogical encounters should be read in terms of Luther's theological motivation: communication of divine agency, of the *otherness* of God. They therefore relate to the *critical* capacity of Protestant rhetoric, its ability to resist becoming a human ideology. Though faith emerges as participation in the Word, faith is not *in possession of* this rhetoric of authority. The Word remains separate from the believer or, in Luther's phrase, *alien* to her. 'The "alien Word" is the Gospel, which is not "my own", but which I must hear "spoken to me"'.[50] In the rebukes of Satan it is never the power of one's own faith, or righteousness, that wins out – it is always one's reference to Christ, usually via scripture.

Alongside his battles with Satan, Luther performs skirmishes with aspects of the believer's own psyche. (His own spiritual experience is translated into that of everyman, rather than exalted as unique – it is turned into material for proclamation.) It is here that faith's basis in the Word alone is most clearly demonstrated, or performed, enacted. We have seen the repudiation of Law (or moralism) and Reason as aspects of the self that seek to colonise faith, to deny its external basis. But for Luther *every* aspect of the self poses a similar threat. 'The flesh' applies to every thinkable component of human existence – none of it has anything approaching divine value; indeed it is all inimical to the Word, standing in need of rebuke. Confusion in this area is, for Luther, the failure at the heart of the Roman Church. It encourages the idea that human works have a role in the attainment of salvation.

---

[47] *Galatians*, p.50.

[48] Luther, Third sermon at Wittenberg, March 11, 1522, in Luther, *Sermons I*, p.80.

[49] Pelikan, Jaroslav, 'The Theology of the Means of Grace', in Kadai ed., 1967, p.128. See also Lindhardt on the exorcistic power of language (Lindhardt, 1986, p.76; pp.162-63).

[50] Oberman 1982, p.226.

Luther's model of faith is based in remembrance of human limitation, and the remembrance is enforced by its agonistic shape. Though these dialogical encounters seem to be Luther at his most violent, I therefore suggest that they contain the seed of self-criticism that redeems his rhetorical violence as a whole. Admittedly, this dynamic obviously remains open to abuse. The demonic voice can be associated with one's enemies and that of the Word used selectively in one's favour. But its primary use in Luther's works is *critical*. It is used against every claim to human sufficiency and authority. The discourse of faith is kept on its toes to a remarkable degree by this inner argument. 'Just as psychiatrists assure us that a healthy personality depends on the ability to conduct a running conversation with oneself, so the life of faith depends on the inner conversation between the man always inclined to rely on himself and the man ready to trust in God... . Because this conversation was conducted so vigorously and, one must add, so consistently, Luther is an example of remarkable spiritual health rather than of a sickly spirituality'.[51] The human voice is always kept in its place by the Word, put down; it always deserves to be contradicted. The voice of faith is only strong when inhabited by the Word, momentarily possessed by it. The Word prevents faith from acquiring independent authority. It enables faith by pre-venting it: in coming first and retaining its agency it frustrates the natural religious impulse; it restrains it and so re-trains it. The Word becomes known through its resistance to the believer, its lofty separateness.

'The Holy Spirit is not a sceptic', we have heard him say against Erasmus. But the apprehension of the Word does entail a sort of scepticism, perhaps the most militant, most manically searching scepticism possible. To assert that faith is based in the Word alone is to deny that it has any human grounding – most obviously in reason or experience. Faith's *certainty* comes from its ungroundedness in the human subject. To defend this alien certainty one must attack all *human* pretensions to religious value. The human subject becomes a dangerous animal, entirely worthy of suspicion. Luther anticipates Nietzsche and Freud here; his thought anticipates the modern discourses of suspicion. (He makes a particularly Freudian comment on the commandment to honour your parents: 'God knows that there lurks in children a poisonous resentment against parents'.[52] There is another Freudian echo in his warning that our greatest danger comes from within ourselves: 'each one of us is himself a great and spacious sea, filled with reptiles and animals...'.)[53]

To acknowledge the exclusive agency of the Word in faith thus entails a surprising degree of scepticism. It becomes acceptable, even laudable, to admit that the entire Christian system is absurd, improbable, too demanding, downright maddening. To admit these things, and *also nevertheless to assert faith*, is to enact faith's extra-human basis, its utopian exorbitance, its distinctness from normal convictions or opinions. This dynamic has been neglected by Protestant piety, to its detriment. Oberman observes that Luther's notion of the alien Word separates

---

[51] E. B. Koenker, 'Man: *Simul Justus et Peccator*', in H. O. Kadai ed., 1967, pp.102-03.
[52] Sermon on the Catechism, Dec 18 1525, in Luther, *Sermons I*, Works vol. 51, ed. and trans. by Doberstein, J. W., Fortress, Philadelphia, 1959, p.89.
[53] Sermon, Feb 24 1517, in ibid., p.37.

him from both his contemporaries and his heirs: 'Modern Protestantism sees faith as individual fulfilment, and the idea of an "alien faith" outside the individual is foreign to it'.[54] (As we shall later see, reviving the notion is essential to Barth's theological agenda.)

Also neglected by Protestant piety is Luther's ethical radicalism, which is also rooted in this scepticism. None of us are significantly better or worse than any others; 'Life is as evil among us as among the papists'. Luther differed from other would-be reformers of the Church by downplaying moral objections, looking instead to the doctrinal core. In relation to ethical discourse, faith is fundamentally sceptical. It wants to expose pretensions to human virtue and worth. To cast doubt on all human values is essential to its advertisement of grace. Part of the dangerous genius of Protestantism is to dissociate religion from morality, or at least to reinvent the connection; to read ethics negatively, in terms of human pretension to authority, and positively, as a form of witness, proclamation's body-language.

Dialogism: General and 'Internal'

Protestantism is a discourse of authority, primarily – its purpose is the communication of the authoritative Word – but it is also a discourse of criticism, including self-criticism. These two elements work together: criticism of the human (including the religious) serves the proclamation of the Word as *God's* Word. The Word must be communicated in its otherness. This entails the endless critique of every human claim to authority, whether through ethics, rational thought or even through piety itself. This dynamic, which is central to my defence of Protestant rhetoric, and will resurface throughout the rest of my study, is a species of 'dialogism'. As suggested earlier in relation to Bakhtin, it may be termed 'internal dialogism'. By this I mean that faith is a conversation between itself, arising from the tension between the Word of God and its human reception (which is also the conversation between the spirit and the flesh). It is this necessary openness that redeems the discourse of faith from authoritarianism, or monologic sterility, and requires reference to the term 'dialogism'. Yet, against most proponents of 'dialogue', I want to distinguish *this* openness from openness in general. Following Buber and others (including Bakhtin, as we have seen), some theologians have identified 'dialogue' as a key element in biblical tradition, and a much-needed antidote to theology's hubristic tendencies.

In a recent book George Pattison, for example, has argued that theology must resist the urge to turn away from other disciplines in a fantasy of ontological gnosis; its true calling is to remain humbly in conversation with them. 'But it does not follow that those who embrace dialogism are sceptics or uncommitted. It is rather that, committed as they are, they recognise that the point of view they seek to represent and promote cannot be realised apart from the process of dialogue'.[55]

---

[54] Ibid., p.242.

[55] George Pattison, *The End of Theology – and the Task of Thinking about God*, SCM, London, 1998, p.41.

Yet the obvious objection duly arises: if faith is so reasonable and open, will it not lose the stomach for its bold truth-claim, and become diluted through conversation? Does not such dialogism exemplify the problem with theological liberalism?

But a later passage may suggest a way out of this impasse. The church, Pattison says, must listen to other voices and so 'subject its own theoretical and practical life to the rigour of disciplined self-reflection... . To achieve the self-reflection needed to do this, believers will have to acquire the ability to establish an imaginative distance from their own beliefs and to look upon themselves as if with the eyes of others... . We don't have to pretend to be "outsiders", since every one of us is, simultaneously, an "outsider/insider"'.[56] Pattison's 'dialogism' here becomes more relevant to the dynamic I am exploring. Here dialogue is not just a case of one position (faith) conversing with another, which it is not. Instead, faith discovers *its own* dialogical nature; it acknowledges that it not a single thing, a fixed position, but that it is *itself* a conversation, a multiple personality. I want to insist that authentic Christian faith necessarily contains within itself the viewpoint of the 'outsider' – for in relation to the Word of God there is no possibility of being an 'insider'.

Also, I want to depart from the conventional understanding of dialogism in suggesting that the conversation is very largely one of tension, of agonistic wrangle, rather than polite conversation. Liberal dialogism suggests an image of Christian Belief moving across the room (a senior common-room, probably) and shaking hands with someone else, and both parties benefiting marvellously. In contrast, what I am calling 'internal dialogism' is defined by Luther's scenes of doubt, dissent, censure, rebuke. Also, of course, liberal dialogism downplays or denies the role of authoritative rhetoric in the economy of faith. Internal dialogism is based in the violent problem of the Word of God's reception and communication.

An objection: is it not rather disingenuous to praise the dialogical openness of Luther, of all people? Surely he is no advertisement for the acceptance of difference – he can hardly be called open-minded, 'a good listener'. Surely his brand of 'dialogism' is just a means to propagating his point of view all the more forcefully. Does he not, like Plato (yet very differently), exploit a dialectical form in order to smother opposition, pretending to have answered it already? Surely it is a parody of dialogism, to set up and lend voice to a caricature of Reason, or whatever? First it must be admitted (again) that Luther is indeed a failure in respect of the virtues of tolerance and so on. His context goes some way to excusing him: polemic is the condition of being heard at all. It is easy, and therefore pointless, for us to sound virtuous in relation to him in this respect. Also, it must be insisted that, despite its polemical agenda, there *is* genuine open-mindedness in Luther's theology, though it is not what we are used to thinking of as open-mindedness. Faith has to deal with the voice of rational objection, constantly take account of what it says. This is perhaps more honest than other points of view, other belief-systems, which assume that they embody reason, that

---

[56] Ibid., p.110.

all wisdom is contained in their single voice. Lutheran faith is supremely against such closure; it is imperfect, unfinished. There is no escaping the endless tension between faith's acceptance of the Word of God, and the flesh's objections. The discourse of faith is the performance of this tension. Faith becomes definable as an inner dialogue based around the necessarily incomplete acceptance of the Christian truth-claim. Consequently, faith is open-minded almost to the point of schizophrenia. It is never reducible to a single viewpoint or voice.

Such dialogism, I suggest, entails a novel account of the relationship between faith and reason. On the surface Lutheran faith is anti-rational; we have seen quotations which seem violently so. Yet it allows rational objection to have its say. In a sense this dissenting voice is to be encouraged, as faith is fuelled by the ensuing argument. And this set-up enables a new sort of honesty concerning 'faith and reason', which respects the integrity of each. The perennial tendency of theology, which is the source of much error and confusion, is to construct a single position in which faith and reason are 'reconciled'. This is the project of medieval scholasticism, and it is echoed throughout modern apologetics. Indeed it is also a feature of fundamentalism, which appeals to historical evidence and to personal experience, even while rejecting secular reason. All such approaches ultimately bring faith into intellectual disrepute. The proofs turn out to be shaky, the 'evidence' flawed.

Luther's model of faith takes a different approach. A conflict is acknowledged between the discourse of faith and the discourse of reason. This is an astonishingly bold move, perhaps unique in the history of thought. The normal tendency of bring faith into intellectual disrepute. The proofs turn out to be shaky, the 'evidence' flawed.

Luther's model of faith takes a different approach. A conflict is acknowledged between the discourse of faith and the discourse of reason. This is an astonishingly bold move, perhaps unique in the history of thought. The normal tendency of thought is to arrogate reason to oneself, to say that this new orthodoxy is the supreme expression of reason. Lutheran faith resists this: it admits a distance between revealed truth, as known to faith, and the rational apprehension of truth. The result would seem to be the rejection of reason, the preference of blind faith – but this is crucially *not* the case. For faith requires the enduring presence of reason, in order to remember its difference from it. Unless the voice of rational objection is constantly on hand, faith will become another human viewpoint, another claim to higher reasonability. Faith *wants* to hear rational objection, for this is used as proof that its basis is not human, but the Word of God. This form of faith, then, necessarily remains in dialogue with reason; it is in its own interest to do so. It includes reason within itself, and not some emasculated form of reason which is in the secret service of faith. It wants the latest, hardest, most relentlessly critical form of reason on the market – such is its fuel and its foil. To 'have' faith, therefore, entails also 'having' reason; being bilingual. We shall explore this further in relation to Barth.

Chapter 5

Protestant Poetics (I):
The Seventeenth Century

'Half of what we mean by poetry
is still the rhetoric Hebrew makes in English.'
(Peter Porter, 'Dragons in their Pleasant Palaces')[1]

Here and in Chapter 7 my scope widens to consider aspects of English poetic tradition in relation to my theme. These chapters constitute a sort of sub-plot to my overall argument. Poetic discourse is, I suggest, an essential concern of Protestant theology. As I have been arguing throughout, Protestantism locates authority in a rhetorical idiom, in a rhetorical performance of authority. It is a rhetorical and literary construction of authority. Modern poetic discourse may be seen as its closest and clearest rival. It too entails a claim to authority which is founded only upon its own linguistic performance. Christian discourse must know this rival in order to know itself.

The difference between them is that Christian discourse is unhappy to be discourse only. It must refer to its limitation, its judgement, which is also its authorisation, which is Christ. It is prevented from becoming aesthetic, or *merely* rhetorical, by Christ. He prevents it in a literal sense: he goes before, comes first, supplies the logic on which this discourse is founded. Christian *discourse* can only signify Christ in an indirect, partial, ironic and parobolic way. In referring to him, it must refer also to its own limitation as discourse. For this reason Christianity is wary of aesthetic value. Yet despite the caveat the Christian rhetoric of authority requires reference to an aesthetic understanding of literature, ie. poetics.

A detailed account of poetics is beyond our scope. But in order to suggest the new relevance of poetics in the Protestant era, we have to backtrack briefly. We have already discussed Plato's scepticism towards rhetoric: this extends to poetry as well. In *The Republic*, poetic discourse entails a rival account of authority to that of the rational state – primarily because it is the vehicle of religious myth. Yet after Plato philosophy develops a more accommodating attitude. For Aristotle, the poet has philosophical purpose; he 'can treat the passions that are dangerous to philosophy, which Socrates had to his great cost ignored. He can arouse these passions in order to flush them out of the soul, leaving the patients...more willing to listen to reason'.[2]

---

[1] Peter Porter, *Dragons in their Pleasant Palaces*, Faber, London, 1999.
[2] Allan Bloom, *The Closing of the American Mind; How Higher Education has Failed Democracy and Impoverished the Souls of Today's Students*, Simon and Schuster, New York, 1987, pp.280-81.

But, like rhetoric, poetic discourse defies Aristotelian intentions. Instead of clearing the way for the march of reason, it seems to entail a supra-rational claim to authority. Plato's rejection seems more realistic. The religious economy of poetry is most clearly and famously apparent in the treatise *On the Sublime* (written by an anonymous Greek known as Longinus in around the first century A.D.). It is an affirmation of poetic discourse in essentially religious terms. For Longinus, the highest form of linguistic expression does not merely persuade or gratify us but *compels* us: '[S]ublime passages exert an irresistible force and mastery, and get the upper hand of every hearer... . [A] well-timed stroke of sublimity scatters everything before it like a thunderbolt, and in a flash reveals the full power of the speaker'.[3] Central to the idea of sublimity is the exercise of a form of unworldly power. It demands reference to religious ideas of possession, enchantment and 'a kind of divine inspiration'.[4] Sublime effects are primarily associated with epic subject-matter, including the representation of the gods. He refers to Homer's depiction of Poseidon, and then, out of the blue, in what is probably a later addition to the text, to the Genesis account of God's creation through his authoritative word.[5] Longinus does not disqualify oratory from the sublime. Indeed it seems that rhetorical authority is of its essence. He commends the 'sublime intensity' of Demosthenes, the master of rhetorical vehemence, whose word is like a 'descending thunderbolt'.[6] Longinus presents poetic grandeur and rhetorical force as the central locus of the divine: 'in literature...we look for something transcending the human'.[7]

From its inception, Christianity of course makes use of poetic speech-forms (as well as classical rhetorical forms). Hymns were a very early vehicle for Christian teaching and worship. And the Hebrew heritage is very largely poetic in form. Yet classical poetry was highly suspect; it was basic to pagan identity and therefore shunned. For Augustine, poetry is an essential part of the classical pagan package; his youthful attachment to Virgil has to be overcome. Because of its mythological and religious function, poetry is a place of demons. The process of exorcism is arduous and uncertain. Very slow progress is made in the religious rehabilitation of poetic form. The Renaissance does not solve the problem: for the humanists, as later for the Romantics, poetry's strongest associations are pagan. The Muse refuses to be baptised in any real sense. (This is despite a longstanding counter-tradition: Augustine's contemporary Prudentius 'could be thought to present the Christian poet as a prophet or apostle delivering salvation through his art... It would take another thousand years before this vision of salvation poetry was realized again by Dante'.)[8]

---

[3] Longinus, *On the Sublime*, in T. S. Dorsch ed. and trans., *Classical Literary Criticism*, Penguin, Middlesex, 1965, p.100.
[4] Ibid., p.109.
[5] Ibid., p.111.
[6] Ibid., p.145-46.
[7] Ibid., p.148.
[8] H. J. Westra, 'Augustine and Poetic Exegesis', in Coward, 1990, p.97.

Despite its pagan provenance, Christianity cannot allow the realm of poetic discourse to be surrendered, left separate. It needs it. For this realm relates to rhetorical authority, and so to the Word. Poetic discourse entails a claim to authority which faith must appropriate (or, if the Word is the source of all truth, *re-appropriate*). Otherwise, the claim of the Word is limited; there remains an area of authoritative speech forbidden it, a language of authority it cannot speak.

With the Renaissance, poetic discourse emerges as an implicit rival to Christian discourse. From one modern perspective, Christian discourse steadily loses ground to this alternative, pagan tradition of authoritative speech (as well as to the other alternative of scientific enlightenment). Yet there is another account, in which poetic discourse becomes gradually and partially subordinate to the Word; the pathos of pagan aesthetics appropriated into the Christian rhetoric of authority. The story of modern Christian poetics is thus essential to my account of Protestantism. Protestantism means the triumph of the Word over all other rhetorics of authority, and by all possible means.

From Humanist to Protestant Poetics

The present chapter is concerned with the Reformation's influence upon English poetry. We shall begin with a brief consideration of Donne, then discuss Herbert and Milton at greater length. Donne's career marks the end of the Renaissance poetic ideal, of which something must first be said.

'For the early sixteenth century', says Greenblatt, 'art does not pretend to autonomy; the written word is self-consciously embedded in specific communities, life situations, structures of power'.[9] For the humanists, literary art is part of a gentleman's cultural repertoire; a reflection of the classical values of order and civility. It is a performance of self-mastery, and indirectly of political dominion: the man of culture must control his errant minions as well as his errant humours. The humanist poetic is therefore decidedly secular: 'The notion of religious literature is alien to the humanist poetics of the sixteenth century, which valued "poesie" for its ethical rather than redemptive force'.[10] It is above all concerned with the values of the *polis*, of course from the perspective of the ruling class, the court. In Castiglione's humanist handbook, *The Book of the Courtier*, the Count extolls literature as essential to nobility. He cites the literary enthusiasm of past military heroes: reading up on them will inspire one to emulation.[11] Courtliness thus has a textual basis; it is a secular religion of the book. The Count goes on:

---

[9] Stephen Greenblatt, *Renaissance Self-fashioning: from More to Shakespeare*, University of Chicago Press, 1980, p.7.

[10] Debora K. Shuger, 'Subversive Fathers and Suffering Subjects; Shakespeare and Christianity', in *Religion, Literature and Politics in Post-Reformation England, 1540-1688*, ed. by Donna B. Hamilton and Richard Strier, Cambridge University Press, 1996, p.46.

[11] Count Baldassare Castiglione, *The Book of the Courtier*, trans. by Sir Thomas Hoby, ed. by V. Cox, Everyman, London, 1994, p.78.

> Let [the courtier] much exercise hym selfe in poets, and no less in Orators and
> Historiographers, and also in writinge both rime and prose, especiallye in this our
> vulgar tunge. For beside the contentation [enjoyment] that he shall receive thereby
> himselfe, he shall by this meanes never want pleasaunt interteinments with women
> which ordinarylye love such matters.[12]

Poetry is a spur to military glory, a high-class leisure pursuit and a sort of foreplay.
It has little more connection with emotional truth than hunting has with hunger.
Thomas Hoby's translation of *The Courtier* in 1561 had a huge influence on
English writers, who had long looked to Italy in matters of taste. Only in
Elizabeth's reign does English writing gain confidence in competing with the likes
of Petrarch, Ariosto and Tasso. From the Italians, English poetry, largely through
Wyatt, learns *terza rima*, the sonnet and epic forms, as well as commitment to the
aesthetic potential of the vernacular. (There is also an older, native tradition, closer
to the Bible, and the people. It continues alongside the humanist poetic of the late
sixteenth century. The 'gospelling' movement, based in prophetic and satirical
forms, 'had greater public appeal than the Petrarchan love songs of the courtiers'.[13]
This tradition was deeply suspicious of the humanist influence, which it associated
with Roman Catholic corruption. The Puritan poetic of Herbert and others largely
derives from this defiantly 'crude' tradition that extends back to Langland.)

Sidney's *Defence of Poesy* (published 1595) defends poetry in rather more
serious terms than Castiglione. As well as being the supreme art-form it is the
primary form of instruction: the Greek philosophers and historians should be seen
as poets. So indeed should the Hebrew prophets and David as psalmist. Sidney
offers a weakly Christianised version of the humanist ideal. Despite offering a
tantalisingly brief theological account of poetry as participation in God,[14] he is
more comfortable relating poetry to the wider notion of 'virtue'. Heroic poetry
'maketh magnanimity and justice to shine through all misty fearfulness and foggy
desire [and] setteth [virtue] out to make her more lovely in her holiday apparel'.[15]
The poet thus serves as moral rhetorician, especially through his portrayal of epic
heroism. Spenser's poetic practice in *The Faerie Queene* (completed 1596) is
related to Sidney's theories (the two men were friends and collaborators). The aim
of the poem, his introduction explains, is 'to fashion a gentleman'; a clear
affirmation of the humanist poetic creed. But Spenser's purpose is also both
national and religious; his epic is a triumphalist celebration of a nation renewed by
its church and queen. Epic discourse in celebration of the Protestant order is a way

---

[12] Ibid., p.80.

[13] John N. King, *English Reformation Literature; the Tudor Origins of the Protestant
Tradition*, Princeton University Press, New Jersey, 1982, p.211.

[14] God, as man's maker (*poieten*), has given him dominion over nature – 'which in nothing
he showeth so much as in Poetry, when with the force of a divine breath he bringeth things
forth surpassing her doings'. This Sidney interprets as a proof of man's original blissful state
(Sir Philip Sidney, *Selected Prose and Poetry*, ed. by R. Kimbrough, University of
Wisconsin Press, 1983, ii, p.109).

[15] Ibid., p.131.

of combining humanist and native-religious poetics: we shall see something similar, but of course different, in Milton.

Donne: Humanism Undone

My concern in this chapter (and Chapter Seven) is the role in English poetry of authoritative rhetoric, particularly of course religious rhetoric. Later on, as we shall see, modern poetry makes a bid for status as the supremely authoritative form of discourse, a progression beyond Protestantism. For the young Donne, however, poetry entails a *refusal* of the authoritative discourses of church and state. Instead the poetic is the realm of wit; of scepticism, play, sensuality, cleverness. The aesthetic is not serious as it later is for Keats, say. Courtly love poetry is for Donne an extended joke – if an occasionally subversive one. Such poems do not take themselves seriously; they deconstruct their own pretensions, their own conceits. Yet within Donne's early frivolity is an intensity and a restless seriousness, which soon 'breaks out' into religious form. A major reason for this self-confinement to the frivolous is surely Donne's Catholic background. His habitual religious allegiance is denied public expression; he is prevented from any *easy* religious response.

Donne comes to think of his early poetry as sinfully trivial and effete. By contrast, the rhetorical arena of faith is serious and manly. It is a bullfight with the devil, an argument with the Almighty. In his religious poems and sermons Donne echoes the rhetorical violence of Luther, and perhaps out-does it. 'Batter my heart, three person'd God', begins one of his religious sonnets. The image of battery is echoed later in a sermon: God's 'Ordinance of preaching batters the soule, and by that breach, the Spirit enters; His Ministers are an *Earth-quake*, and shake an earthly soule; They are the *sonnes of thunder* and scatter a cloudy conscience...'.[16] 'Earnest prayer hath the nature of Importunity... . Wee threaten God in prayer... . Prayer hath the nature of Violence; In the publique Prayers of the Congregation, we beseige God, saies Tertullian, and we take God Prisoner, and God is glad to be straitned by us in that seige'.[17] Verbal force is at the heart of faith, but for Donne this does not preclude subtlety, eloquence, rhetorical cunning.

The Holy Sonnet beginning 'Death be not proud' is a taunt, a threat. Despite the debt to humanist eloquence and logic-chopping cleverness, it is a passionate, even a primitive utterance. The basic Christian speech-act of asserting victory over death is reperformed in humanist guise. But humanist individualism dominates: even though this poem is a gloss on Paul's remark, and so refers to a common Christian experience, it seems to insist that *this* religious utterance is more intense and effective than Paul's, or anyone else's. In the manner of Hamlet, the humanist self is exalted through turmoil, desperately seeking significance in its pain.[18] In

---

[16] John Donne, Sermon XXVII (May 6th 1627), in Donne, *Complete Poetry and Selected Prose*, ed. John Hayward, Bloomsbury, 1929, p.697.

[17] Donne, *Sermons*, V, p.364, quoted in Patrides ed., *The English Poems of George Herbert*, Everyman, London, 1974, p.70.

[18] The breakdown of the humanist ideal is also one of the central concerns of *Hamlet*. He is

faith as in love, the poet remains the centre of the universe, the criterion of all meaning. In Sonnet XIX he is the victim of his own inconstancy of faith: 'Oh, to vex me, contraryes meet in one:/Inconstancy unnaturally hath begott/A constant habit…'. The psychological labour of faith seems to have been designed to punish him alone. 'As humorous [i.e., changeable] is my conditione/As my prophane Love, and as soone forgott…', he continues. There is a hint of boasting here: how can I (being who I am) be expected to be constant? Donne's ego dominates these poems. As Patrides says, Donne's idea of devotional poetry was to 'rear his mighty ego in order to exorcise it before his angry God'.[19] Related to the problem of ego is the theme of restlessness, inconstancy, dis-ease (famously expressed in XVII: 'A holy thirsty dropsy melts mee yett'). This concern is an inversion of the humanist ideal of self-control, mastery of one's humours. Donne wants to rub his nose (and ours) in the gulf between that old ideal and what to him is Christian reality. Here the self is dependent, yearning, unhappily passionate. Yet despite this inversion of the humanist ethos of self-control he retains the centrality of the self that it assumes. The result is a self-centred piety in which obsessive anxiety becomes the main means of proclamation.

Herbert's Psychodrama

Herbert is a religious poet in a new and distinctively Protestant sense. His poetry is based in an assumption of the authority of the Word. This entails a fuller rejection of the humanist poetic self than is achieved by Donne. In *The Temple* (published posthumously in 1634), faith is not a personal crisis but an objective pattern or dynamic that fits every human psyche.

Herbert's poetry is strikingly close to the concerns of early Reformation theology. His style at first seems quaintly over-simplistic: in language of biblical plainness, he seems to approach complex religious issues with a Sunday-school naivety: 'well-nigh every aspect of Herbert's poetry is traceable to the Bible'; this includes 'the omnipresent propensity toward understatement'.[20] Yet his poems have great theological and dramatic depth. The childlike simplicity emerges as an act, a deliberate construction which reflects the 'second naivety' of faith. And this performance has polyphonic depth; the poems 'share with the poems of Donne, and Marvell and Milton a natural inclination to dramatise in order to achieve an optimum of tonal range'.[21] Herbert offers an anatomy of faith's basis in competing voices of authority. The rhetorical drama is based in Lutheran psychomachy as mediated by Calvin's theology: the voices of the flesh must be imitated and

---

the Renaissance prince, and Castiglione's courtier: 'The courtier's, soldier's, scholar's, eye, tongue, sword' (3.1.159). Or rather, he is not this; for the humanist model of selfhood cannot contain his angst.

[19] C. A. Patrides, '*A Crown of Praise*: The Poetry of Herbert', in *The English Poems of George Herbert*, Everyman, London, 1974, p.8.

[20] Ibid., p.9.

[21] Patrides, 1974, p.22.

rebuked; faith's agonistic adherence to the Word must be reperformed. Mortification, Herbert reflects in *The Country Parson*, means 'the stupifying and deadening of all the clamorous powers of the soul'.[22]

Let us begin with one of his most dramatic and rhetorically astute poems, 'The Collar'. It dramatises the ideal of autonomy. 'I struck the board, and cry'd, No more./I will abroad./What? shall I ever sigh and pine?'. This indignant complaint against service, or being 'in suit' is further enacted and then subverted:

> But as I rav'd and grew more fierce and wilde
> > At every worde
> Methought I heard one calling, *Child!*
> And I replied, *My Lord.*

The main rhetorical force of the poem is the complaint against religious heteronomy, expressed through the metaphor of feudal fealty. This outburst seems more natural to the speaker, more 'his own voice', than his faithful assent at the end. Here, not in faith, is passion, energy, expansiveness. The contradictory climax is an anti-climax; it offers no superior passion but is the cursory cessation of his strident rebellion. There is something deeply unsatisfactory about the poem's dutiful preference of heteronomy to the vigour and zest of autonomy. This is as it should be: the truth of faith is not based in feeling – at least, not in a conventional account of it. There is a similar dynamic in the well-known poem 'The Pearl': faith emerges not as a superior passion but as an alternative to passion; a preference of sobriety and submission to authority.

For Herbert, as a good Protestant, the Word has authority over the words that constitute the dynamics of human worldly meaning and life. The Christian self is the arena of violently competing claims to authority; faith is the open-ended, unsettled argument, divinely won only in eternity. Just as the argument is *unsettled*, so is the self: it lacks self-sufficiency and stability. The self is constituted by voices and powers beyond it; it is radically 'de-centred'. (This account of the self is echoed by certain 'structuralist' trends in recent thought.) According to this conception, and in striking contrast to the modern assumption, 'being oneself' is a demonic ideal; for one's self is a constant danger to one's soul. Subjectivity is condemnation to an anarchy of troublesome thoughts and passions (the political image of anarchy figures highly in these poems, as does its opposite: absolute rule). Such is the Protestant view on selfhood, which is perhaps more effectively communicated in religious poetry, with its capacity for dramatisation, than anywhere else.

Consciousness itself is a major danger. In the second stanza of 'Affliction (IV)', the speaker complains: 'My thoughts are all a case of knives,/Wounding my heart... Nothing their furie can control,/While they do wound and prick my soul'. Thoughts become hostile external powers: 'their furie' recalls the classical Furies, the demons who wreak vengeance through mental disturbance. The 'inner' thus

---

[22] George Herbert, *The Country Parson, The Temple*, ed. by J. N. Wall, SPCK, 1981, iii, p.56.

speaks of the agency of external powers. 'The Familie' similarly complains at 'this noise of thoughts within my heart', at 'these loud complaints and pulling fears' which it is God's role to set in order: these constitute 'the Familie' of which God is the presently absent father, or lord – the image again invokes an ideal of courtly order. The machinery of consciousness, what Herbert calls 'thoughts', is not, as humanist optimism suggests, man's surest claim to dignity but his burden, snare and curse. (Herbert is more pessimistic, humanly speaking, than Donne – there is little indication in *The Temple* that reason is 'God's viceroy' in oneself, albeit incapacitated, held captive by sin.)

Man without God (which even in faith he humanly remains) is in a state of psychological disorder, which is represented in vocal and rhetorical terms. The self is the medium of the voices which are to be silenced, rebuked, defied. Sometimes the destructive voices are presented as purely external: in 'Self-Condemnation', the world is ascribed a murderously 'enchanting voice'.[23] Because one lives in the world and the world lives in one (as the Scottish Confession puts it), there is no absolute distinction between one's natural 'inner dialogue' and external demonic voices. For faith, the real distinction is not between 'self' and 'world' but between both of these and the Word of God, the genuine 'other'. Also, the humanist distinction between thought (good) and passion (bad) is refuted: all of one's human nature is the servant of sin; the only good is the *external* intelligence of the Word. The Word must order one's inner chaos, counter the call of the world.

Herbert's dramatisation of the self belongs to the dialogical structure of faith: these worldly voices are only known in relation to the Word which opposes them. In turn, the latter is only known and expressed through its dialogic interaction with the powers it opposes. This rhetorical situation can be addressed in different ways, by different strategies. The speaker may represent the Word's authority in his own voice. Or he may demand divine action, which is also to threaten his opponents with it: there is therefore aggression in this imprecation.

Some of Herbert's poems resemble Luther's violent dramatisations of *Anfechtung*, in which personifications are unmasked as cronies of the devil.[24] In 'The Size', the dialogue is between the soul and the 'greedie heart', the personification of fleshy disobedience: 'Wouldst thou [God's] laws of fasting disanull?' it is asked. And it is told (in a particularly Lutheran touch) to 'sit down, good heart...'. Likewise in 'Conscience' the speaker censures another personification of his own humanity: 'Peace pratler, do not lowre.../If thou persistest, I will tell thee,/That I have a physick to expell thee'. This antidote is his 'Saviours bloud'; if it is not sufficient, the threat descends to physical violence:

> Yet if thou talkest still,
> Besides my physick, know there's some for thee:
> Some wood and nails to make a staffe or bill

---

[23] Also, in 'The British Church' Rome becomes the 'painted' seductress of souls, calling out from her hilltop.

[24] In 'Avarice', 'Time' and 'Death' eponymous personifications are defied. See also 'The Bag', a rebuke and counter-taunting of despair.

For those that trouble me:
The bloudie crosse of my dear Lord
Is both my physick and my sword.

Faith doesn't get much more rhetorically violent than this; even Luther does not go so far as to transform the cross into a gruesome weapon. Ironically, of course, the cross originally *is* a gruesome weapon of torture: this image re-invents, or re-directs that violence.

Like Luther Herbert seeks to communicate the *alien* Word, and is thus concerned to criticise the rhetoric of piety. Even the 'voice of faith' remains a human voice, subject to worldly dangers. This is explored in 'The Holdfast': the speaker's own religious zeal emerges as a barrier to God; even 'to confesse/That we have nought' is illegitimate. Faith's dependence upon divine agency means that it cannot stand as a special form of human passion or sensibility. Religious poetry must continually undermine the speaker's voice; this is precisely *not* the locus of meaning or truth. The most the poet can do is to point to the agency of another voice, the posited Word of God. (Fish relates the rhetorical strategies of the poems to catechistical theory, in which Herbert was very interested: 'Because the aim of the discourse is always the realisation of one's dependence on Jesus Christ, the reader's success will be inseparable from an acknowledgement of personal inadequacy'.)[25]

For Herbert as for Luther and Calvin, faith is an assurance of divine victory which is nevertheless obliged to fight: the doctrine of assurance is at the root of the drama. This strange situation lends the rhetorical militancy of faith a very particular *tone of voice*. It is informed by the already victorious Word, yet faith *is* not this word of infinite assurance but refers to it, signifies it, clings to it. The dramatic depth of these poems is a reflection of eschatological faith, of the dramatic irony entailed in the divine reversal. The speaker's voice is both weaker than the demonic assaults *and stronger* – through reliance on the Word. The rebuke of the powers of the world is ultimately God's task, not ours: 'Assurance' dramatises the expectation of God's final, definitive rebuke. Faith's victory lies in reference to the victory which precedes its struggle.

In many of the poems the authoritative word is graphic rather than vocal. In contrast to insubstantial human noises, God is a writer. 'Nature' refers to the prophetic image of scriptural open-heart-surgery (eg. Jer. 31.33): 'O smooth my rugged heart, and there/Engrave thy rev'rend law and fear...'. Likewise 'The Sinner' concludes, 'And though my hard heart scarce to thee can grone,/Remember that thou once didst write in stone'. Man's scriptural ability is derivative of God's: he is 'Secretarie of thy praise' ('Providence'). God's authorship precedes, and in a sense precludes, the poet's: the only truly significant word has been uttered or penned (or *carved*) already and we must refer to it; authorial originality is the original sin. In 'Jordan (II)', a reflection on his poetic calling, he relates the painstaking artistry of his original poetic method, and is interrupted by a voice

---

[25] Stanley Eugene Fish, *The Living Temple; George Herbert and Catechizing*, University of California Press, 1978, p.47.

telling him instead to copy what is '*readie penn'd*'. The authoritative word of command and assurance, then, already exists – the poet *sub-scribes* to it rather than conjures it up from scratch. This deference to the Word's priority, so basic to Protestant faith, is repeatedly enacted in the structure of Herbert's lyrics. A significant proportion of the poems conclude with an italicised voice which breaks into the frame of the poem, signifying the external resolution of its particular problematic. This is often a direct scriptural quotation but may also be (as in the above) a sort of sacred *skaz*, or stylisation of divine assurance (also in 'Love bade me welcome'/'Love III'). We have already noted the inverting conclusion of 'The Collar' in which the simple apostrophe '*My child*!' punctures the rhetoric of freedom. Such poems represent a sudden entry of the Spirit into the speaker's psyche. He at last speaks with a voice beyond his own; a new and strange rhetorical strength descends on him. It is an account of faith as rhetorical possession by the Spirit.

The many poems of dereliction generally conclude with a certainty that feels falsely imported, forced. What is unfelt is instead asserted; the reality of loving grace both *cannot* be and *must* be vouched for. The height of devotion *de profundis* is, in a sense, forcing oneself to comply with what is manifestly *disingenuous*; the idiom of unfelt divine assurance. 'The Method' relates the effort to infer that one's dereliction speaks not of God's absence but one's own sin. It concludes with instruction as to the penitent's proper procedure:

> Then once more pray:
> Down with thy knees, up with thy voice.
> Seek pardon first and God will say,
> > *Glad heart rejoyce.*

The final affirmation is not quite the speaker's own; the poem's mood is not blankly inverted by a fortuitous change of heart and the reality of loss revoked. Instead there is an abiding dialogue between the speaker's voice of near despair and his formal submission to, or subscription to, the voice of divine assurance (there is a similar dynamic in 'The Crosse'). Faith is big enough to embrace both; its affirmation should not be labelled insincere, at least not in the normal sense.

Because the locus of faith's certainty is not of this world, there is, humanly speaking, an *inauthenticity* about it. In faith we assert (as if with clenched teeth) *what we fail to feel*, but what we know (inexplicably, by grace) to be the truth. We shall see this again in relation to both Kierkegaard and Barth. A nondialectical conviction of faith, with which reason and feeling concurred, would not be Christian faith. Truly eschatological faith necessarily has this dialogical structure in which the believer is conscious of assuming a voice of definitive authority that is not her own, that is not rooted in her experience. To the secular mind this smells of insincerity if not mild schizophrenia. Herbert warns us against sharing the assumption.

We should finally take note of Herbert's new confidence towards the aesthetic. He insists that faith surpasses aesthetics, and that aesthetics belongs to faith. Poetry must be baptised (the theme of the 'Jordan' poems). 'Is there in truth no beautie?', he asks, and the question is confidently rhetorical. This application of Protestant confidence to the realm of aesthetics is also apparent in an early sonnet he wrote for his mother:

> My God, where is that ancient heat towards Thee
> Wherewith whole shoals of martyrs once did burn,
> Besides their other flames? Doth Poetry
> Wear Venus' livery? Only serve her turn?
> Why are not sonnets made of Thee, and lays
> Upon Thine altar burnt? Cannot Thy love
> Heighten a spirit to sound out Thy praise
> As well as any she?

Here the baptism of poetry is presented as essential to the task of proclamation, to the rediscovery of 'that ancient heat'. True and inspired proclamation of the Word depends upon the insistence that poetry is *not* essentially and necessarily pagan. This insistence, I would argue, is more essential to the Protestant cause than anything going on in church governance.

Herbert is clear that his poetry is implicated in Christian proclamation. It is stated in the first poem of *The Temple*, 'The Church-porch': 'A verse may finde him, who a sermon flies,/And turn delight into a sacrifice'. Aesthetic delight is not an end in itself but serves the purposes of the Word. To literary purists, this is anathema. It is a modernist truism that true poetry refrains from preaching at us; in Keats' phrase, it should have no 'palpable design on us'. This is echoed by the major moderns – Yeats, Pound and (with some misgivings) T. S. Eliot (he wants 'unconsciously Christian' literature). It has become a key piece of literary orthodoxy, which one almost fears to argue with. But Protestantism challenges the autonomy of poetic discourse, scenting a proclamatory rival.

Before we turn from Herbert to Milton it should be acknowledged that these poets exist in a wider religious context. The central emphasis of early English Protestantism, in which high and low were fairly united, was upon the Word as an actual historical power. Puritan writers in particular were 'concerned with recovering the original simplicity of the Word of God and conveying what they perceived to be its extraordinary power to transform the individual and society';[26] '"plain and powerful" became a Puritan formula for describing effective preaching'.[27] A fuller study than mine might discuss Bunyan in this context. In *Pilgrim's Progress* faith takes the form of dialogic encounters with demonic voices, in which it has constant recourse to the arsenal of Scripture. In *Grace Abounding to the Chief of Sinners*, conversion takes the form of learning how to deploy this arsenal against the foe. But it is to the grandest and strangest of the Puritan proclaimers that we now turn.

---

[26] John R. Knott, *The Sword of the Spirit; Puritan Responses to the Bible*, University of Chicago Press, 1980, p.4.

[27] Ibid., p.5. He also cites Hooker's insistence that the Word should be preached with 'a holy violence' (p.39), and this from Baxter: 'Let us...speak to our people as if for their lives, and save them as by violence, pulling them out of the fire' (p.73).

Milton's Theodrama

Milton is regarded by poets and critics rather as Luther is by liberal theologians: with grudging respect, reluctant reverence. Though he practically invents modern English poetry he is charged with problematising it unduly. He commits the cardinal sin of modern aestheticism: ideological motivation. Even worse, in the form of religious fanaticism. Modern critics can muster little affection for Milton the man; the consensus is that his self-importance 'would be intolerable but for his genius'.[28] But even as it berates his motivation and character, modern criticism cannot deny the force of his style, his invention of a new poetic language which combines lofty grandeur with plainness.

I am here concerned with Milton not as a poet *per se* (nor as a theologian *per se*) but as a Protestant voice in the context of my thesis, a practitioner of the Protestant rhetoric of authority. In his epic poems Milton constructs one of the most compelling representations of divine rhetoric in Christian history. As with Luther, the achievement is ambiguous. He too was at times guilty of associating Christian rhetoric with a political cause. It is little excuse that he thought this political cause more than just a political cause, that he thought it the final overthrow of tyranny. (In fact, his epic poetry is written after his political involvement. In its repudiation of worldly power, it seems to constitute a sort of repentance for his political enthusiasm.)

Unlike Donne, Milton knows from the first that poetry is serious. In 1629, aged twenty-one, he wrote his first important poems (published in 1645), including 'On The Morning of Christ's Nativity'. This is a very Protestant celebration of *Christus Victor*. Though it is classical in form, and in its reference to the infant Hercules, its primary concern is with the exorcism of pagan deities. (The idea of a Nativity exorcism is a traditional one, extending back to Ignatius of Antioch.)[29] The usurping spirits flee from the world in fear of his power: 'Our babe, to show His Godhead true,/Can in His swaddling bands control the damned crew.' It is a celebration of the downfall of classical religion (and not, as some have said, an elegy to it). The classical oracles are suddenly spent forces, struck dumb. Milton's point, of course, is that they are made redundant by Christ, the new and exclusive locus of divine power and significance. Yet one form of magical oracular power survives the purge: Milton's prophetic Muse. In the new religious order divine power resides only in Christ *and the voice that proclaims him*. The Christian religion establishes prophetic speech (in which Christ is proclaimed) as the new form of divine power. In celebrating Christ, Milton thus also celebrates himself as poet-prophet.[30]

---

[28] A. L. Rowse, *Milton the Puritan; Portrait of a Mind*, Macmillan, 1977, p.22. 'As a man, he is antipathetic' (T. S. Eliot, 'Milton' (1936), *Selected Prose*, Penguin, Middlesex, 1953, p.123).

[29] Ignatius of Antioch, 'Epistle to the Ephesians', p.19, in *Early Christian Writings: the Apostolic Fathers*, trans. by M. Staniforth, ed. by A. Louth, Penguin, Middlesex, 1987, p.66.

[30] Bloom goes further: 'Milton's major desire was to assert his own identity as poet-prophet, far surpassing Moses and Isaiah and the authors of the New Testament' (Harold Bloom,

The fusion of classical pastoral and Protestant theology continues in the two major works of his youth: *Comus* and 'Lycidas'. The former is a masque, a drama performed at a country house. It is set in a fairy-tale forest. But the resemblance to Shakespearean comedy ends there. It concerns the attempted seduction of the chaste Lady by the rhetorical assault of the Bacchic enchanter Comus. A sketch for Satan, Comus is a voice of seductive evil that is doomed to failure. He finally admits rhetorical defeat: 'I feel that I do fear/Her words set off by some superior power'(800). Like a Shakespearean villain, his energy is the source of the entire drama. But unlike Shakespeare, Milton supplies the opposite voice, that of divine authority, and stages its triumph. The plot emerges as a vehicle for the Lady's Word-inspired rhetoric of militant fortitude: 'She is as strong as Milton's Jesus in *Paradise Lost* in saying the equivalent of "Get thee behind me, Satan"'.[31]

Alongside his poetic development, Milton imbibed the radical Protestantism of the day, and became a leading critic of the Laudian church. Even Anglican writers such as Donne and Herbert were deemed guilty of ecclesiastical incorrectness; of failing to prevent a backsliding towards Rome. 'Lycidas', written in 1637, was to be his last English poem for twenty years. It is a pastoral elegy for a drowned acquaintance from Cambridge. Within the classical form he sets out a polemical agenda. The vulpine clergy are stripped of their shepherd's clothing, their 'blind mouths' are cursed, retribution is promised. This promise or threat of violent reversal is essential to his faith. Rather like Communist faith, its expression is necessarily violently polemical (in fact this passage adumbrates the political poems of Shelley). Milton's early religious zeal gives political reference to eschatological rhetoric, which is hardly avoidable in an age for which ecclesiastical reform is the hottest political issue.

Much of his prose work is devoted to justification of his poetic and rhetorical practice. In 'The Reason of Church Government' (1642) he warns his audience 'not suddenly to condemn all things which are sharply spoken, or vehemently written, as proceeding out of stomach, virulence and ill nature...'.[32] '[N]either envy nor gall hath entered me upon this controversy', he says – his conscience bids him speak; he can do no other.[33] He proceeds to relate his prophetic commission to his poetic training. His poetic gifts 'are of power beside the office of a pulpit, to inbreed and cherish in a great people the seeds of virtu, and publick civility, to allay the peturbations of the mind, and set the affections in right tune, to celebrate in glorious and lofty Hymns the throne and equipage of God's Almightinesse..., to sing the victorious agonies of Martyrs and Saints, the deeds and triumphs of just and pious Nations doing valiantly through faith against the enemies of Christ, to deplore the general relapses of kingdoms and states from

---

Ruin the Sacred Truths; Poetry and Belief from the Bible to the Present, Harvard University Press, New Jersey, 1987, p.112).
[31] Ibid., p.29.
[32] Milton, *Complete Poetry and Selected Prose*, ed. by E. H. Visiak, Nonesuch Press, London, 1938, p.53.
[33] Ibid., p.53.

justice and Gods true worship'.[34] It was a staple of Protestant rhetoric to present religious reform as England's special calling. The aim of culture is 'that the call of wisdom and virtu may be heard every where, as *Salomon* saith, *She crieth without, she uttereth her voice in the streets*...'.[35] The nation is called to call; its primary vocation is to proclaim God's word. (This is echoed in 'Areopagitica' of 1644: 'Why else was this Nation chos'n before any other, that out of her, as out of *Sion*, should be proclam'd and sounded forth the first tidings and trumpet of Reformation of all *Europ*?')[36]

He declares the religious-cultural legitimacy of all forms of literature, even the theatre, and returns to his exemplary calling. He has been planning a work 'not to be rays'd from the heat of youth, or the vapours of wine, like that which flows at wast from the pen of some vulgar Amorist..., nor to be obtain'd by the invocation of Dame Memory and her Siren daughters, but by devout prayer to that eternall Spirit who can enrich with all utterance and knowledge, and sends out his Seraphim with the hallow'd fire of his Altar to touch and purify the lips of whom he pleases... .'[37] He thus asserts the superiority of prophetic over pagan literature, which includes its *aesthetic* superiority. The poet of Sinai breathes rarer, purer air than that of Parnassus.

In *An Apology against Smectymnuus* (1642) he returns to the theological justification of rhetorical vehemence. The Prelates' plea for tactful restraint is dismissed. The present stalling of reform calls for us to 'imitate the method God uses; *with the froward to be froward, and to throw scorne upon the scorner*... .'[38] The task of opposing the Prelaty deceivers, 'openly and earnestly', goes to 'whomsoever God shall give apparently the will, the Spirit, and the utterance'.[39] He knows that the question will arise of his authority so to speak. With exhaustive allusion he points to the biblical sanction for righteous protest. He denies the charge of libel, unless libel 'is to speak freely of religious abuses'. And now the rhetorical debt to Luther becomes explicit: 'I see not how *Wickleffe* and *Luther*, with all the first Martyrs, and reformers, could avoid the imputation of libelling'.[40] The reformers' use of rhetorical vehemence follows naturally from biblical tradition. 'Our Saviour...was Lord to expresse his indoctrinating power in what sort him best seem'd', which was sometimes 'with bitter and irefull rebukes... .'[41] Biblical witness entails 'Zeal whose substance is ethereal', as figured in the lion of Ezekiel and John, signifying 'power, high autority and indignation'.[42]

Milton anticipates the objection that these instances of 'sanctified bitterness' are special cases of direct inspiration, 'not to be tried at home'. In

---

[34] Ibid., p.57.
[35] Ibid., p.58.
[36] Milton, 'Areopagitica', in ibid., p.236.
[37] Ibid., pp.58-59.
[38] Milton, 'Apology against a Pamphlet...', in ibid., p.573.
[39] Ibid.
[40] Ibid., p.575.
[41] Ibid., p.590.
[42] Ibid., p.591.

response he argues that rhetorical violence is a human capacity like any other; able by grace to serve the Word. Here he cites the example of Luther, who 'not [out] of revelation, but of judgement writ so vehemently against [Rome]'.[43] His verbal force was an appropriate rhetorical strategy, '*seeing that matters quietly handled, were quickly forgot*'. God decided to make use of 'his tart rhetorick in the Churches cause'.[44] Milton now returns to the more certain proof of the prophets; through them the Spirit has spoken against idolaters in terms that strike us as offensive. For Milton, Protestantism is based in a new prophetic situation, in which prophetic speech must be consciously deployed as a human rhetorical strategy. His reading of Luther foregrounds the style of his speech-act: it is of *theological* relevance that '*he could not write a dull stile*'.[45] Milton understands that the legitimisation of rhetorical violence is an essential task of early Protestantism. (It is also a theme privileged in Foxe's *Book of Martyrs*.)[46]

Before and during Cromwell's reign, Milton's authorship was strongly political. In 1649, the year of the king's trial, he was appointed Secretary for Foreign Tongues to the Council of State. He was apologist and propagandist for the regime, denouncing the immediate royalist reaction in an official publication. At the Restoration he was lucky to evade punishment. Yet his major poetry is written in response to the defeat of his political cause rather than in support of it. It is written in the knowledge that the ideal Christian commonwealth has failed to emerge, that the opportunity has passed. Yet what matters more than this historical failure is that its theoretical basis is eternally secure. In the Word of God we have the blueprint for human liberation.

Paradise Lost and its sequel are about the possibility of liberation. Its possibility depends on the knowledge of its original loss. 'Man's first disobedience' means the loss of both liberty and reason, in its fullest, spiritual sense. Entailed in this is a failure of language to convey true meaning: 'Just as Original Sin had entailed the fall of speech, so spiritual and verbal redemption are linked'.[47] The Word of God is now only knowable through its contrast with normal human language, which is to various extents possessed by the devil. The poem is largely concerned with a false ideal of liberation, a false claim to authority. Satan's rebellion entails a perversion of language. He peddles the powerful lie that God's authority is objectionable, that it is a form of tyranny. And reflecting on his fate, he sees no way back from this wilful error:

> ...but by submission; and that word
> Disdain forbids me, and my dread of shame

---

[43] Ibid.

[44] Ibid., p.592.

[45] Ibid.

[46] Wycliffe's translation of the Bible is 'the unsheathing of the sword of the Spirit, which is the Word of God'; his preface was 'written in a bold and uncompromising spirit' (John Foxe, *Book of Martyrs*, ed. Rev. W. Bramley-Moore, Cassell, Petter and Galpin, London 1886, p.220).

[47] Robert L. Entzminger, *Divine Word: Milton and the Redemption of Language*, Duquesne Univerity Press, Pittsburgh, 1985, p.2.

> Among the Spirits beneath, whom I seduced
> With other promises and other vaunts
> Than to submit, boasting I could subdue
> Th'Omnipotent..' (4.81).

Satan has founded a rival discourse whereby God is conceivable as tyrant (he calls him 'Punisher' later in the speech). It entails an aesthetic: 'submission' has acquired a contemptible sound. It is a rival rhetoric of authority whose falsity Satan tries to drown in relativism and linguistic obfuscation. It is false by definition; for instance in the above boast of overcoming 'Th'Omnipotent'. But Satan is seduced by it himself, he cannot abandon his invention, delete it. It is an aesthetic form of temptation; a new form of self-expression is deemed self-justifying, its falsity redeemed by its vitality. He must constantly emit this new and self-contradictory language: 'Evil, be thou my Good' (4.110). On one level there is something commendable in this linguistic ingenuity, and in Satan's general rhetorical vitality. But that is Milton's whole point: the attractiveness of falsity, its seductive linguistic power. The Fall is our falling for it.

As Stanley Fish has shown, most critics make the mistake of forgetting what this poem is about.[48] It is not about a form of human authority but about God. Any reading of it which questions the goodness of divine authority is condemned from within the text as contradictory, even as rooted in Satanic logic. But for Satan's lie, there is no possibility of questioning divine authority. In the world of the poem, the identity of goodness and power is simply a fact. Yet it is a difficult fact, in which the reader is gradually trained: 'Submitting to the style of the poem is an act of self-humiliation... . By accepting the challenge of self-criticism and self-knowledge, one learns how to read, and by extension how to live, and becomes finally the Christian hero who is, after all, the only fit reader'.[49]

What of the rhetoric of divine authority? It sounds cold, distant, formal, excessively orderly.[50] It is rather inhuman. Surveying the cosmic scene in Book Three, God is the image (or rather the voice) of regal self-assurance; he calmly condemns the rebellion of the 'ingrate' Satan, excuses himself from possible blame, and predicts the fall and rise of mankind. The Son is more enthusiastic, more involved in the unfolding story but still seems to lack Satan's passion. Offering his life for humanity's redemption he sets out a rather too orderly theory of atonement, as if brooking a business deal. The plan is approved and a very orderly celebration of angelic hymns ensues. It is easy to criticise Milton's heaven as cold and sinister, the dream of a control-freak rational Puritan, but hard to imagine how else it could have been done. Also, of course, it is part of Milton's

---

[48] Most readers 'end by accusing God or by writing volumes to expose the illogic of His ways' (Stanley Fish, *Surprised by Sin, the Reader in Paradise Lost*, second edition, Macmillan, London, 1997, p.272).

[49] Ibid., p.207.

[50] Bloom is scathing: 'I cannot explain the disaster of Milton's God, who resembles, say, Ronald Reagan more than he does, say, Sigmund Freud' (Bloom, 1987, p.106).

point that we are inclined to find fault with God's apparent shortcomings, therefore revealing our own.

It is a form of rhetoric that fell us and it is a form of rhetoric that can save us. While *Paradise Lost* narrated the limited triumph of Satanic rhetoric, *Paradise Regained* enacts the larger counter-triumph of the Word. A rhetoric of disobedience and false logic is met with a new rhetoric of obedience which restores meaning to language. In *Paradise Regained* Milton seeks to convey the entire import of the New Testament through focusing on one scene from the Gospels: the temptation of Christ in the wilderness. It is a very Protestant choice. He uses it to portray Christ as the Word, whose definitive rebuke of Satan effects the victory of faith. As in *Comus*, the rhetorical drama is centered around the conflict between the Word (and faith's apprehension of it) and the demonic voices which seek to undermine it. In the case of *Paradise Regained*, of course, the Word himself is on stage, and so the victory is entirely assured, almost absurdly easy: Satanic rhetoric cannot constitute even the slightest threat; it is reduced to a foil. As in John's Gospel, Christ is forceful without recourse to violence or even to passion in the normal sense.

Part of Satan's defeat at the hands of Christ is aesthetic. Beside the rhetorical presence of Christ, Satan lacks his former pathos; his rhetoric is stale and predictable, his sophism tedious. It is now Christ's voice of obedience that is endowed with heroic daring, or at least heroic fortitude. In its Christic instance, obedience entails Promethean defiance, heroic resistance. These qualities are wrested from Satan, restored to truth; redeemed. *Paradise Lost* must be read in the light of its sequel for Satan's character to be understood. His earlier appearance as rebel-hero is exposed as a temporary aberration by the true heroism of Christ. The Romantic refusal of such a reading is almost strange. Especially as Milton's Christ has certain characteristics associated with Romantic thought. Though obedient to God he is proudly independent of worldly authorities – there is a hint of Promethean daring here. And his individualism has aesthetic affinities, for instance when he scorns the praise of the mob. He is full of righteous pride, of assurance in his God-given strength, and of course, as the Word, he is the embodiment of forceful speech. The religious truth of this speech consists at least partly in its stylistic force.

Christ's responses refer back to the idea of the Satanic perversion of language. The messianic-related ideals that Satan raises are rejected and redefined by Christ; the concept is restored to meaning. Also of course Satan perverts scripture, wilfully interpreting it to his own ends. Christ restores its spiritual sense. As we have seen in the preceding epic, Satan tempts through the attractive rhetorical presentation of false ideals. Christ responds by deconstructing them. On one level he shares Plato's scepticism of rhetoric. But only on one level: the Word is an alternative rhetorical force, a true enchantment. And it is known as the infinitely stronger force. The narrator finally warns Satan against it:

> Hereafter learn with awe
> To dread the Son of God: he all unarmed

> Shall chase thee with the terror of his voice
> From thy demoniac holds, possession foul...
>   (4.625-9)

Here we neatly return to the demonic exorcism of the Nativity Ode. In Milton's poetic theology, faith consists in the apprehension and appropriation of the Word's rhetorical victory. It is known through its agonistic encounter with what opposes it. *Samson Agonistes* reflects the same dynamic. Samson has fallen from grace through yielding to the verbal assaults, the 'tongue-batteries' of Delilah. His recovery of faith comes with his recovery of a polemical voice. The presence of real rhetorical opposition, in the form of Delilah and then Harapha, reminds him of his cause, re-trains him in the verbal idiom of faith.

Milton is not concerned simply to perform a booming rhetoric of divine authority. In *Paradise Lost* especially, his is a dialectical strategy: to expose the ideological tendencies of all power-related rhetoric, and thereby to represent the alien otherness of the Word. This is his common ground with Herbert. In its first wave of poets, then, Protestantism performs its capacity for dialogical self-criticism as well as its proclamatory force.

Milton's lasting influence was not where he would have wanted it: in poetic style. For Saintsbury and Dryden he was the master of lofty diction, the grand style. Johnson agreed: 'The characteristic quality of [*Paradise Lost*] is sublimity'.[51] Milton's aim was to subject poetic sublimity to Christianity, to put it in the service of the Word. Instead the poetic grand style becomes itself endowed with pseudo-religious weight. The message is lost in the medium. This is the recurring problem with Christian art: art has a tendency to proclaim itself. In the next chapter devoted to poetry, we shall return to this point.

---

[51] Samuel Johnson, from *The Lives of the Most Eminent English Poets* (1783), in Milton, *Paradise Lost*, ed. by S. Elledge, Norton Critical Edition, New York, 1993, p.485.

Chapter 6

Kierkegaard and the Crisis of Authority

This chapter returns to theology in its stricter sense, and so to the Continent. As we move from the sixteenth to the nineteenth century, the intellectual context of theology becomes markedly different, of course. Although Luther was already aware of humanism as a potential danger to theological method, as we saw in his response to Erasmus, the recovery of learning was more often seen as an ally and a spur to the Reformers' cause. By the time of Kierkegaard's authorship, however, Protestant theological discourse has long been subsumed by the rise of the Enlightenment discourse of reason, progress and human sovereignty. It has opted to justify itself in relation to the discourse of the Enlightenment – and also of its Romantic supplement (most obviously in Schleiermacher). Thus begins the central argument of modern theology: between the 'liberal' mediators of Christian discourse and secular thought, and the stubborn opponents of this. To set it out thus is to invoke Barth and probably to side with him. This modern narrative is most clearly identified by Barth, and of course it serves his own polemical purposes. Although Barth is the master-narrator of this story, of the surrender of theology to secular liberalism, it extends back to Kierkegaard – and, as we shall presently see, before him.

I argue that Kierkegaard anticipates Barth not only in objecting to this surrender but also in the alternative conception of faith he develops in response. In contrast to the 'speculative' approach of modern philosophy, particularly Hegel, Christian truth is conceived in rhetorical terms, as a voice of authority in which faith participates. As 'speculative' suggests, the Enlightenment prefers looking to hearing. Lash laments 'the early modern subsumption of the whole grammar of revelation and religious belief into that "spectatorial" model of the process of knowledge which came so to dominate the Western imagination'.[1] Theology must think against modernity; it must deconstruct the dominant structures of thought so that the voice of Christian witness can again be endowed with passionate meaning.

Before Kierkegaard

Before we get on to Kierkegaard himself let us briefly consider the Enlightenment's effect upon theological discourse as it relates to our theme. For Kierkegaard's reaction against Hegelian thought is really a rejection of the dominant intellectual trends of the last century or more. The eighteenth century

---

[1] Nicholas Lash, *The Beginning and End of 'Religion'*, Cambridge University Press, 1996, p.79. Such a model is necessarily inimical to 'the doctrine that God *is* utterance, *verbum*, Word' (ibid., p.91).

sees the rapid rise of a discourse of the sovereignty of human reason, and the consequent marginalisation of the discourse of faith. The movement is traceable back to the seventeenth century, of course; to Descartes, Locke and others.

One of the earliest relevant texts is Hobbes' *Leviathan* (1651). Hobbes is the first to extend the spirit of Galileo and Descartes to the subject of politics. In doing so he establishes the trend that culminates in Hegel: the social becomes the central category of reflection. Hobbes begins with Man, with an anatomy of his various qualities, among which is the religious. He proceeds to show that human society is based on the idea of voluntary submission to soveriegn power. Unless this power is single and unrivalled the state will fall into the chaos of civil war (as in England at the time of writing). His thesis is based in the claim that all power is amenable to human reason. It is comprehended in terms of its social necessity. And this extends to religion. Because religion must not disrupt civil order (Hobbes' bottom line), its account of authority must be subsumed into civil authority. It can have no rhetorical power of its own, if order is to be upheld. The sovereign must have a monopoly on authoritative rhetoric: it is therefore his duty to control Christian rhetoric, to make it refer primarily to himself. He, rather than an independent church, must be seen as God's true prophet, and as the true judge of heresy.[2]

Though Hobbes professes to Protestant orthodoxy, his effect is to identify the voice of God with the will of the absolutist Christian state. The relationship of this position to Protestantism is ambiguous. On one hand it is enabled by Luther's rejection of Rome: Hobbes thus applauds the Tudor 'Exorcisme' of Rome, 'the Kingdome of Fairies'.[3] Also, Hobbes is following Luther in his stark political realism, his secularisation of politics. For Luther, to try to rule by the gospel would be to 'loose the bands and chains of the wild and savage beasts, and let them tear and mangle every one...';[4] civil order is unthinkable unless 'power and authority are honoured and feared'.[5] Yet, on the other hand, Hobbes has no conception of the Word of God as an independent sovereign power. For Luther, the ruler exists to serve the progress of the Word of God. For Hobbes, in effect, religion exists to augment the ruler's hold on power.

Hobbes may be seen as a true parent of Enlightenment theology. In Deism the notion of religious truth becomes both socialised and rationalised. Deism is soon the conventional religious discourse in England; Locke's *Reasonableness of Christianity* (1695) and Toland's *Christianity Not Mysterious* (1696) are representative of a trend that continues through to Paley's *Evidences of Christianity* (1794), and beyond. It takes Hume to give the lie to this in philosophical terms; to deny that religious belief has a rational basis. But the intellectual tide is against him. The dominant tendency, which culminates in Kant and Hegel, is to force reason and religion together. This tendency of course has socio-political implications. To rationalise religion is also to socialise it, to

---

[2] Thomas Hobbes, *Leviathan*, ed. by C. B. Macpherson, Penguin, Middlesex, 1978, 3.36, p.469; 3.42, p.605.
[3] Ibid., 4.47, p.714.
[4] Luther, *On Secular Authority: to what extent it should be obeyed*, in Dillenberger ed., 1961, p.370.
[5] Ibid., p.374.

conform it to an account of rational civil order, in this case bourgeois progress. Against this tide it becomes almost impossible to forge an alternative account of religious discourse; one in keeping with the Reformation, with the rhetorical extremity of Luther.

One reaction to this process, which is to influence Kierkegaard over a century later, comes from Jonathan Swift. A prime target of his satire is the emergent discourse of bourgeois utilitarianism, and its tendency to arrogate all authority to itself, a tendency he associated with Hobbes.[6] The tendency is apparent in Gulliver's arrogant Enlightenment voice, and in that of his ironic tracts. Most relevant to our purposes is his defence of Christianity: 'An Argument to prove that the Abolishing of Christianity in England, may as Things now stand, be attended with some Inconveniences, and perhaps not produce those many good Effects proposed thereby'. The title contains the main point: the polite, reasonable style is an absurdly inappropriate one in which to defend the faith from extinction. With an allusion to Hobbesian thinking he acknowledges 'the fundamental Law that makes Majority of Opinion the Voice of God', and that this opinion is broadly in favour of Christianity's abolition.[7] He insists that he is not out to defend 'Real Christianity, such as used in primitive Times...to have an Influence on Mens Belief and Actions': this would be 'to destroy at one Blow all the Wit, and half the Learning of the Kingdom; to break the entire Frame and Constitution of Things, to ruin Trade, extinguish Arts and Sciences with the Professors of them... .'[8] Instead his discourse is 'intended only in Defence of Nominal Christianity, the other having been for some time wholly laid aside by general Consent, as utterly inconsistent with all our present schemes of Wealth and Power'.[9] The idea of the social good has moved on from Hobbes' exaltation of peaceful order: here are the more familiar bourgeois goods of economic progress and 'culture'. Swift pretends to accept that these are now the criteria of truth and goodness, and to advocate nominal Christianity as a useful opiate and diversion.

In *A Letter of Advice to a Young Poet* (1721) Swift's irony returns to the marginalisation of religious discourse, in this case in relation to poetry. The young poet is urged to overcome any childish prejudice in favour of religious belief, 'so far as to think it better to be a *great Wit* than a *good Christian*'.[10] The doctrinal baggage of religion is 'a wonderful check to Wit and Humour, and such as a true Poet cannot possibly give into with a saving of his Poetical License'.[11] He is urged to read the scriptures, but only as a resource for poetic invention: 'Far be it from me to desire you to believe them, or lay any great stress upon their Authority'.[12] Accompanying the bourgeois ideal of economic freedom is that of aesthetic and intellectual freedom. Swift, like Kierkegaard after him, satirises the arrogance of

---

[6] As its Preface explains, *A Tale of a Tub*'s title is a rejoinder to Hobbes' *Leviathan*.

[7] Jonathan Swift, 'An Argument...', in Swift, *Gulliver's Travels and Selected Writings in Prose and Verse*, ed. by John Hayward, Random House, New York, 1949, p.383.

[8] Ibid., p.384.

[9] Ibid., p.385.

[10] Swift, 1949, p.422.

[11] Ibid., p.423.

[12] Ibid., p.424.

these secular ideals, their colonisation of public speech. The new discourse of
bourgeois reason arrogates all authority to itself. It delegitimises any other voice,
any other tone; it writes off all other rhetoric – as dangerous, erratic, mad.
Religious utterance is subtly consigned to the latter category; it is a manifestation
of 'enthusiasm' or 'passion'. Hobbes helps to establish this Platonic suspicion; for
him the verbal expression of passion is inferior to rational discourse because
potentially false. Passionate expressions do not qualify as 'certain signes'; and the
most extreme are entirely disqualified: 'Cursing, Swearing, Reviling, and the like,
do not signifie as speech; but as the actions of a tongue accustomed'.[13] Such
strictures are intended to reduce the possibility of prophetic claims, to disqualify
would-be Luthers or Miltons. The discourse of faith is thus subjected to the more
'real' authority of social reason. (In the next chapter we shall consider this in
relation to poetry.)

Pascal is another useful witness to the origins of Enlightenment theology.
Against the rationalization of religion he defends the idea of God's miraculous
grace as the basis of faith. Thus his famous rejection of the God of 'philosophers
and scholars' in favour of the God of Abraham, Isaac, Jacob and Jesus Christ.[14]
Entailed in this decision for the particularity and mystery of revelation is a will to
retain a privileged role for authority in the economy of faith. 'There are two ways
of persuading men of the truths of our religion; one by the power of reason, the
other by the authority of the speaker'. Present theology uses the former, and the
result is 'feeble arguments, because reason can be bent in any direction'.[15] Like
Montaigne before him, Pascal uses scepticism in the service of theology; and
thereby rediscovers the role of authority in the grammar of faith: 'Our religion did
not come to us through reasoned arguments or from our own intelligence: it came
to us from outside authority, by commandments'.[16] Because human reason
provides no adequate basis for a metaphysic, Christianity remains fully reliant
upon *faith* – and so upon revelation, and the rhetoric of authority that mediates it.
Yet Pascal is by no means a fideist, contemptuous of reason. He seeks to show that
Christianity is alone reasonable, despite its appeal beyond reason. Faith's
submission to authority must exist *alongside* reason, not in place of it: 'Submission
and use of reason; that is what makes true Christianity'.[17] This coexistence may
result in dialogical tension akin to Luther's: '[Man] carries on an inner dialogue
with himself, which it is important to keep under proper control... . We must keep
silence as far as we can and only talk to ourselves about God, whom we know to be
true, and thus convince ourselves that he is.'[18]

---

[13] Hobbes, 1978, 1.6, p.129.
[14] This is from a document known as the Memorial, found upon Pascal's death sewn into his
clothing. In Pascal, *Pensées,* trans. with an introduction by A. J. Krailsheimer, Middlesex,
1976, p.309.
[15] Ibid., no. 820, p. 273 – also eg. 418, 449, 588, 769, 781.
[16] Michel de Montaigne, *An Apology for Raymond Sebond,* trans., ed., with intro. by M. A.
Screech, Penguin, Middlesex, 1987, p.66.
[17] Ibid., 167 (269), p.83.
[18] Ibid., 99 (536), p.55.

The rise of scientific and bourgeois liberalism creates a new discourse of human authority, which is to say that it constitutes a new discourse of power. Religion seems happy to be recruited to this process: its social relevance is guaranteed by its alliance with the dominant discourse. It forgets that is based in an alternative discourse of authority. Readers of Barth will recognise this as an adaptation of his argument. Barth's study of Enlightenment and Romantic religious thought is an extended indictment of *hubris*. His preliminary assessment of the eighteenth century extrapolates from political absolutism in its characterisation of the age. 'Absolute man' discovers the potential of his own humanity 'and looks upon it as the final, the real and absolute, I mean as something 'detached', self-justifying, with its own authority and power'.[19] As we shall see in later chapters, Barth's critique of modernity is an accusation of auto-idolatry, of aping God.

The discourse of bourgeois liberalism culminates in Hegelian thought. Here, Hobbes' exaltation of rational-social order is developed; it is now endowed with spiritual and historical dynamism. Hegel starts with the presupposition that Christianity is essentially rational, and therefore a force of human freedom. He joins Kant in the idea that Christianity must free itself from its 'positivity', its irrationality and authoritarianism (ascribed to its Jewish roots). But previous attempts to rationalise Christianity have forgotten that religion is *social*. Following Herder's conception of 'folk religion', Hegel puts this 'expressivist' concern at the centre of his thought. 'Even the purest religion of reason must become incarnate in the souls of individuals, and all the more so in the people as a whole', he declared early on.[20] Christianity has become socially alienated, culturally impotent, even *frigid*: at holy communion, 'which is supposed to be a celebration of human brotherhood, we fear we might contract venereal disease from the brother who drank out of the communal chalice before'.[21] Religion must be the expression of the popular, national spirit, not the concern of a few pious intellectuals. Ancient Greece is Hegel's model; or rather an idealised image of its ethical-social cohesion (*Sittlichkeit*). Historically, Christianity has worked *against* the achievement of social cohesion; it has encouraged isolated individuality, alienation, what Hegel calls 'the Unhappy Consciousness'. This tendency works against human freedom, because human freedom is necessarily social. Yet this tendency is not the whole Christian story, just the preliminary unfolding of the dialectic. Despite first appearances, there is social life in Christianity. Indeed Hegel declares that its true logic is social, rational and historical. Hegel thus fits Christianity into a narrative of the historical achievement of social liberty, a narrative in which the modern state plays a starring role: 'Everything that man is he owes to the state; only in it can he find his essence. All value that a man has, all spiritual reality, he has only through the state'.[22] Hegel is the nodal point in modern thought – he is rational *and*

---

[19] Karl Barth, *From Rousseau to Ritschl, being the translation of Die Protestantische Theologie Im 19. Jahrhundert*, ed. by J. McIntyre and A. McIntyre, trans. by B. Cozens, SCM Press, London, 1959, p.15.

[20] G. W. F. Hegel, 'The Tubingen Essay', in Hegel, *Three Essays 1793-1795*, ed. and trans. by P. Fuss and J. Dobbins, Notre Dame University Press, Indiana, 1984, p.51.

[21] Ibid., p.56.

[22] Hegel, *Die Vernunft in der Geschichte*, ed. J. Hoffmeister, Hamburg 1955 (p.111), quoted

romantic, his theory of history and society helps to inspire both Marxism *and* fascism. The contradictions of secular modernity are united in his establishment of the social as the criterion of 'religious' value. He takes the religious tendency of the age and steps it up a gear, teaches it faith in itself.

Kierkegaard has just one objection to this ingenious new system of thought: despite pretences it bears no relation to Christianity. Indeed it strikes him as Christianity's very antithesis. Before we consider this, however, one more of his predecessors deserves a mention. Georg Hamann was Kierkegaard's most important recent intellectual and religious influence.[23] (Ironically, Hegel too was influenced by him.) Hamann was a sworn enemy of rationalism in general and rational theology in particular. Those who tried to prove religion's truth he declared even bigger fools than the biblical atheist.[24] He admired Hume's attack on natural religion, especially his famous opinion that Christianity cannot be believed by any reasonable person without a miracle: 'He may have said this with a scornful and critical air, yet all the same it is orthodoxy and a witness to the truth from the mouth of an enemy and persecutor'.[25] Though a strong Lutheran, Hamann's opposition to religious rationalism was not merely reactionary. Indeed he was an innovator of expressivist linguistic theory and thus a founder of German Romanticism – Herder and Jacobi were both his followers. Hamann's theology was based in the presupposition of God's linguistic authority and originative power. He called God 'a powerful speaker', whose 'counsel is immediately translated into deed'. He thus rediscovered the Semitic idea of word as event (*dabar*), and of revelation as a *poetic* phenomenon.[26] Instead of trying to prove God, theology's business was reflection on its own linguistic inheritance. He noted that Luther called theology 'the grammar for the language of Scripture', an idea he took further: 'Holy Scripture ought to be our dictionary, our art of rhetoric, so that all a Christian's ideas and speech would be based on it, would consist and be composed of it'.[27]

---

in Charles Taylor, *Hegel and Modern Society*, Cambridge University Press, 1979, p.86.

[23] According to Leibrecht (who supplies no reference) Kierkegaard called him his 'only master' (Leibrecht, W., *God and Man in the Thought of Hamann*, trans. by J. H. Stam and M. H. Bertram, Philadelphia, 1966, p.5).

[24] J. G. Hamann, *Leben und Schriften*, vol. 5, quoted in ibid., p.34.

[25] J. G. Hamann, *Briefwechsel* I, p.356, quoted in ibid., p.14.

[26] Berlin suggests an affinity with William Blake here, for instance in the latter's comment: 'Jesus & his Apostles & Disciples were all Artists' (Blake, *Jerusalem*, plate 4, l.20, quoted in Isaiah Berlin, *The Magus of the North: J. G. Hamann and the Origins of Modern Irrationalism*, Fontana, 1993, p.64). As we shall see, there is a danger in Blake's corrective intention: the sacralisation of the artist.

[27] Hamann, *Bibl. Betrachtungen*, N I,243, quoted in Von Balthasar, 1984, p.277. He anticipates Wittgenstein's idea that different forms of life generate distinctive 'languages' (see Berlin, 1993, p.77).

'Away from the "Poet"!': Towards a Theology of Authority

I am largely passing over Kierkegaard's earlier, dominantly pseudonymous authorship. Here, rather like Swift, he is concerned with attacking liberal discourse from within, by doing its voices. In 'The Seducer's Diary', part of *Either/Or*, he exposes the psychopathology within the aesthetic attitude. Then, through Judge Wilhelm's voice, he considers bourgeois religious morality as an alternative 'gaze'. From around 1847, both the philosophical and aesthetic idioms begin to recede before the increasingly bold expression of theological purpose, which may increasingly be seen as his 'own' theological position. This chapter emphasises the role of authority in Kierkegaard's conception of Christianity's truth, and analyses the rhetorical construction of religious authority in his authorship.

The concept of authority is basic to Kierkegaard's unique theological approach. *The Point of View for my Work as an Author* (completed in 1848, though unpublished until after his death) provides useful evidence to this effect. He explains that his aesthetic authorship was intended to address the illusion of Christendom, which is rooted in the fact that most people who call themselves Christians 'live in categories quite foreign to Christianity... . [They are] People upon whom it has never dawned that they might have any obligation to God...'.[28] As we shall see, this pathos of obligation is for Kierkegaard essential to the genuine reassertion of the Christian idiom.

Chapter Three of *The Point of View* is called 'The Share Divine Governance had in my Authorship', which sounds rather like the chapter headings of Nietzsche's *Ecce Homo* – though its content could hardly be more different. His authorship is designed to reflect the process of education, or 'instruction' by divine governance in which the aesthetic is overcome. 'If with one word I were to express my judgement of this age, I would say that it lacks religious education (understanding this word in the broadest and deepest sense)'.[29] The religious educator's task is to oppose the spirit of the age: 'The task which has to be proposed to the majority of people in Christendom is: Away from the "poet"!... . Away from speculation!... . The movement is Back! And although it is all done "without authority", there is, nevertheless, something in the accent which recalls a policeman when he faces a riot and says, Back!'.[30] His 'accent', or tone of voice, will express urgency in a situation of dangerous chaos, where the re-establishment of order is the first necessity. We note that he both does and does not claim authority for himself in this passage. It is a characteristic ambiguity. The phrase 'without authority' first appeared in the Preface to his *Two Edifying Discourses* of 1843. In a late *Journal* entry he expands on it: 'I am not an apostle bringing something from God with authority. No, I am serving God, but without authority. My task is to make room for God to come... . I am a policeman, if you like. But in this world the police come with power and arrest the others, whereas the higher

---

[28] Kierkegaard, *The Point of View for my Work as an Author: a Report to History and Related Writings*, trans. by W. Lowrie, Harper & Row, New York, 1962, p.22.

[29] Ibid., p.74.

[30] Ibid., p.75.

police come suffering, and rather ask themselves to be arrested'.[31] At first he denies that he has apostolic authority; then suggests that he lacks authority in the worldly sense, which is surely true of the apostle also.

Authorial authority is constantly problematised in his work: his use of pseudonyms contributes to this.[32] Unlike Luther or Barth, he does not lay claim to priestly authority, does not speak from and for the Church (later on, he speaks directly against it). There is thus a constant tension surrounding this lay voice which both exalts and undermines the official voice of the Church. His denial of his own authority is often a way of highlighting the absoluteness of the authority of Christian proclamation: 'To preach true Christianity, New Testament Christianity is in a sense beyond man's powers, divine authority is required, or rather, divine lostness in the Absolute'.[33] Elsewhere he explains that whereas '[t]he Christian discourse has some degree of involvement in doubt, the sermon operates absolutely, solely with authority: scriptural, or of the apostles'.[34] He thus 'raises the stakes' of official Church proclamation. His dissatisfaction with the Church is born out of a stubborn perfectionism: a naïve expectation that the Word will be delivered here with appropriate authority.

Kierkegaard recounts his own (unsentimental) education towards obedience. His upbringing, he tells us, was religiously strict to the point of 'the most inhuman cruelty'.[35] Though his father infected him with religious melancholy, he has accepted the pathos of 'obedience absolute' rather than rebelled against it.[36] This is of course an unusual attitude to an excessively religious upbringing. Like liberal apostates he recognises the excess and its danger yet he refuses to react against it. Unlike Edmund Gosse, in *Father and Son*, aestheticism offers him no lasting refuge from his formative influence. This inhuman sternness is accepted and affirmed as the core of faith and as the germ of his authorship. Kierkegaard surely knows that he is hereby exposing himself to the Enlightenment retort that such faith is an infantile hang-over. He invites our suspicions of pathological excess, dares us to 'take offence'. (Had Nietzsche fulfilled his intention of reading Kierkegaard, such passages would surely have shocked him more than anything he found in Pascal.)

Continuing his analysis of his authorship, he turns to his category of 'the individual' and his polemic against 'the crowd'. I suggest that this (easily-misinterpreted) theme of his authorship is also based in his conception of religious authority. It is even a device by which to proclaim a theology of authority.

---

[31] Kierkegaard, *The Last Years: Journals 1853-55* (*LY* hereafter), ed. and trans. by R. Gregor Smith, Collins, London, 1965, p.303, XIA, 250.

[32] See Kirmmse, Bruce, "'Out with it!': Kierkegaard and Golden Age Denmark', in Hannay and Marino 1998. Kirmmse usefully traces Kierkegaard's psychological struggle against the authority of the established Church, which is rooted in the drama between Mynster and his father.

[33] *LY* p.206, XIA 45.

[34] Kierkegaard, *a Selection from his Journals and Papers* (*JP* hereafter), ed. by Hannay, Penguin, Middlesex, 1996, p.254, 47 VIII I. A6.

[35] Ibid., p.76.

[36] Ibid., p.82.

His complaint is against 'the view of life which conceives that where the crowd is, there also is the truth, and that in truth itself there is need of having the crowd on its side': instead, 'a "crowd" is untruth'.[37] In an important footnote to this he insists that his polemic against the crowd is specifically religious: 'it goes without saying…that in relation to all temporal, earthly, worldly matters the crowd may have…decisive competency as a court of last resort… . But…I am affirming the untruth of the crowd…when it is treated as a criterion for what "truth" is'. In another note he denies that his aversion to 'the crowd' 'is meant as an invidious qualification, the distinction which human selfishness irreligiously erects between "the crowd" and superior persons… . No, "crowd" stands for number, the numerical…'.[38]

The evil of 'the crowd' is thus its implicit claim to authority in all matters including the religious. And the essence of the religious is that normal criteria of truth or authority, such as reason, consent and utility, are entirely renounced in order that a distinctive authority may be known. This aversion to 'the crowd' is not misanthropy, he protests, for to love one's neighbour is commanded of us, but 'never have I read in Holy Scripture the commandment, Thou shalt love the crowd – and still less, Thou shalt recognise, ethico-religiously, in the crowd the supreme authority in matters of "truth"'.[39]

Kierkegaard does not try to give an account of how and why Christian revelation is the true authority in ethico-religious matters. He is only insisting that, according to its own logic, Christian discourse cannot be compromised by the introduction of human criteria of truth – and remain Christian discourse. If we are to bother with it at all, we must accept it as a discourse of *authority*. And his polemic is primarily against the 'category mistake' of liberal theology, which adapts Christianity to the requirements of modern thought. (As that phrase suggests, there is a link with Wittgenstein here.)[40] This confusion constitutes rebellion against God:

> [Christendom] treat[s] Christianity, not as something which *in obedient subservience to God's majesty* must be believed, but as something which in order to be acceptable must try by the aid of *reasons* to satisfy 'the age', 'the public', &c. [41]

The way forward (or, as Kierkegaard prefers, back) from this confusion is to replace the category of 'the race' with 'the single individual'. In the isolation of individuality, the speculative hubris of Hegel *et al* simply dissolves. But this position is only minimally related to the Romantic belief in the *dignity* of the individual. Christianity must tirelessly exalt 'the individual' because the individual

---

[37] Ibid., p.110.

[38] Ibid., p.112.

[39] Ibid., p.118.

[40] They 'both saw philosophy as having [a] positive role to play in clarifying the "logic of concepts"…in the practices and concerns of belief and faith' (Gouwens, D. J., *Kierkegaard as Religious Thinker*, Cambridge University Press, 1996, p.18). See also Cavell, Stanley, 'Kierkegaard's *On Authority and Revelation*', in Thompson, 1987, p.384.

[41] Ibid., p.133.

is, as it were, the weak link in the human chain, defenceless against the sovereignty of God, cornered into obedience. 'A person can relate to God in the truest way only as an individual, for one always best acquires the conception of one's own worthlessness alone'.[42] (His exaltation of the 'vulnerability' of individuality relates to his particular brand of misogyny. Though the man is weaker in this world without the support of the woman, 'from the Christian standpoint [such] weakness...is indispensable for strength for eternity'.)[43]

And this obedience, engendered by individuation, must be the foundation of Christian discourse: 'If the "race" is to be the court of last resort or even have subordinate jurisdiction, Christianity is abolished – if in no other way, at least by the *wrong and unchristian form* one gives the *Christian* message'.[44] Central to the question of proper authority in Christianity is *how one speaks of it* (in Chapter Four we have seen this in relation to Luther, and we shall see it again in relation to Barth).[45] In the final section of *The Sickness Unto Death* he explains: 'The trouble is not that Christianity is not voiced...but that it is voiced in such a way that the majority eventually think it utterly inconsequential'.[46] In a late Journal entry he observes that 'almost everyone nowadays speaks of Christianity as a critic of something he feels superior to'.[47] The pathos of obedience is essential to the grammar of Christian speech.[48]

Kierkegaard's polemic is thus concerned with the *rhetorical* apostasy of a debased Christendom. In faith the key issue is *how* one relates to God, and rhetoric is the arena of this 'how'. 'Rhetoric' must be handled with care in relation to Kierkegaard, however. In one sense, 'rhetoric' relates to the aesthetic illusion of Christendom. For example he warns the student of faith of the danger of 'taking a wrong turn into a rhetorical or poetical exposition instead of into action'.[49] Yet in another sense 'rhetoric' is positively fundamental to Kierkegaard's theological agenda. As Pattison says, he 'was concerned to redirect the task of Christian dogmatics by giving the kind of foundational role to rhetoric which had previously been given to metaphysics (or, sometimes, history)'.[50] The following journal entry backs this up:

---

[42] *JP* p.336, 48 I X A 318.

[43] *LY* p.148, XIA 426.

[44] Ibid., p.134.

[45] Barth, we shall see, speaks of a true 'ancestral line' in theology (which includes Luther and Kierkegaard) which is defined by its appropriate 'way of speaking' of God.

[46] Kierkegaard, *The Sickness Unto Death*, ed. and trans. by Howard V. Hong and Edna H. Hong, Princeton University Press, 1980, p.103.

[47] *LY* p.242, XIA 48.

[48] "Grammar' has regard, not only for the concepts of the faith ('dogma'), but also for 'rhetoric', not in the sense of 'oratory' alone unrelated to conviction, but the language of faith as it is used in the situation of existence' (Gouwens, 1997, p.21).

[49] Kierkegaard, *Judge For Yourself!* in Kierkegaard, *For Self-Examination and Judge for Yourself*, ed. and trans. by Howard V. Hong and Edna H. Hong, Princeton University Press, 1990, p.136.

[50] Pattison, 1992, pp.157-58.

In an older journal...(when I was reading Aristotle's *Rhetoric*), I wrote that I thought that instead of dogmatics one should introduce a Christian rhetoric. It would relate to *pistis*. *Pistis* in classical Greek is the conviction (more than *doxe*, opinion) which relates to what is probable. But Christianity, which always turns the natural man's concepts upside down and extracts the opposite, lets *pistis* relate to the improbable.[51]

This reflects our discussion of rhetoric in Chapter Two, and more particularly Kennedy's insistence that Christianity reinvents rhetoric, substituting authority for probability. It is even the *inversion* of normal rhetoric, which remains in the realm of the rational and the probable. Because it is 'improbable', such rhetoric must compel rather than convince; it relies upon its representation of the authority of its source.

Kierkegaard explicitly identifies the truth of revelation with its authority. For example he explains that *The Book on Adler* 'is essentially an ethical investigation of the concept of revelation... . Or, what comes to the same thing, the whole book is an investigation of the concept of authority, about the confusion involved in the fact that the concept of authority has been entirely forgotten in our confused age.'[52] Elsewhere he laments that Augustine's insistence that 'the perfection of Christianity consists precisely in its authority' is now forgotten, or explicitly rejected. Now 'theology seeks to establish the authority of Christianity by means of reasons, which is worse than any attack, since it confesses indirectly that there is no authority'.[53] Yet what, for Kierkegaard, is the locus of this authority? Obviously not the Church, which is presently an embarrassing parody of itself. Nor is scripture a reliable alternative: Kierkegaard was aware of the beginnings of biblical criticism and knew better than to make naïve claims in this area. I suggest that for Kierkegaard the Gospel's authority can only be located in the event of its reassertion, its reconstruction. To explore this further we must look in more detail at his polemics against the false rhetorics of authority that threaten faith.

We have already seen that the evil of 'the crowd' consists in its implicit claim to authority in *all* spheres. The democratic principle, what he calls 'the ballot', is a function of this danger: 'as eternal truth Christianity is entirely indifferent as to whether something has the majority or not but in the abracadabra of the ballot the majority is the test of truth'.[54] Elsewhere he makes the Swiftian proposal that a new public office be instituted: 'the teller', whose job is to announce the results of all votes. 'The idea is that whatever wins is the truth. The whole assembly falls down in adoration and says: It is the will of God. The teller should also be a holy person, since in him the state embodies its maxim. Accordingly, he is a kind of deity, or at least a mythological person who could be worshipped in oriental style and an annual festival held in his honour'.[55] Democracy is potentially

---

[51] *JP* p.462, 50 X 2 A 354.
[52] Kierkegaard, *On Authority and Revelation: The Book on Adler, or a Cycle of Ethico-Religious Essays*, trans. by W. Lowrie, Harper & Row, New York, 1955, p.lii.
[53] *LY* p.150, XIA, 436.
[54] *JP* p.305, 1848 ix A4.
[55] Ibid., p.472, 1850, x 2A 463.

the usurpation of the *voice* of God: '*vox populi vox Dei*' is the blasphemy of the age.

Scientific method is another such danger: it too refuses to recognise any limitation to its sphere of competence.

> Let them treat plants, animals, and stars in that way, but to treat the human spirit thus is a blasphemy which only weakens the passion of the ethical and the religious... . Nor is praying to God something inferior to making observations but absolutely the highest of all.[56]

The concern is not that science may have negative applications but that it constitutes an implicit claim to authority which can only marginalise the 'voice' of Christianity, and discredit the speech-act of faith. This new surfeit of knowledge 'fools people out of the simple, deep, passionate wonder and admiration which gives impetus to the ethical. *The only certainty is the ethico-religious*. It says: "Believe, you shall believe"'.[57] Though the ethico-religious lacks the mundane certainty of science, it must lay claim to a *rhetoric* of higher certainty, of authority and absoluteness. Indeed, in his refusal to justify faith in neutral terms, Kierkegaard shows a 'postmodern' awareness that this rhetoric of certainty is all that it has.

The authority of Christian discourse must be polemically constructed anew. There is no simple source of authority to which to appeal (neither the Church nor scripture). In Lutheran fashion, the Word's authority is only known as it is *proclaimed*. Of course his method of proclamation is more awkwardly self-conscious than Luther's. It is distanced from the authoritative space of the church, and so lacks all institutional paraphernalia of authority. All he has is a voice. Yet instead of claiming direct identity with the proclamatory voice, he *assumes* it as one possibility of discourse among others. Despite his disclaimers, Kierkegaard seeks to confront his reader with a re-enactment of the 'scandal' and the 'moment' in which faith is founded. He seeks to impress his reader with this rhetorical performance which plays with different voices of religious authority.

This raises the question of the aesthetic. Is the Christian voice of authority just an aesthetic construct, on a level with the voice of the Seducer in *Either/Or*? It would certainly seem that the aesthetic tendency towards *performance* abides in his religious works. His first religious voice, that of Judge Wilhelm in *Either/Or*, is consciously performed; he is imitating this (rather bourgeois) religious attitude. Despite its theological shortcomings, he is largely in sympathy with the rigour of this voice: it is echoed in subsequent signed works such as *Works of Love*. His 'own' theological voice is thus in part an imitation of his religious personae. The locus of religious authority becomes the rhetorical performance of the religious voice. By distancing this religious voice from himself and experimenting with various forms of it, Kierkegaard draws our attention to its performative agency. His aim is not to convey religious authority as a static given but as an event which demands contemporary repetition.

---

[56] Ibid.
[57] Ibid.

Kierkegaard as Lutheran Performer

The distinctive logic of faith is its acknowledgement of the authority of the Word of God over all other 'voices'. And Kierkegaard's discourse largely consists in the performance of this preference. This rhetorical performance owes a great deal to Luther. In general Kierkegaard is ambiguous about Luther. Though a Lutheran, his entire theology is an argument with Danish Lutheranism, which is typical of modern Christendom, and for which he often blames Luther himself. He protests that Luther's 'corrective' purpose has become falsely established as a new norm: everyone feels justified by an experience of 'Lutheran' angst, whereas in fact 'scarcely one individual in every generation experiences it in this way'.[58]

In his refutation of conventional apologetics, Kierkegaard revitalises the Lutheran dialogic of faith, discussed in Chapter Four. The desire for rational proof is cast as one voice in a dramatic dialogue in which the voice of the Word (or of faith) is shown to triumph. The only positive solution to the post-Enlightenment sceptical impasse is to re-cast it in specifically Christian fashion as the struggle of faith with unbelief – and in which faith triumphs 'by definition'.

The discourse of faith presupposes an authority-situation which entails the drastic refiguring of all intellectual categories. For example: 'The misfortune of our age...is disobedience... . And one deceives oneself and others by wishing to make us imagine that it is doubt. No, it is insubordination [rather than] doubt which is the fault in our misfortune and the cause of it'.[59] Doubt is thus *re-named* according to the perspective of faith. It is no longer an abstract concept, but is dramatised as a demonic force, requiring to be vanquished. In *For Self-Examination*, he likens doubt to a beast which feeds off reasons: 'one must not offer reasons to doubt – not if one's intention is to kill it – but one must do as Luther did, *order it to shut its mouth*'.[60] In defiance of Enlightenment discourse he thus subscribes to the Lutheran *style* of violent assertion. In the *Journals* he depicts faith as self-imposed torment, and wonders: 'Why should [anyone] be a Christian when it is so hard? The first answer to this might be: Shut up! Christianity is the absolute, you just have to!'.[61] This 'Shut up!' is directly Lutheran; as in Luther the voices of the world must be silenced and rebuked by an assertive tone of voice which strongly resembles normal rudeness, and so breaks the stylistics of civil discourse. This Lutheran idiom repeatedly surfaces in the *Journals*: 'Just now my melancholy raises so many horrendous possibilities that I neither can nor want to record them. The only way to fight such things is to say: Hold your tongue, and look away from them and look only to God'.[62] The locus of faith becomes the act of saying 'I believe', the assumption of the defiantly certain tone of simple testimony. This is an entirely different category of speech-act from the speculative tendency: 'Off with all this

---

[58] *LY* p.319, quoted in Koenker, E. B., 'S. Kierkegaard on Luther', in Pelikan ed. 1968, p.234.
[59] Kierkegaard, *On Authority and Revelation: The Book on Adler, or a Cycle of Ethico-Religious Essays*, trans. by W. Lowrie, Harper & Row, New York, 1955, p.liv.
[60] Kierkegaard, *For Self-Examination and Judge for Yourself*, p.88.
[61] *JP* p.342, 48, X I A 414.
[62] Ibid., p.359, 49, X I A 74.

world history and reasons and proofs for the truth of Christianity: there's just one proof – that of faith... . [T]here is nothing higher I can say than "*I* believe"... . Reasons are reduced to the ranks and that, again, is the opposite of all modern objectivity'.[63] Central to faith is this rhetorical moment in which the objections of reason are expelled by appeal to the Word. As in Luther the simple, primal speech-act of faith thus takes on an exorcistic force. Despite his reservations about Luther's legacy, the rhetorical debt is fundamental. For Luther, as we began to see in Chapter Four, theological discourse is founded not in reason or experience but in the tone of voice which is capable of communicating divine authority, and thus participating in divine agency. In the following journal entry Kierkegaard acknowledges an ambiguity in this tone:

> Reading Luther gives one the clear impression of a wise and assured spirit speaking with a decisiveness which is *gewaltig* [with the force of authority] (*er predigte gewaltig* [he preached authoritatively] – *ekousia* – Matthew 7). And yet this assurance strikes me as having something tumultuous about it, indeed precisely an uncertainty... . This is not some kind of deception; it is a pious effort.[64]

To endow the utterance of faith with authority is 'a pious effort': as we remarked of Herbert's poems and as we shall also see in Barth's *Romans* commentary, there is an element of conscious falsity, of *inauthenticity* in faith. For in preferring a received tradition of speech to all else it ventures beyond the pale of mere experience. Faith's task is to endow the unheard Word with authority over all heard words, all worldly rhetorics. As in the pseudonyms, this entails the assumption of a voice not fully one's own.

The *Edifying Discourses* often read as a handbook for such an endeavour. Though these discourses claim to lack the authority of a sermon, their preoccupation is with the struggle to apprehend authority in the Word. As one critic says, his 'response to...dogmatic Christology's loss of authority is to use the literary form of the discourses to sharpen and intensify the scandal of the crucified God-man... . For the philosophical-historical argumentation employed by the current theology, he substitutes the poetically imaginative power of the discourses... .'[65] The discourse entitled 'The Expectation of Faith' is a dramatisation of the rhetorical struggle of faith. The believer learns to resist the 'voice' of doubting realism.

> When the world begins its sharp testing...then the believer looks with sadness and pain at himself and at life but still he says: 'There is an expectation which all the world cannot take from me; it is the expectation of faith, and this is victory... . This expectation is not deceived; even in this moment I feel its victory more gloriously and more joyfully than all the pain of loss... .[66]

---

[63] Ibid., p.388-9, 49, X I A 481.

[64] Ibid., p.193, 45, V I A 108.

[65] Deuser, Hermann, 'Religious Dialectics and Christology', in Hannay and Marino, 1998, p.387.

[66] Kierkegaard, *Edifying Discourses*, 1843, p.38.

How faith speaks, in defiant response to the voices that besiege it, is the best description of *what faith is*. It consists in a tone of simple certainty, which, in Lutheran fashion, continually refers to the datum of the promise, the Word. And again we note the element of inauthenticity in this tone: its cold resolution sounds forced and, one level, false; as if through gritted teeth. We are told that it is said by the believer who 'looks with sadness and pain at himself and at life'. We are not told that he *feels* the certainty of victory but that he *says that he does*. Is he 'only saying' this, then? The pejorative implication is inappropriate, for the locus of faith is its adherence to the Word in spite of contradictory experience; what humanly seems inauthentic speech becomes transformed into something more than human. The human locus of the miracle of faith lies in this tone of voice, this 'putting on' of the *persona* of faith. As we have seen in Luther (and will see in Barth), faith is located in the utterance, in the speech-act's conformity to the received rhetorical idiom, and not in any sort of inner experience. As we argued in relation to Luther, the agent in faith is the Word of God, who remains external to the believer.

For Kierkegaard, to preach, or to speak with ecclesial authority, would be to assume a consistently authoritative religious voice as one's own voice; to claim too rigid an identity with it. His psychological analysis of Luther's authoritative speech implies that he cannot naively do the same. Ironic distance has become inevitable. Yet it is used to positive effect: in clarifying the pneumatological logic of Protestant rhetoric. His authorship thus anticipates the central tenet of Barth's 'dialectical theology' (to be discussed shortly): the communication of God's Word must primarily be understood as a human impossibility.

Kierkegaard's conception of the Christ-event as a paradox incapable of rational appropriation is of course reminiscent of Luther (it also anticipates Barth's *Romans*, as we shall see). In *Philosophical Fragments* he presents revelation as the overturning of the Socratic model of knowledge (the discovery or remembering of what is innately known). Though this work generally conforms to a philosophical, analytical style, it recalls Luther in its account of faith as defiant scandal and folly. At one point this debt comes to the surface: 'The paradox is so paradoxical as to declare the Reason a blockhead and a dunce'.[67] 'The paradox' here emerges as more than a philosophical category: it is a vocalisation of the Word's authority. We shall return to Kierkegaard briefly in Chapter Eight, in order to show the extent of Barth's debt to him.

---

[67] Kierkegaard, *Philosophical Fragments*, ed. and trans. by Howard V. Hong and Edna H. Hong, Princeton University Press, 1987, p.66.

Chapter 7

Protestant Poetics (II): Romanticism and After

This chapter returns to the literary 'sub-plot' of my thesis, begun in Chapter 5. Yet now we see a reversal in the relationship between Protestantism and English poetry. The confident appropriation of poetics for Protestant proclamation does not last beyond Milton. Poetic discourse reasserts its autonomy. And, in the period we are now discussing, it does more: it becomes an alternative discourse of authority which borrows heavily, and dangerously, from the Christian prophetic tradition.

Most of the writers assigned the Romantic label have little else in common, making Romanticism a notoriously elusive category. Yet one common factor is a concern with our theme: the rhetorical construction of authority, as it features in religious, political and of course aesthetic discourse. Romanticism begins as a variable mixture of religious, philosophical and political radicalism, under the aegis of the aesthetic. After Blake and early Coleridge, religious radicalism features less strongly, and political enthusiasm becomes narrower, in Shelley. The dominant factor becomes the aesthetic itself. In very different ways it triumphs in both Byron and Keats (who have little else in common). And it is the lasting legacy of Romanticism; it persists into the Modernism of Yeats, Eliot, Pound and others. And in these Modernists is exposed the political dangers in this aesthetic triumph: Romanticism ends in the aesthetic of fascism. (We shall later return to this theme in relation to Nietzsche.)

Romanticism is the desire for a new discourse of authority. In contrast to anaemic Enlightenment-speak, the affective and the aesthetic become instrumental to the new utterance. A fuller study would discuss the origins of Romantic thought in the Continental Enlightenment (Rousseau etc.) and eighteenth-century aesthetics (Burke etc.). I am limiting my brief survey to a few English writers, and passing over large questions of influence and genealogy. The story I want to illustrate, however sketchily, is this: poetic discourse imitates prophetic speech. 'Spilt religion' is the best definition of Romanticism, at least for our purposes (it is T. E. Hulme's). The relevance of this to my overall study should perhaps be underlined at this point. I am trying to expound the difference of 'the Christian rhetoric of authority' from ideological violence, to exonerate it as the uniquely nonviolent discourse of authority. To this end, it must be understood in the context of its modern alternatives.

The literary context must first be briefly recounted. In the Augustan poetic of the eighteenth century, moderation and order reassert themselves after the religious excess of the Interregnum. Milton gives way to Dryden, who sets the poetic tone for the following century. Pope is its figurehead; his is a poetic of social decorum, of civilised value, of taste. As we began to see in the last chapter, in relation to Hobbes and Swift, religious passion is again suspect, *infra dig*. This neo-classical poetic has such cultural force that its opposition is tantamount to madness. Christopher Smart, born 1722, defies his age for a proclamatory poetic, citing King David as his inspiration and precedent. He is patronised (in the modern sense) and institutionalised. William Cowper meets a similar fate (he is an important Romantic influence, in his puritan introspection, conversational style and spiritual recourse to nature). Blake is the most famous poetic rebel of this time, and for him too prophetic resistance blurs with madness.

Conventionally enough, I want to begin with Wordsworth and Coleridge. Their *Lyrical Ballads* of 1799 contains a Preface by Wordsworth, in which he is first concerned to justify his subject-matter's basis in 'humble and rustic life'. Here, he explains, human passions 'speak a plainer and more emphatic language' in which 'our elementary feelings...may be more accurately contemplated, and more forcibly communicated'.[1] This directness is a corrective against a cultural spirit of triviality and pretension. It has been forgotten that a poet is 'a man speaking to men'. Despite its seeming earthy lack of pretension, this formula entails large claims. For the poet is not an average man; he has exceptional sensitivity and insight, 'whence...he has acquired a greater readiness and power in expressing what he thinks and feels'.[2] Wordsworth objects to the idea that poetry is a gentleman's hobby: 'its object is truth, not individual and local, but general, and operative; not standing upon external testimony, but... its own testimony'.[3] This is an account of poetic truth informed by Enlightenment and democracy, as Hazlitt was the first to stress: 'the political changes of the day were the model upon which [Wordsworth] formed and conducted his poetical experiments. His Muse...is a levelling one'.[4] The poet, Wordsworth insists, is the representative and spokesman of Democratic Man; he 'binds together by passion and knowledge the vast empire of human society'.[5]

His stylistic innovation is a means of renewing poetry's power of utterance. Traditional poetry, he explains, soon developed a linguistic strangeness, a distance from how people speak. This 'distorted language' now obstructs poetry's purpose: 'The Poet must descend from this supposed height; and, in order to excite rational sympathy, he must express himself as other men express themselves'.[6] This linguistic 'descent', however, does not lead to a renunciation of the poetic claim to authority. It is reinvented as consciously and self-righteously modern. It is endowed with the new authorities of science and democracy. And a form of religious authority is retained, and developed.[7] This is clear from his poetic

---

[1] William Wordsworth, 'Preface to the Lyrical Ballads', in Russell Noyes ed., *English Romantic Poetry and Prose*, Oxford University Press, 1956, p.358.

[2] Ibid., p.361.

[3] Ibid., p.362.

[4] William Hazlitt, 'Mr. Wordsworth', in Hazlitt, *Selected Writings*, ed. by R. Blythe, Penguin, Middlesex, 1987, p.220.

[5] Noyes, 1956, p.363.

[6] Ibid., p.364.

[7] 'Wordsworth is really the first...to offer a new kind of religious sentiment which it seemed the peculiar prerogative of the poet to interpret' (T. S. Eliot, 'Shelley and Keats', in Eliot,

practice. 'Lines Composed A Few Miles Above Tintern Abbey'(1798) reports hearing in nature 'The still, sad music of humanity,/Nor harsh nor grating, though of ample power/To chasten and subdue'. This is the nature-religion of a lapsed Protestant, not a real pagan. A Calvinist voice of divine guidance and discipline underlies the scenery, a voice surely influenced by Milton. Nature's God-like *voice* is a major theme of the *Prelude* (1798-1805). It is a hymn of thanksgiving to this vocal power, for guiding him to adult wisdom. Rather as Augustine does, he traces the story of his subjection to vocal influence, his aural passion. At its heart is an equivalent of the Word. He learns to compare himself with 'the ancient Prophets': 'So, did a portion of that spirit/Fall on me'(10.458). He joins this tradition by a new means: the new authority of personal experience, minutely reflected on. Thus has he 'dared to tread this holy ground,/Speaking no dream, but things oracular'(13.253). He communicates his discovery of the new spiritual terrain, of '– if here the words of Holy Writ May with fit reverence be applied – that peace/ Which passeth understanding...'(14.125).

Fairly explicitly, then, he claims the status of religious poet, Milton's heir. 'What else is the authentic burden of Wordsworth's poetry, unless it be his sense of election to be the prophet of nature, as he calls it, in succession to Milton as prophet of Protestantism?'[8] In 'London, 1802', he imprecates Milton as if he is God (or, to Milton's horror, a saint); 'O raise us up, return to us again'. Milton's spirit replaces Milton's Spirit, who is alone worthy of such imprecation.

> Thou hadst a voice whose sound was like the sea:
> Pure as the naked heavens, majestic, free... .

Milton would reply that anything laudable in his voice was due to the agency of the Word. His prophetic status is humanised in this poem, its delicate theological logic undone. Wordsworth has come to praise him but buries him in Romantic confusion of categories. Other Romantics follow suit: Shelley declares that Milton 'stood alone, illuminating an age unworthy of him'.[9] Here too Milton becomes the source of illumination rather than God's reflector, or prophetic mouthpiece. The heroic pathos of standing alone is also misleading. As his two lesser epics attest, true heroism entailed for him dependence and obedience – words which Shelley like Satan holds in disdain (*PL* 4.81). Milton himself conceives his 'standing alone' in humbler terms: 'They also serve who only stand and wait'. Milton becomes a type of the Romantic ideal of poet as righteous victim, misprized by 'the ingrate world', as Keats says of Chatterton.

Coleridge is warier than Wordsworth of investing poetry with religious weight. He later responds to Wordsworth's *Preface*, questioning the notion that poetry's object is truth. As 'an immediate object', this is better pursued 'in sermons or moral essays, than in an elevated poem'.[10] Poetry only relates to truth indirectly,

---

The Use of Poetry and the Use of Criticism; Studies in the relation of Criticism to Poetry in England, Faber, London, 1933, p.87).

[8] Bloom, 1987, p.137.

[9] Shelley, *A Defence of Poetry*, in Noyes, 1956, p.1103.

[10] S. T. Coleridge, *Biographia Literaria*, 22, Noyes, 1956, p.437.

by means of aesthetic pleasure. Yet despite this caution, an interest in neo-prophetic speech underlies Coleridge's poetry as well. For him too, the new poetic agenda is rooted in recent historical events. To the young Unitarian preacher, the French Revolution was a sign of the Kingdom's coming, and poetry an essential response. The revolutionary faith waned but the interest in prophetic rhetoric remained central to his poetry. It is apparent in his best known poem, 'The Ancient Mariner'. The mariner's voice is possessed of a sort of monstrous authority, a terrible echo of the Word. The Wedding-Guest 'cannot choose but hear', and the teller concludes by reflecting on his 'strange power of speech' and his compulsion to speak to rare receptive souls, a Romantic elect.

'Fears in Solitude, Written in April, 1798, During the Alarm of an Invasion' is a pastoral 'conversation poem' which becomes a report on the spiritual state of the nation. It must repent. 'We have offended, Oh! my countrymen!'. There is an earnest authority in his tone of repentance which recalls Cowper. The problem is that public speech has become debased (an echo of the Psalmic complaint at wrong speech as the root of all social evil). The Press familiarises everyone with brutal talk of war, but such words are 'empty sounds to which/We join no feeling and attach no form!'. All forms of official language have lost the power of emotional reference. Politics is 'A vain, speech-mouthing, speech-reporting guild', and religious discourse is similarly impotent:

> ...The sweet words
> Of Christian promise, words that even yet
> Might stem destruction, were they wisely preached,
> Are muttered o'er by men... .

The Bible is reduced to a 'superstitious instrument' by its political and legal function, and the Church is politically compromised. But its words 'might yet stem destruction': is Coleridge pursuing this possibility, finding a new medium for the words of promise? Is poetry a means of preaching them more 'wisely'? It seems that poetry's first task is one of diagnosis. And the form of the diagnosis suggests the cure: a discourse of new sincerity and force. The poem begins and ends with scenes of rural domestic peace, into which the political and prophetic content is a rude intrusion. Special circumstances force pastoral poetry, and its conversational style, to take on a prophetic role. It is here, in the speech of one friend or lover to another, that language retains credibility and purity. This speech-form must transcend its parochial limitations and speak high and hard words, 'most bitter truth'. The almost childish earnestness and simplicity reflects a neo-Puritan faith in 'plainness' as antidote to worldly corruption.

Coleridge becomes a voice of English Toryism; like Wordsworth he subscribes to and develops a rhetoric of political and ecclesiastical authority, updating such a rhetoric with the insights of German Romantic philosophy. This influences theologians such as F. D. Maurice, and secular prophets such as Carlyle and Ruskin. Also, Wordsworth is an important influence on the High Church revival.[11]

---

[11] See Sheridan Gilley, 'John Keble and the Victorian Churching of Romanticism', in *An*

Of the English Romantics, Shelley is the most interested in political radicalism and its philosophical basis. He is also the most forthright advocate of poetry as the new prophecy. 'Ozymandias' (1817) heralds an end to oppressive authority. It tells of a broken statue in the desert, a monument to a forgotten tyrant. His decapitated face maintains its 'frown,/And wrinkled lip, and sneer of cold command'. The legend on the pedestal is quoted: 'My name is Ozymandias, king of kings:/Look on my works, ye Mighty, and despair!'. This motto represents all political rhetoric of authority, all use of words to impress and cow. Shelley offers a critique of such rhetoric – more, he proclaims judgement on it. The poem depicts the fall of a voice. It echoes the Psalms and prophets: the bold and threatening words of worldly rulers will pass and receive their comeuppance, whereas the word of God will abide for ever. (It also echoes Daniel's vision of a political statue's destruction.) For Shelley, of course, it is not the Word of God that triumphs but the political freedom of humanity. The writing is on the wall for tyrants, but it is for human fingers to write it. The problem with this historical eschatology, of course, is that it calls for a new form of *political* triumphalism: new and grander statues in place of the old.

Shelley's 'Ode to the West Wind' (1819) also concerns the political change presently in the air. With implicit reference to the biblical equation of wind, breath and spirit (*ruah*), Shelley's wind is a divine force effecting renewal and liberation, largely through destruction. It is also a Voice, at which the 'oozy woods...suddenly grow grey with fear'. The ode is a psalmic imprecation to this power: 'oh, hear!', he begs a number of times. It seems that the spirit does hear, for it soon emboldens the speaker. By the end it inspires (breathes into) and possesses him, and perhaps he possesses it, for its locus is now 'the incantation of this verse'. The force that is at first distantly observed becomes by the end of the poem equated with the poetic voice: 'Be through my lips to unawakened earth/The trumpet of a prophecy'. This resolution feels too easy, and one is tempted to read the poem against Shelley's intentions. The closer it comes to the poet's voice, the less freely the spirit ranges. It feels more like he traps it than it up-buoys him. The claim to inspiration is at the cost of the spirit's limitation to one man's verbal will. Religious prophecy contains a similar danger, yet Christian tradition entails a narrative account of the Spirit's otherness, and provides rules for claims about inspiration. In 'Adonais' (1821), his elegy for Keats, the Orphic idea of the poet as nature's voice returns: 'He is made one with Nature: there is heard/His voice in all her music...'. The Power is later referred to as 'That Benediction which the eclipsing Curse/Of birth can quench not'. It is a power of blessing, a rhetoric of authoritative affirmation, a secular Word.

Shelley's *Defence of Poetry* is a useful insight into the new intellectual landscape. Prophecy is 'an attribute of poetry. A poet participates in the eternal, the infinite, and the one'.[12] Poetry comes first; it underlies all truth-claiming discourse. It would surprise Plato to hear that he 'was essentially a poet'.[13] Any virtue in

---

Infinite Complexity; Essays on Romanticism, ed. by J. R. Watson, Edinburgh University Press, 1983, p.233.

[12] Shelley, *A Defence of Poetry*, in Noyes, 1956, pp.1100-1101.

[13] Ibid., p.1099.

religious systems is attributable to the spirit of poetry. After the demise of the classical era, 'the world would have fallen into utter anarchy and darkness, but that there were found poets among the authors of the Christian and chivalric systems'. Poetry thus emerges as a sort of secret church, keeping the flame alive amid centuries of darkness. This flame largely consists in classical values, political and moral, though it is also capable of enlightening Christianity. The supreme religious reformer is Dante: 'Luther surpassed him rather in the rudeness and acrimony, than in the boldness of his censures'.[14] Luther's rhetoric is uncouth; he offends against the standards of classical speech. This compares interestingly with Milton's validation of Luther's prophetic rhetoric – it reveals Shelley's affinity with old-fashioned humanism.

Shelley waxes famously lyrical about the spiritual nature of poetry. 'The mind in creation is as a fading coal, which some invisible influence, like an inconstant wind, awakens to transitory brightness...'.[15] This wind, again, is an echo of the biblical spirit, which is also the breath of God which inspires us. Further on he tells us that the poets are themselves astonished by the working of the 'spirit' in them: 'for it is less their spirit than the spirit of the age'.[16] Here is an explicit example of the spiritualisation of the secular, of the *saeculum*, the present age. Poetry, he goes on, 'makes us the inhabitant of a world to which the familiar world is a chaos'[17]: i.e., it creates a realm of value which stands in opposition to 'this world'. But the secular has just been declared good. He seems to want to preserve an aura of otherworldliness even as he affirms the historical as the true locus of value. Such confusion is hardly uncommon in Romantic thought. Like its philosopher Hegel, it wants to see the spiritual in the secular; a contradiction in terms.

Keats has more faith in the realm of aesthetics than of history. 'On First Looking into Chapman's Homer' (1816) directly proclaims such a realm. The speaker first recounts his familiarity with certain 'realms', 'states', and 'kingdoms', referring to imaginative landscapes, encountered through reading.

> Oft of one wide expanse had I been told
>   That deep-brow'd Homer ruled as his demesne;
>   Yet did I never breathe its pure serene
> Till I heard Chapman speak out loud and bold... .

Homer is a sort of prophet-king, maybe a god. We have just been told of islands 'Which bards in fealty to Apollo hold'. Homer, however, is not 'in fealty' to anyone: he rules it as his own. His authority is more divine than prophetic. Indeed he *has* a prophet and his name is Chapman. Upon 'hearing' the translation, the poem's speaker also breathes it; is inspired by it. Here again is the biblical fusion of word, spirit and wind or breath. The second half of the sonnet presents this discovery in terms of astronomy ('When a new planet swims into his ken'),

---

[14] Ibid., p.1107.
[15] Ibid., p.1109.
[16] Ibid., p.1112.
[17] Ibid., p.1110.

and of exploration (Cortez on his peak in Darien). These are images of revelation, of breathless wonder at new intelligence, at the lifting of the veil – and by means, of course, of verbal communication, bold speech.

'Ode on a Grecian Urn' (1819) is also concerned with an aesthetic proclamation. The urn is a 'historian, who canst thus express/A flowery tale more sweetly than our rhyme'. Despite its 'chaste' silence, the urn *tells* a story better than words can. The poet struggles to interpret this 'speech', largely through asking questions, thereby telling us what is (or is not) happening. The theme of speech returns in the famous ending. In future ages the urn will remain 'a friend to man, to whom thou say'st,/"Beauty is truth, truth beauty," – that is all/Ye know on earth, and all ye need to know.' This silent aesthetic space is suddenly interpreted in the terms of oracular utterance. Through the speaker's mediation, the aesthetic realm constitutes a claim to vocal authority; it wants to be a truth-telling voice, an alternative rhetoric of authority, commanding human assent. At first sight the poem is about poetry wanting to become a plastic art, to escape the burden of truth-telling. But the result is the reverse. The aesthetic realm of eternal silence wants to become a form of prophetic discourse.

From this brief sketch it emerges that all these major Romantics, Wordsworth, Coleridge, Shelley and Keats, are engaged in forging a new discourse of authority, basic to which is a secularised theology of the Word. The danger in this move becomes clearer when we turn to one of the leading prose writers of the Romantic era: Thomas Carlyle. He is the first of the Victorian prophet-thinkers, the Dover Beach-combers. His history of the French Revolution (of 1837) defined political right-thinking for the generation, influencing Dickens among others. Its message was that true political progress needs spiritual foundations, in a wide sense of 'spiritual' of course. Established religion is not up to the job; it cannot command the truly visceral respect of the people (an echo of Hegel). No form of Christianity quite gets Carlyle's vote, it seems a spent force in all its traditional forms; he was impatient with Coleridge for not admitting the fact. Yet he was no simple atheist or agnostic; his strange response to religion's demise was to speak as if he was the prophet of a new religion, as if passionate speech about spiritual needs could will a new faith into being. What might this new faith be? He follows the literary Romantics in exalting the imaginative faculty and criticising the philosophical materialism of the age. But, although he idolises Goethe, Romanticism is no real solution; it is too rarefied, unworldly: 'For us in these days *Prophecy* (well understood), not Poetry is the thing wanted'.[18] For Carlyle the Romantic appropriation of prophecy ought to be fuller, more explicit; it ought to make an outright take-over bid rather than mincing around on the margins.

Carlyle's 'hero-worship' is a particularly Romantic form of humanism; an attempt to invest human affirmation with religious passion. He analyses the principle of heroism in religion, culture and politics. Heroism is what unites and underlies these falsely separated areas; it is the true religion. 'No nobler feeling than this of admiration for one higher than himself dwells in the breasts of man.... .

[18] Thomas Carlyle, *Letters*, in LaValley, A. J., *Carlyle and the Idea of the Modern: Studies in Carlyle's Prophetic Literature and its Relation to Blake, Nietzsche, Marx and Others*, Yale University Press, New Haven, 1968, p.1.

Religion I find stand upon it; not Paganism only, but...all religion hitherto known. Hero-worship, heartfelt prostrate admiration, submission, burning, boundless, for a noblest godlike Form of Man, – is not that the germ of Christianity itself?'[19] Nietzsche at least had the self-awareness to declare himself Christianity's enemy. The emphasis on authority and obedience clearly derives from his native Calvinism; he attempts to secularise it. Yet the Calvinist pathos becomes more dangerous when detached from its antihumanist pessimism, when reference to God is expunged.

Though Carlyle analyses the hero as divinity, prophet, poet, priest, man of letters and king, *prophet* is the dominant category of heroism, which re-invents itself in the forms of poet and the rest. Luther is a priestly prophet, whose stand was the germ of modern political progress.[20] The entire Reformation had a prophetic-heroic basis: it took 'only the passionate voice of one man'. As with the Romantic reception of Milton, this humanises Luther's rhetoric. It neglects the constant reference in Luther's voice to God; the insistence that 'the Word did it all' – and of course it evades his anti-hagiolatry.

Carlyle gradually loses interest in the intellectual, religious and artistic aspects of heroism, in favour of the 'man of action': Cromwell, Mirabeau and Frederick eclipse his admiration for Goethe and Luther. The actual political cause that his heroes fought for is immaterial beside their effectiveness as leaders, and above all their power to reinvent morals, create values. This is a clear anticipation of Nietzsche's *Ubermensch*, of the lethal idea that prophetic speech finds its true referent in human power.

Carlyle exhibits most clearly what I want to identify as the key danger of Romanticism. He detaches the idea of prophetic speech from its Christian roots and tries to make a religion out of prophecy *per se*. The authoritative tone of the prophet is taken to be a solution in itself, the only feasible form of religion for a modern enlightened age. The righteous tones of a preacher are applied to a creed of *realpolitique*. His thought, like Nietzsche's after him, helps to inspire modern fascism. In their doomed bunker, Goebbels was cheering up his boss by reading Carlyle's *Frederick the Great* to him. Of course, Carlyle is not alone in such influence; he merely displays the logic of Romanticism with especial clarity. For this process is a crucial element in the definition of Romanticism: through secularising prophetic rhetoric it leads to the aggrandisement of a political rhetoric of authority.

Marxism too has a heavy debt to the Romantic appropriation of the prophetic, largely by means of Hegel's philosophy of history. Marx develops Hegel by identifying the proletariat as the true agent of History. Though he presents this as a scientific discovery, it is also a prophetic insight into a form of 'salvation history' – or a parody of the doctrine of election.[21] The proletariat 'has a

---

[19] Thomas Carlyle, *On Heroes, Hero-Worship and the Heroic in History*, ed. by Carl Niemeyer, University of Nebraska Press, 1966, p.11.

[20] Carlyle, 1966, p.135. Protestantism, he ventures, lives on in the forms of 'German literature and the French Revolution' (ibid., p.137).

[21] This was Barth's assessment of both the myth of the proletariat and that of the nation-state (see Gorringe, 1999, p.148).

universal character by reason of the universality of its sufferings... . It stands for the total ruin of man, and can recover itself only by his total redemption'.[22] The language of religious absoluteness finds its true application in this new proclamation. Marx himself was more than a bit of a Romantic, fond of likening himself to Prometheus, a lover of heroic literature. He also thought of himself in prophetic terms (perhaps Carlyle helped to inspire the self-image). The rhetoric of *The Communist Manifesto* has an obvious debt to Marx's Jewish inheritance, but what enables the translation is the Romantic climate in philosophy and political thought. This is Romanticism's key legacy: the secularisation of prophetic rhetoric. It underlies the ideological horror of the twentieth century. In Nazism, the pseudo-prophetic is barely disguised: for example, Goebbels presented Hitler as a prophet-saviour, calling him the only man 'capable, by means of fate-given perception and the power of the word, of creating political works for the future. Many are called, but few are chosen... .'[23]

All pseudo-prophetic rhetoric ends in fascism, in the wide sense of political violence, which of course includes Communism. For such rhetoric of authority cannot be prevented from reference to political authoritarianism; it naturally gravitates towards it. Only the Christian rhetoric of authority is exempt from this fate. For it is 'Christian' in as far as it refers to Christ, and it fails to refer to Christ if it supports political authoritarianism. By definition, if you like, Christian rhetoric is opposed to political authoritarianism. My study is attempting to trumpet this as essential to its uniqueness: it is a rhetoric of authority uniquely opposed to worldly power. And, in this chapter at least, the argument is predominantly negative. The secular reinvention of authoritative rhetoric can be shown to be dangerously wanting, even doomed to violence.

Even the 'pure' aestheticism of Keats contains a form of pseudo-prophecy. It locates spiritual value in a form of literary discourse, endowing it with unwarranted weight. Even if it seems to abjure politics, all such discourse remains open to political exploitation. All strong speech that is unanchored in the Christic model tends towards the glorification of some form of political strength.[24] Wordsworth and Coleridge back off from political radicalism, but in their reaction they become open to the charge of using poetic discourse to bolster the Tory-imperial ideology. Romanticism cannot avoid this complicity in political ideology because it is essentially secular; its secularisation of the spiritual in the name of poetry leads to the sanctification of the secular.

---

[22] Karl Marx, 'Introduction to a Critique of Hegel's Philosophy of Right' (1843), quoted in Leszek Kolakowski, *Main Currents of Marxism, Its Origins, Growth and Dissolution; 1 – The Founders*, trans. by P. S. Falla, Oxford University Press, 1978, pp.129-30.

[23] Quoted in Gorringe, 1999, p.129.

[24] What about the 'strong speech' of other religious traditions? It is justified only to the extent that it echoes the Christic pattern of the refusal of violence.

After Romanticism

What is called literary Modernism has an ambiguous relationship to Romanticism. Its aesthetic novelty is undeniable, but this novelty has Romantic parentage. And it inherits and develops the assumption of poetic discourse as the locus of post-religious authority. Perhaps the relationship is best expressed by the famously ambiguous German word *Aufhebüng*, which means both cancellation and preservation. It is in Modernism that the political dangers inherent in Romanticism most clearly emerge. Many critics have discussed the fascist tendencies of Yeats, Pound, Eliot, Lawrence and others. Relating these tendencies to my overall argument, I am going to focus on W. B. Yeats, and then, more briefly, on T. S. Eliot.

W. B. Yeats

Yeats is perhaps the clearest instance of the *Aufhebüng* of Romanticism. Even before he is influenced by Ezra Pound, the high-priest of poetic Modernism, he has already learned to take selectively from Romanticism, opposing its weakness for abstract ideas, such as mars the poetry of Shelley, in favour of the particularity of symbol (following the French Symbolists). True poetry rises above ideological interest: 'We make out of the quarrel with others, rhetoric, but of the quarrel with ourselves, poetry'.[25] This sounds like a healthy disavowal of ideology, but, as we shall see, the arguments that Yeats has with himself are ultimately one-sided and serve to promote a distinct rhetorical position. Though poetry is exalted as the supreme calling, there are for Yeats certain values it 'naturally' celebrates. His poetry too is implicated in the political logic of all secular authoritative rhetoric.

In his youth he was involved in the Celtic Twilight movement which combined Irish nationalism with aestheticism. 'There is no fine nationality without literature, and therefore no fine literature without nationality', he declared in 1890.[26] Inspired by Maude Gonne he sought to revive the myths of Ireland's pagan past, which would constitute the basis of a new national religion: a clear inheritance of Romantic thought.

Alongside his early nationalist concern, Yeats is influenced by the wider trend of intense aestheticism, particularly the French Symbolist movement. His early symbolism amounts to a form of magical belief; through incantatory rhythms poetry becomes a potentially revelatory medium: it 'keep[s] us in that state of perhaps real trance, in which the mind liberated from the pressure of the will is unfolded in symbols'.[27] This mysticism is the abiding context for his increasing tendency towards authoritative, even dogmatic, utterance. The effect is to suggest to the reader that such statement is more than just one man's opinion; almost that it utters itself through the poet as mouthpiece. To an extent perhaps unparalleled in

---

[25] W. B. Yeats, 'Anima Hominis' (1917), in *Yeats, Selected Criticism*, Norman A. Jeffares ed., Macmillan, London, 1964, p.170.
[26] Quoted in Keith Aldritt, *W. B. Yeats*, 1998, p.89.
[27] Yeats, 'The Symbolism of Poetry', in Brown 1999, p.77.

modern poetry, Yeats seems to believe in this shamanistic myth, and with infectious force.

Yeats' cultural nationalism did not lead him to the frontline of political activism. Shocked by the violence of the Easter rising of 1916, he realised that he must keep his art at a distance from political immediacy, from 'The seeming needs of my fool-driven land'.[28] Political developments thus serve to intensify his belief in *poetry* as the supreme vocation. It is nothing short of a faith. He concludes his 'Meditations in Time of Civil War' (1923) with one such profession of faith. He has been surveying the world from his tower-top, depicting its violence in images of apocalyptic terror. Descending, he questions his vocation, wondering 'how many times I could have proved my worth/In something that all others understand or share':

> But O! ambitious heart, had such a proof drawn forth
> A company of friends, a conscience set at ease,
> It had but made us pine the more. The abstract joy,
> The half-read wisdom of daemonic images,
> Suffice the ageing man as once the growing boy.

This is perhaps his strongest profession of faith in his poetic calling. It is grandiloquent ('O! ambitious heart'); it dares the reader to find it foolish. Indeed its potential absurdity is crucial to the pathos. It resembles the willed naivety of Kierkegaard's faith – also in its renunciation of 'company' and 'conscience'. And it has a similar dialectical structure: it is strengthened through doubt, through confronting the voice of realism; a version of Lutheran *Anfechtung*. In 'The Tower' (1926) he declares that, though he is now ageing, 'Never had I more/Excited, passionate, fantastical/Imagination, nor an ear and eye/That more expected the impossible...'. This too suggests the willed naivety of Christian faith, for which 'all things are possible'. This theme intensifies in his late poems. 'The Circus Animals' Desertion' (*Last Poems 1936-9*) recalls the mythological basis of his faith in the manner of an incantation; Oisin and company are trooped out like verbal icons. His personal mythology is thus presented with a pathos indebted to Christian faith: it is adhered to in the teeth of modern thought, political fashion and common sense. It is a faith in 'things not seen'.

This faith is not limited to a realm of poetic individuality; it also has social and political reference. Though poetry is distanced from politics in a narrow sense, true poetry remains political for Yeats. It is political in the widest sense of having unique power to communicate the value of a tradition, to endow a way of life with authority, to celebrate it. It thus underlies politics, moulding rather than serving the national spirit. It creates and determines value. As this description suggests, Yeats' political poetic emerges as essentially conservative, indeed radically so. Though it sits rather uneasily with his Irish nationalism, he identifies himself above all with the Anglo-Irish aristocracy, whose power has all but expired. Aristocracy and art are asserted to be radically linked: artists are 'the only aristocracy that has never

---

[28] From 'All Things Can Tempt Me' ('..from this craft of verse'), in *The Green Helmet and Other Poems*, 1910.

been sold in the market or seen the people rise up against it'.[29] And the present weakness of his political allegiance is crucial to its pseudo-religious pathos. This nobly defeated aristocracy is the 'we' of the conclusion to 'Coole Park and Ballylee' (1931): 'We were the last romantics – chose for theme/Traditional sanctity and loveliness..' The demise of this form of civilisation is accepted, even embraced. The previous stanza contrasts the noble ideal of ancestral rootedness with modern reality in which 'We shift about – all that great glory spent – /Like some poor Arab tribesman and his tent'. This cultural aesthetic of aristocratic elitism is heavily indebted to Nietzsche, whom he excitedly discovers in 1902.[30] Nietzsche also decrees the right response to the crisis: tragic joy, Dionysian acceptance, the willing of eternal recurrence. The old order need not be defended in any narrow political way: despite its defeat it is stronger than the world. This is paganised eschatology, proclaimed by a paganised prophecy adapted from Nietzsche. There are often signs of a paganised theology of the Word. The late poem 'The Gyres' forsees apocalypse and asks: 'What matter? Out of cavern comes a voice,/And all it knows is that one word "Rejoice!"'. In an appropriation of Christian tradition, Yeats mediates (and constructs) this *voice* of cosmic affirmation.

Yeats' voice, founded in this aesthetic of 'natural authority', constitutes perhaps the supreme instance of authoritative discourse in modern poetry. It asks that its utterance should be accorded special status, received in a spirit of reverence. In all prophetic rhetoric, the hearer is judged by her response; she is forced to choose for or against this account of authority. (This decision concerning Yeats' authority is a real issue for subsequent English poetry, central to Eliot, as we shall see, and also to Auden and others.)

Yeats' poetic locates authority in aesthetic excellence, traditional social structures and a cultural vitality based in a shared mythology. It says that divine revelation operates within this matrix, primarily in its inspiration of the poet-visionary, the shamanistic voicer of the communal spirit. In the conclusion to 'Under Ben Bulben' future Irish poets are urged to 'Sing whatever is well made,/ Scorn the sort now growing up/All out of shape from toe to top... .' Here poetry has an explicit religious function – to celebrate and to scorn, to allot value by the force of the word.

The account of authority implied in Yeats' cultural-prophetic voice reflects two religious impulses at once. Firstly it expresses the religious power of community and tradition, distilling and translating it into a modern faith. But this translation transforms it. Tradition becomes self-conscious, reactionary; the opposite of its traditional self. Like Nietzsche's faith, Yeats' combines worldly glory with otherworldly yearning. Their shared contempt for 'the crowd' is partly a Christian inheritance (here Yeats is also influenced by Swift's misanthropy). More

---

[29] Yeats, 1962, p.125.

[30] Nietzsche 'is exaggerated and violent but has helped me very greatly to build up in my mind an imagination of the heroic life' (Yeats, letter to Quinn, *CL 3*.313, in Brown, 1999, p.152). As Brown observes, Yeats seeks in the Italian Renaissance, particularly Castiglione, a humanised form of the Nietzschean ideal (ibid., p.171). The violence of his late poems (and prose) suggests only limited success.

basically, the claim to speak truth against the wanton spirit of the age is a borrowing from the Judeo-Christian dynamic of prophecy. If Yeats really *belonged* to a traditional culture, which took his aristocratic values for granted, this pathos, this agonistic intensity would be unavailable to him. The power of this voice relies on a particular cultural situation in which a traditional source of power is threatened, perhaps doomed. Yet this voice may acquire real political influence, in the reconfiguration of that power. Modern conservatism is strongly indebted to this rhetorical strategy.

Part of Yeats' strength is that he does not go all the way with Nietzsche. His attitude to Christianity has little of his mentor's strident hostility. Instead, the Christian God may be invoked alongside the neo-pagan mythology. His tactic, conscious or not, is to conflate Christianity with myth in general, to honour it as one instance of mythological power. The final section of 'Vacillation' (1932) addresses the Catholic thinker Von Hügel: 'Must we part, Von Hügel, though much alike, for we/Accept the miracles of the saints and honour sanctity?' It seems they must: 'I – though heart might find relief/Did I become a Christian man and choose for my belief/What seems most welcome in the tomb – play a predestined part./Homer is my example and his unchristened heart.' There is an echo here of 'O! ambitious heart...': though normal faith would be easier, he has had another calling, he did it his way. It is a case not of holier than thou, but of lonelier than thou. Poetic paganism is the superior pathos because rarer, more dramatically poignant. There is even a claim to selflessness, self-sacrifice (a theme which obsesses Yeats).[31] The possibility of salvation is something he must renounce in his even narrower way. The idea returns in 'The Choice', which is between 'Perfection of the life, or of the work'. The opposition of work and life, or art and morality, is a particularly modern malady. To faith it is a false alternative, a demonic trick.

Yeats called Nietzsche 'that strong enchanter',[32] but he is maybe a more powerful because a subtler one. (Nietzsche warns us away from himself through his excess.) His relevance to my study is that he constructs perhaps the most compelling 'prophetic' voice in English of the century. Aristocratic and neo-pagan value is so persuasively identified with aesthetic force that mere argument against these principles is useless – we shall also discuss this in relation to Nietzsche. We are dealing not with ideas about values but with a rhetorical performance of value.

T. S. Eliot

Despite acknowledging his importance, Eliot is highly wary of the influence of Yeats. His anti-Romantic principle of 'impersonality' entails criticism of Yeats as a Romantic throwback.[33] And his move to a 'traditional' Christian position on one level confirms this. Yet on another level Eliot's trajectory echoes Yeats'. Eliot too

---

[31] A number of his plays are concerned with heroic self-sacrifice for the noble cultural cause (see Brown, 1999, p.135).

[32] Yeats, letter to Lady Gregory, *CL3*: p.284, in Brown, 1999, p.151.

[33] 'Tradition and the Individual Talent' (1919), in T. S. Eliot, *The Sacred Wood*, Methuen, London, 1950, p.58.

wants a poetry organically related to culture and tradition. His cultural ideal is not pagan Ireland but Christian Europe, but this ideal is similarly charged with nostalgia and elitism.

But the affinity is not really acknowledged. In 'After Strange Gods' (1934) he depicts Yeats as an erratic genius, outside the real intellectual tradition. His home-made neo-paganism fails to arrive at 'a central and universal philosophy'.[34] He belongs with the 'heretics'. Yet the influence remains apparent. For instance Yeats informs the ghostly voice of authority in 'Little Gidding' (1942). During an air-raid, the speaker, in Dantean fashion, meets 'some long dead master', 'a familiar compound ghost'. Like Hamlet, he charges it speak. Its spiritual tone is suggestive of Milton, yet in other respects (including its counsel to 'purify the dialect of the tribe') there are hints of Yeats.[35]

The passage is evidence of one of Eliot's primary preoccupations: poetry's relationship to voices of authority. His early work involves a worrying and questioning of what a contemporary prophetic voice would be, and his later work involves an attempted answer.

He first confronts the problem in 'The Love Song of J. Alfred Prufrock' (1917). 'Let us go then, you and I' echoes of one of Yeats' most famous openings: 'I will arise and go now...' (from 'The Lake Isle of Innisfree'). But here the going is not to a pastoral idyll but through a surreal cityscape, and to no clear destination. And the voice is correspondingly uncertain. It is a voice of urgency lacking content, of urgent discontent. It unravels into cosmic anxiety and comic insecurity. 'Do I dare/Disturb the universe?' Such questions intercut with surreal urban detail.

At the root of 'Prufrock' is the yearning for a transcendent finality of utterance that can never emerge. The only strong statement that emerges is negative, desperate: 'I should have been a pair of ragged claws/Scuttling across the floors of silent seas'. The image is both wistfully romantic and dark, like a detail from Hieronomus Bosch.[36] But such forceful speech cannot relate itself to the real, the social. This becomes the central theme: the impossibility of significant utterance amidst contemporary reality. The endless surreal images search for meaning in the visual, the actual. But the surface complexity of the daily world militates against significant speech. It intimidates the oral into silence or appropriates it into mere triviality: '(They will say: "How his hair is growing thin!")...(They will say: "But how his arms and legs are thin!")'. Also, of course, 'the women come and go/Talking of Michelangelo'. Religious art, which once had the power to 'speak' to us, is now occasion for the chatter of lunching ladies.

The speaker's own possibility of significant speech is mocked by the dominance of the superficial: 'Should I, after tea and cake and ices,/Have the strength to force the moment to its crisis?' Though he has 'wept and fasted, wept

---

[34] Eliot, *After Strange Gods; a Primer of Modern Heresy*, Faber, London, 1933, p.47. Yeats, he announces, 'chooses the wrong supernatural world' (ibid., p.46).

[35] In conversation, 'Eliot is said to have more or less identified [the ghost] with W. B. Yeats' (Hugh Kenner, *The Invisible Poet, T. S. Eliot*, Allen, London, 1960, p.27).

[36] Kenner observes that the couplet 'is not quite at home in the context of the poem', ibid., p.31.

and prayed', he says, he is 'no prophet'. He is, however, haunted by the possibility of prophetic speech. Would it have been worth while, he wonders,

> ...To have squeezed the universe into a ball
> To roll it towards some overwhelming question,
> To say: 'I am Lazarus, come from the dead,
> Come back to tell you all, I shall tell you all' –
> If one, settling a pillow by her head,
>   Should say: 'That is not what I meant at all.
>   That is not it, at all.'

How can there be authoritative utterance? That is the question. Speech in the prophetic mode would be rendered ridiculous by any real context, any real recipient. The speaker's existence seems to demand such speech. But in practice it prevents his full existence, this possibility, this lack.

The haunting memory of prophetic speech devalues actual communication. The memory is thus a torment, a disaffection, an awareness of radical insufficiency. The poem ends with the image of mermaids' song, which fuses religious and artistic inspiration: 'I have heard the mermaids singing, each to each./I do not think that they will sing to me'. There is awareness of supernatural discourse but without *hearing*, in the sense of being addressed. There is no message to man, only the tantalising overhearing of mermaid-speak, which is not good for us.

> We have lingered in the chambers of the sea
> By sea-girls wreathed with seaweed red and brown
> Till human voices wake us, and we drown.

The very idea of inspiration, in relation to art or religion, has become dangerous, incompatible with life, a snare.

I do not want to trespass too far into *The Waste Land* (1922), except to suggest that it follows the logic of 'Prufrock', and develops it. Here there is not even a speaker, only a collage of voices, and an impression of their incongruity. Again the poem is haunted by the possibility of prophetic speech. The first section includes an imitation of Ezekiel: 'Son of man,/You cannot say, or guess, for you know only/A heap of broken images... .' The 'message' here is that no message is possible, that we lack the cultural depth to receive one. Then comes Madame Sosostris' Tarot reading, an alternative claim to prophetic speech (which in this case is by means of the visual and symbolic). The ominous speech ('Fear death by water', etc.) is framed by circumstantial banality. She has 'a bad cold', we are first told, which presumably affects her allegedly exalted voice, and after the visionary intelligence we overhear her small-talk.

There are snatches of speech whose 'meaning' is their failure to communicate. We seem to overhear a failing relationship: 'Speak to me. Why do you never speak. Speak'. Then we hear a woman in a pub, telling of advice she has given a friend about her marriage; but it is a voice of casual deception and self-justification. Soon we have a speech from Tiresias; he relates, in the grand style, a scene of casual sex between alienated moderns. The effect is unpleasantly voyeuristic. Is this what the prophetic vision is for; to gaze disgusted on people's personal lives? To hypostasize disdain? The final section is called 'What the Thunder Said'. But there is no revelation, despite a desperate-feeling inclusion of transliterations from Sanskrit: 'DA' etc. There are only fragments. The only revelation is negative: the negativity of vocal dissonance is presented in the terms of a revelation of sorts.

What significant utterance remains for us? Poetry, Eliot implies, must at least pose the question, confront the crisis, keep the wound open. Elsewhere Eliot constructs further dramatic personae to this end. 'Gerontion' (1920) is a voice of experience but without substantial wisdom; 'The Hollow Men' (1925) presents a voice from beyond death (like Lazarus'), which ought to have authority but has chosen to renounce it.

In 1927 he came out as a classicist in literature, an Anglo-Catholic in religion, and a royalist in politics. After this declaration his poetic output is minimal. Literary and social criticism becomes his primary platform, or pulpit; the arena for a new voice of cultural authority. Why this retreat from poetry? An answer is suggested in *After Strange Gods*. Poetic authority has been usurped by the 'heretics' (Hardy and Lawrence are charged, as well as Yeats and Pound), and the cultural climate is duly tainted. For true art requires the basis of a common religious culture. So he largely retreats to criticism, which becomes more social and religious than literary.

The voice of authority Eliot comes to assume is strongly politically partisan. Just as Yeats claims his voice is essentially artistic, Eliot claims his voice is essentially religious; but both are rooted in socio-political principles, and indeed in similar ones. Although Eliot called himself a classicist and associated Romanticism with wanton liberalism, he in fact shared many of the core values of Yeats' 'last romanticism'. Value lies in the cultural tradition of a homogenous people, and is explicitly opposed to the forces of modern 'levelling'. Part of 'the struggle of our time', he said, which is the struggle 'against Liberalism', is 'to re-establish a vital connection between the individual and the race'. [37]

A neat example of the Yeatsian ingredient in his 'Christian' position is his fear of unrootedness. We have already noted Yeats' image of the modern individual 'shifting about', 'like some poor Arab tribesman and his tent'. Consciously or not, Eliot echoes it a number of times. He warns that the result of equal education 'might be to produce a race of spiritual nomads', and elsewhere laments that 'we are destroying our ancient edifices to make ready the ground upon which the barbarian nomads of the future will encamp in their mechanised caravans'. [38] There is a Christian response to this image, which remembers the story of Abraham and the theme of pilgrimage, and Jesus' warning that the Son of Man has nowhere to lay his head. The urge for a stable cultural home is essentially pagan. To quote Eliot against himself, he belongs with those 'clutching at their gods'.

---

[37] Eliot, *After Strange Gods*, p.48.

[38] In Robbins, *The T.S. Eliot Myth*, Henry Schuman, New York, 1951, p.69; Eliot, *Notes Toward the Definition of Culture*, Faber, London, 1948, p.108.

Does the Modernist aesthetic tend toward fascism? The further evidence of Ezra Pound strengthens the case. His *Literary Essays* offer some useful hints. In 'A Retrospect' (1918), the poetry of the nineteenth century is dismissed as artificial and sentimental. Twentieth century poetry 'will be harder and saner... . [I]t will be as much like granite as it can be, its force will lie in its truth... . At least for myself I want it so, austere, direct, free from emotional slither'.[39] Pound retains a high conception of literature; it maintains 'the very cleanliness of the tools, the health of the very matter of thought itself'.[40] It has a scientific, medicinal function; purifying language and thought, keeping it 'efficient'. Great literature is moral in that it 'bears true witness', delivers true and precise reports of the nature of human life.[41] In a sense Pound's literary theory follows the logic of Wordsworth's. What seems a down-to-earth lack of pretension conceals a new sort of claim to authority, based in a form of science. And now there is an additional rhetoric of efficiency, hardness, cleanliness, purity – throughout his work he seeks models of this ideal in Renaissance Italy, ancient China and elsewhere. As with Yeats, the aesthetic ideal is also an 'aristocratic' protest against modern democracy. He declares that 'the aristocracy of the arts' is to regain its birthright of power.[42] During the 30's his aestheticism begins to find political embodiment, above all in Mussolini, 'a male of the species', and an artist.[43] He also admires Lenin: in a piece of adulation reminiscent of Carlyle he says that he 'evolved almost a new medium, a sort of expression half way between writing and action'.[44] Also in these years his neo-pagan distaste for Christianity becomes explicitly anti-Semitic. In his advocacy of Confucius he attacks 'the semitic component in Christianity'.[45] And he accuses Milton of being a Semitic influence on literary culture, an 'Anglican Hebrew'.[46]

Modernism inherits the Romantic appropriation of prophetic rhetoric – one could illustrate this further, for example in relation to Lawrence.[47] Like Romanticism it wants a new rhetoric of authority, heedless of the violence entailed in the venture. (There is a similar blindness in some of the philosophy of the period. There is a particularly clear philosophical parallel in Heidegger's notorious dalliance with National Socialism in 1933. He even echoes Poundian rhetoric in celebrating the 'hard clarity' of the emergent regime.)[48]

---

[39] Ezra Pound, 'A Retrospect', in *Literary Essays of Ezra Pound*, ed. by T. S. Eliot, Faber, London, 1954, p.12.

[40] Ezra Pound, 'How to Read' (1928), ibid., p.21.

[41] Ezra Pound, 'The Serious Artist' (1913), ibid., p.44.

[42] Ezra Pound, 'The New Sculpture', in *The Egoist*, 16 February 1914, in Noel Stock, *The Life of Ezra Pound*, Penguin, Middlesex, 1985, p.198.

[43] Ezra Pound, 'Date Line', in *Selected Essays*, in Stock, 1985, p.408.

[44] Ezra Pound, from the *Exile* 1928, quoted in Stock, 1985, p.353.

[45] Ezra Pound, 'Mang Tze (the Ethics of Mencius)', the *Criterion*, July 1938, in ibid., p.441.

[46] Ibid., p.508.

[47] Lawrence closely fits this trajectory of secularised prophecy feeding into a fascist aesthetic. 'Preaching out of an evangelical culture of moral fervour and plain speaking, he often resembles a demonic version of John Bunyan' (Tom Paulin, 'Lawrence and Decency' in Paulin 1996, p.202).

[48] Quoted in George Steiner, *Heidegger*, Fontana, 1992, p.118.

This detour into modern literature is not an instance of theology straying from its remit. Literature has necessitated the widening of scope, by itself straying onto theological ground, in its quest for a secular theology of the Word. Its pseudo-prophetic adventures provide useful evidence for theology: that, away from the Christian idiom, the will to 'authoritative discourse' ends in the logic of fascism.

Chapter 8

The Rhetorical Theology of Karl Barth

'[S]tyle is not an external matter, not a matter of form but of content.'
(Barth, *The Göttingen Dogmatics*, p.71).

'In each really Christian utterance there is something of an absoluteness such as cannot
belong to any non-Christian language.'
(Barth, *Dogmatics in Outline*, p.83).

It is strange that one has to introduce the name of Karl Barth (1886-1968) to non-theologians. In any other century, it has been said of him, he would have been world-famous. But the biggest name of twentieth-century theology (even Catholics might concur) has less currency than Roland Barthes and probably John Barth, not to mention Bart Simpson.

Although Barth's theology is in one sense a hugely complex structure (especially as mediated by his expositors), its proclamatory and prophetic basis makes it also essentially simple. Like the first Reformers, and unlike most modern intellectuals, he is concerned with *communication*. But his theology of prophetic affirmation is not simply a rehash of Luther and Calvin: in Barth the Protestant rhetorical tradition becomes modernised. Not in the sense of diluted with modern secular thought, but rather – remarkably – the opposite: clarified by means of it, restored to integrity. In my brief reading of him (mostly of his early work), Barth shows that theology can reaffirm its authoritative rhetorical basis and be fully self-critical about the potential dangers of religious rhetoric. Indeed the two things necessarily go together: true proclamation of the Word demands an endless critical awareness associated with modern 'suspicion'.

With so much written on Barth by so many theologians, it may seem strange to begin with a novelist. Yet the nature of the appeal of Barth's theology is perhaps more vividly conveyed in the novels of John Updike than in the work of any theologian. His novelistic treatment of Barth is free from the stylistic constraints of academic theology: fiction affords him a space in which to reflect on the importance of Barth's style without also affirming the rights of intellectual liberalism. Updike's most consistent central character is a semi-lapsed Protestant surprised to find that there remains a sense in which the Word is heard. In defiance of the agnostic indifference of his family and acquaintances, to whom his faith appears neurotic, he remains drawn to the pathos of theological concerns and to the antique orderliness of churchgoing. And his stubborn attachment to faith often takes the form of a largely aesthetic weakness for the rhetorical strength of Barth's theology. One character re-finds a book by Barth and remembers feeling that here, in Barth's prose, he had found 'the path, the voice, the style, and the method to save within himself and to present to others the Christian faith. Just glancing through the pages, I felt the superb irony of Barth's paragraphs, his magnificent seamless integrity and energy in this realm of prose – the specifically Christian – usually conspicuous for intellectual limpness and dishonesty'.[1] Similarly, the narrator of *A Month of Sundays* reflects on the origins of his faith: 'My father's house bred into me a belief in God which has made my life one long glad feast of inconvenience and unreason... . I became a Barthian in reaction against his liberalism, a smiling, fumbling shadow of German Pietism'.[2] Yet he goes on to tell us that he 'did not become a Barthian in blank recoil, but in positive love of Barth's voice, his wholly masculine, wholly informed, wholly unfrightened prose... . In Barth I heard, at the age of eighteen, the voice my father should have had'.[3]

Much mainstream Barth criticism is attentive to the issue of his style. 'Without a doubt, Barth's theology had style, great style', says Jüngel.[4]

> The writings of Karl Barth were seductive from the beginning. They have remained so. One reason for this is the extraordinarily expressive power of their language, which characteristically distinguishes it from the language of scholarly discourse. Barth's writings are also anything but one-dimensional in content. They impress; they attract and repel; they seduce both their defenders and their detractors.[5]

Jüngel emphasises the stylistic unity of Barth's life and work. His theological existence was bold, polemical, confident, cheerful. He epitomised *Menschlichkeit*, he 'lived intensely', and 'with enthusiasm'.[6] Von Balthasar is another critic who is attentive to the importance of style in Barth's theology:

> For Barth the encounter of revelation inevitably raised the question of *style* in theology. He knew that the task of theology was not only to say something proper about the content of revelation, but also somehow to convey to us how utterly, stupendously dramatic the event was that is now reaching our ears. Even style, indeed style above all, belongs to the truth of what is being said.[7]

To begin with in this chapter I am engaged in a partial reading of Barth's early radicalism. I suggest that it consists in a new theology of the Word – which is to say, a new theology of rhetorical authority. What obsesses Barth in the years surrounding the *Romans* commentaries is the quest for the appropriate style for a truly God-referent theology. It is *how theology speaks* of God, and revelation, that determines its worth. Amidst his flirtation with religious socialism he rediscovers the Reformation rhetoric of the Word of God as an actual power. This force is initially expressed through the metaphor of political revolution: 'God's Word is a

---

[1] John Updike, *Roger's Version*, Penguin, Middlesex, 1986, p.40.

[2] John Updike, *A Month of Sundays*, Penguin, Middlesex, 1976, p.24.

[3] Ibid., p.25.

[4] Jüngel, E., *Karl Barth, A Theological Legacy*, trans. by G. E. Paul, Westminster Press, Philadelphia, 1986, p.12.

[5] Ibid., p.11.

[6] Ibid., p.16.

[7] Von Balthasar, H. U., *The Theology of Karl Barth: Exposition and Interpretation*, trans. by Edward T. Oakes, Communio Books, San Francisco, 1992, p.82.

divine worldwide revolution'[8] which includes 'the revolution of what is today called "revolution"';[9] 'the little phrase "God is" amounts to a revolution'[10]; 'The Kingdom of God is…the revolution *before* all revolutions'.[11] The rhetorical idiom of faith is *über*-revolutionary. To God alone belongs revolutionary superiority (to borrow Trotsky's phrase). McCormack identifies 1913 as the highpoint of his religious socialist sermons, and traces the way in which these anticipate the themes of his imminent radicalism. 'Most striking perhaps is the prominence of the theme of the judgement and wrath of God'.[12] By 1915 he has firmly come out on the side of theology's priority to socialist politics, and the articulation of this priority is the genesis of his theological radicalism.

Barth's 'socialism' is one of excess; it dispenses with political realism in favour of utopian absoluteness: 'The revolution envisaged by Socialism is no more and no less than a conversion of the entire world, a conversion of the whole of humanity. Less is nothing'.[13] Conventional socialism is charged with the same failing as conventional Protestantism: it lacks a passion for the impossible. The full realisation of this comes to him on the famous 'black day' of 1914. *Die Christliche Welt*, the bastion of the theological liberalism upon which Barth was raised, had come out in uncritical support for Germany in the war. In a letter to his former mentor, Martin Rade, Barth angrily deconstructs the pretension of the journal's name: 'That is the disappointment for us…that we have to see the *Chr. W.*, in this decisive hour, cease to be *Christian*, but rather simply place itself on the same level with *this* world'.[14]

The central influence of these years is a subsidiary element within Swiss religious socialism. Kutter's *Sie Müssen*, published in 1903, was the founding text of Swiss religious socialism; it heralded socialism as the 'hammer of God' through which the Church's complacency is judged. Though Barth admired Kutter's daring (he called him a 'prophetic thinker and preacher…who at that time…represented the insight that the sphere of God's power is really greater than the sphere of the church…'),[15] he soon found him too narrowly political. By 1915 he seemed to Barth 'to have nothing to do with theology at all'.[16] Yet Kutter was central to Barth's prophetic apprenticeship: 'From Kutter I simply learned to speak the great

---

[8] Barth, *Der Römerbrief* 1919, 387; quoted in Jüngel, 1986, p.33.

[9] Ibid., p.234; in ibid.

[10] Barth, Sermons, 1914, quoted in Busch, E., *Karl Barth: his Life from Letters and Autobiographical Texts*, trans. by John Bowden, SCM, London, 1976, p.80.

[11] Barth, 'The Christian in Society' (1919), in Barth, *The Word of God and the Word of Man*, trans. by Douglas Horton, Hodder and Stoughton, London, 1928, p.299.

[12] McCormack, B. L. (1995), *Karl Barth's Critically Realistic Dialectical Theology: its Genesis and Development, 1909-1936* , Clarendon Press, Oxford, p.93.

[13] Barth, 'Das was nicht geschehen soll', July 1919, quoted in McCormack 1995, p.193. He soon declares that Christianity is *'more* than Leninism…'all or nothing'' (Barth, *The Epistle to the Romans*, first edition, quoted in Gorringe, T., *Against Hegemony: The Theology of Karl Barth in Context*, Cambridge University Press, 1999, p.45.)

[14] Quoted in McCormack, 1995, p.111.

[15] Barth, *The Church Dogmatics* 1.1, p.74.

[16] Barth, 'Nachwort', in Bolli, *Schleiermacher-Auswahl*, p.294; quoted in Jüngel, 1986, p.31. This is also directed at Leonard Ragaz, the other pillar of Swiss religious socialism.

word 'God' seriously, responsibly and with a sense of its importance';[17] 'When he preached, and indeed in private conversation, he could impress on one that this was a deadly serious matter, which could not be taken lightly';[18] he spoke 'like an uncanny volcano'.[19]

The influence of the Blumhardts (an eccentric father-and-son team of Lutheran preachers) should also be seen in these terms. In the midst of the 'hopeless confusion' of all theological and political options at the outbreak of the war, 'it was the message of the two Blumhardts with its orientation on Christian hope which above all began to make sense to me'.[20] In the year following his visit to them, Barth suggests that he has found a new starting-point: 'Blumhardt always begins right away with God's presence, might, and purpose: he starts out with God; he does not begin by climbing upwards to Him by means of contemplation and deliberation'.[21] This debt is restated at the very end of his theological career: these men, he says, 'stood out in contrast to all the academic theology of their day. They did not so much teach as testify, in sermons, meditations, and other "edifying" utterances – but still with the highest theological relevance – of the reality contained in the word and concept of the "Kingdom of God"'.[22] When they spoke 'of the Kingdom of God...they meant very naively, but for that reason very surely, the...Jesus who...acts, creates, and speaks as a real, quite specific, agent'.[23] There is in the Blumhardts' ministry a very Lutheran exaltation of the power of utterance – it is associated with exorcism.[24] The phrase 'Jesus is Victor!' is endowed with actual force (Barth calls it a 'challenge'). This saying remains at the heart of Barth's theology: 'the doctrine of reconciliation in *The Church Dogmatics* was expounded under the elder Blumhardt's watchword "Jesus is Victor!"'.[25] The phrase originates from an actual exorcism conducted by the elder Blumhardt in 1843; it is the cry of the demon expelled from the young woman. This story seems to have fascinated Barth from his earliest days as a parish pastor. Whether or not he literally believed it, he is at least attracted by the militant pathos of such faith, directly judging himself by this standard: 'Alongside such a man I see how very small I am', he writes to Thurneysen in 1914, having read Blumhardt's biography; and recounts a confrontation he recently had with an abusive drunk; 'The elder Blumhardt would at once have struck up a song of praise in that situation and would have driven the devil out of him'.[26]

Barth's break with liberal theology is in favour of one based in the rhetoric of divine authority. He later recounts that he was seeking to establish a better

---

[17] Barth, ibid., p.113-14, quoted in Busch, 1976, p.76.

[18] Barth, Interview, 1964, quoted in ibid.

[19] Barth, letter to Thurneysen, in ibid.

[20] Barth, 'Autobiographical Sketch' 1927, in Busch, 1976, p.84.

[21] Barth, 'Action in Waiting', in McCormack, 1995, p.123.

[22] Barth, *CD 4.3*, p.276.

[23] Barth, *Das Christliche Leben*, 447f.; in Jüngel, 1986, p.64.

[24] 'Exorcism was not understood as a fringe activity but as related to the whole world of forces which oppress human beings, including the political' (Gorringe, 1999, p.28).

[25] Jüngel 1986, 32; see *CD* 4.3, p.168ff.

[26] Barth, 1974, p.30.

theology than that of liberalism – 'better in the sense that in it *God*, in his unique position over against man, and especially religious man, might clearly be given that honour which we believed we found him to have in the Bible'.[27]

McCormack argues that, from the end of 1915 on, Barth's theology is dominated by a new, 'critically realistic' starting-point. 'Where nineteenth-century theology originated in a "turn to the subject", Barth's course now clearly gave evidence of a "turn to theological objectivism"'.[28] This, for McCormack, is the only truly decisive shift in Barth's theology, which 'from this point on represented a more-or-less continuous unfolding of a single theme: God is God. No further major breaks in his thought would take place'.[29] The 'realism' in question is to be understood in a very strictly *Christian* sense, which simply contradicts idealism and empiricism: '[t]he truly "real" is the wholly otherness of the *Self*-revealing God in comparison with whom the empirical world is mere shadow and appearance'.[30] It entails a radical distinction, or *diastasis*, between God and the world, and the 'impossible' attempt to think from the side of God (*'ein Denken von Gott aus'*). While accepting McCormack's thesis, that this realistic starting-point is indeed the basis of all of Barth's future theology, I am offering a new reading of it – as a reassertion of the authoritative-rhetorical basis of Protestant tradition.

This is the central theme of his early lectures. 'The Righteousness of God' of 1916 heralds a voice of authority which breaks in upon the conscience: 'As with a blare of trumpets from another world it interrupts one's reflections concerning himself and his life...It comes with its message, now as a bitter, pressing accusation, now as a quiet, firm assertion, now as an imperious task set for the will... .'[31] In a lecture later in 1916, this voice of authority returns, now in relation to the Bible: 'We are with Abraham in Haran. We hear a call which commands him... . We hear a promise... .'. This vocative force culminates in Christ, in whom it is incarnated: 'his words cause alarm, for he speaks with authority and not as we ministers. With compelling power he calls to each one: Follow me!... . [T]hrough his whole being peals one triumphant note: "I am the resurrection and the life! Because I live – ye shall live also!"'[32] This 'note' is echoed elsewhere: 'The whole Bible authoritatively announces that God must be all in all... .'.[33]

The first edition of his commentary on Romans is the first major exposition of this new 'theological realism', intended to 'overcome every attempt to ground theology in the human subject (whether idealistic, pietistic, or Religious

---

[27] Barth, 'A Thankyou and a Bow: Kierkegaard's Reveille', in *Canadian Journal of Theology* vol. XI (1965), p.209.

[28] McCormack, 1995, p.130.

[29] Ibid., p.134.

[30] Ibid., p.130.

[31] Barth, 'The Righteousness of God' in *The Word of God and the Word of Man*, trans. by Douglas Horton, Hodder and Stoughton, London, 1928, pp.10-11.

[32] 'The Strange New World Within the Bible', ibid., pp.30-31. Cf: 'The life of Jesus was the one tremendous proclamation: Fear thou not' ('Good Friday', in Barth and Thurneysen, Eduard, *Come Holy Spirit: Sermons 1920-1924*, p.137).

[33] Ibid., p.49.

Socialist)'.[34] It is structured around the breakthrough of 'real history', which is based in the act of God's speaking, into 'so-called history'.[35] As McCormack says, 'The vehicle of God's creative activity was everywhere understood by Barth to be the Word (the personal creative speech of God)'[36]; 'Ultimately, Barth resolved the question of how the new world was created and inaugurated in Christ by appeal to the creative power of the Word as exemplified in the Genesis account of the first creation: "God spoke: Let there be light! and there was light"'.[37]

The Tambach lecture of 1919, 'The Christian in Society', is a powerful summary of Barth's new position. To the religious socialist audience, Barth would have incurred the charge of quietism in his relativisation of all political options. Yet it is the most stridently militant 'quietism' conceivable. 'God in history is *a priori* victory in history. This is the banner under which we march'.[38]

What was so new about Barth's emphasis upon divine authority, the Word of God? Partly such an emphasis simply stood out from its academic context. Theology was now established as *Wissenschaft*, a kosher liberal science. And it was still on the defensive from the recent advances in biblical criticism, as well as secular sociology, cautiously wondering how to deal with them. Bold, seemingly brash, proclamation seemed hugely inappropriate. Also, more importantly, there is novelty in Barth's positive attitude to modern critical thought. His naïve-seeming theology is accompanied by a very modern critical intelligence. He learns from the modern masters of suspicion, especially Feuerbach, Marx and Nietzsche, and knows that all religious rhetoric had to be judged by the sharpest human standards. It is this conjunction of proclamatory confidence with critical acuity that underlies Barth's 'dialectical theology' (as his early phase is known).

To illustrate this further let us jump ahead to a lecture of 1927. Here he famously sums up the 'dialectical' impossibility of speaking of God: '*As ministers we ought to speak of God. We are human however and so cannot speak of God. We ought therefore to recognise both our obligation and our inability and by that very recognition give God the glory*'.[39] 'Dialectical theology' concerns the problem of theology's basis in the Word of God. The problem is that the divine rhetoric of authority in which faith is based cannot be expressed in a human rhetoric of authority without being falsified, betrayed. The primary task is to advertise this very difference between them, and so to convey the *otherness* of God. This can only be done through a self-contradictory rhetoric which wants to communicate divine authority with one hand and knock down the pretence with the other. Yet what necessarily comes first in 'dialectical theology' is the positive aspect; the need to speak. Barth's priority is to revive a rhetoric of proclamation; to dust down the verbal gestures of the Reformers. To this end, further on in the lecture of 1926, he identifies 'an ancestral line which runs back through *Kierkegaard* to *Luther* and

---

[34] McCormack, 1995, p.182.

[35] See ibid., p.144.

[36] Ibid., p.149.

[37] Ibid., p.152.

[38] Barth, 'The Christian in Society', in Barth, 1928, p.297.

[39] 'The Word of God and the Task of the Ministry', ibid., p.186.

Calvin, and so to *Paul* and *Jeremiah…*', but which does not include Schleiermacher.

> The very names Kierkegaard, Luther, Calvin, Paul, and Jeremiah suggest what Schleiermacher never possessed, a clear and direct apprehension of the truth that man is made to serve *God* and not God to serve man. [Their various prophetic ministries] are all characteristic of a certain way of speaking of *God* which Schleiermacher never arrived at.[40]

Barth's theological radicalism is rooted in this concern with 'a certain way of speaking of God'. Theology's post-liberal basis is this rhetorical audacity.

The Epistle to the Romans

The abiding radicalism of the second edition of Barth's *Romans* commentary[41] (*Romans* hereafter) consists in a theology of the Word as consistent and compelling as Luther's. God is known as a voice of authority, and theology's task is primarily rhetorical: to mediate this voice of authority. And, as we have begun to see, this entails the critical task of distinguishing this 'voice' from merely human rhetoric. What results is a dialogical rhetorical performance, in which faith is shown to abjure any single position, any single voice.

Barth's hermeneutic is, by modern standards, almost as strange as if he had written the entire commentary in ancient Greek. In defiance of his liberal schooling he declares that the 'historical-critical method of Biblical investigation' must be subordinated to 'the venerable doctrine of Inspiration'(1); his aim is 'to see through and beyond history into the spirit of the Bible, which is the Eternal Spirit'(1). Barth's approach is consciously theologically reactionary. Due to a theologically misguided age, '[t]he mighty voice of Paul'(2) will be new to us. It consequently flirts with an appearance of arrogance. Barth's earliest critics highlight its strange and strident appearance: in a review of the first edition Brunner declares it as anomalous as 'a faithful yeoman with a halberd and a suit of armor in a machine gun company. It may seem at first to some a "naïve" book in the common sense that the author is not quite "up with the times"… . Naturally, with so well-equipped a theologian as Barth that can be only appearance'.[42]

The second Preface explains the rewriting of the commentary but does not retract the bold naivety of the hermeneutical method. The inevitable protests of the historical critics that greeted the first edition are rebuffed; do these learned men, he asks, 'fail to recognize the existence of any real substance at all [in the text], of any underlying problem, of any Word in the words?'(9). Such critics are ignorant of the anguish of the minister mounting the steps of his pulpit, needing to *say something*.

---

[40] Ibid., p.197.

[41] Barth, *Der Römerbrief*, 1922 , Theologischer Verlag Zurich, 1989. ET: *The Epistle to the Romans*, trans. by Edwyn C. Hoskyns, Oxford University Press, 1933/1968.

[42] Brunner, Emil, 'The Epistle to the Romans by Karl Barth: An Up-to-Date, Unmodern Paraphrase', in Robinson, 1968, p.63.

The third Preface announces that the central question for the commentator 'is whether or no he is to place himself in a relation to his author of utter loyalty... . Anything short of utter loyalty means a commentary *on* Paul's Epistle to the Romans, not a commentary so far as is possible *with* him – even to his last word'(17). Through this loyalty the commentator will seek to render audible 'the dominant tones of the Spirit of Christ'.

> The Word ought to be exposed in the words. Intelligent comment means that I am driven on till I stand with nothing before me but the enigma of the matter; till the document seems hardly to exist as a document; till I have almost forgotten that I am not its author; till I know the author so well that I allow him to speak in my name and am even able to speak in his name myself (8).

The degree to which – as the Prefaces promise – Barth speaks *with* Paul rather than about him is striking. The voice of the commentary is one of the achievements of modern literature, let alone theology. Over hundreds of pages its energy never slackens; its engagement of the reader is sustained. It is often a preaching voice, yet what sermon would hold one's attention for the equivalent of five hundred pages? It is a strong voice, often polemical, strident, insistent, as well as poetic, ironic and even comic, yet it is never blaring, opinionated, 'preachy'. It is also a critical, analytical voice, yet never descends into bloodless theorizing. The vitality of the spoken voice lives in this text as in perhaps no other sustained work of complex critical analysis.

This is in defiance of the logic of textual commentary, which constitutes a distinct level of discourse from that of its text, an entirely different 'voice'. Indeed, in its lack of oratorical presence it can hardly be called a voice at all – for it does not compete with the original discourse. It typically appears as small-print, and places itself *under* its original text, marginalised. Yet in another sense it stands above its text; it invokes the encyclopaedic authority of fact. The normal commentary claims *a different sort of authority* from its text. (Barth does make a number of textual comments, in the conventional tone of academic rigour, yet these are few and brief, and relegated to footnotes. In his response to the first edition, Jülicher declares that these 'would all have been better left out, because they clash with the style of this work and offer nothing new'.)[43]

The purpose of Barth's commentary is not to explain its text: its purpose is the purpose of its text. Author and commentator are united in purpose; they constitute, in a sense, *one voice*. Barth is not in awe of the apostolic voice. In his act of identification with Paul the traditional category of 'Apostle' is deconstructed, dissolved. It is because Paul serves the authority of God that his voice has authority. This is the first point that Barth makes in the commentary proper. 'The man who is now speaking is an emissary, bound to perform his duty; the minister of his King; a servant, not a master'(27). Though no ambiguity is probably intended, this is true of Barth also; he too is 'the man who is now speaking [*es, der hier das Wort ergreift*]', and, in its hermeneutic of obedience, Barth's discourse is similarly unfree. The water-tight apartness of 'Paul the

---

[43] Jülicher, 'A Modern Interpreter of Paul', in Robinson, 1968, p.75.

Apostle' is theologically broken: 'The distinction between Paul and other Christians can be a matter of degree only. For, where the grace of God is, men participate in proclaiming...the Resurrection – however reservedly and with whatever scepticism they proclaim it'(31). All human proclamation of the Gospel is – potentially – the locus of grace, of divine authority; if true proclamation occurs, the real Speaker or Author is the Spirit himself.

Barth of course risks seeming arrogant in his identification with Paul. Ironically, this only serves to heighten the comparison. In fidelity to his theme, Barth assumes a voice of authoritative assurance, and of authoritative assertion. Yet I suggest that this 'inspired' voice is conscious of being a literary construct which invites the reader's deconstruction of it. Consider the following, from the introductory section:

> 'Unto faith' is revealed that which God reveals from His faithfulness. To those who have abandoned direct communication, the communication is made.... . Those who take upon them the divine 'No' shall themselves be borne by the greater divine 'Yes'. Those who labour and are heavy laden shall be refreshed (41).

Whose voice is this? On one level, very much Barth's; a good example of the idiom of 'dialectical theology': the paradoxes, the 'No' and the 'Yes'. Yet not only does it incorporate biblical parallelism, but there is suddenly an unacknowledged quotation from Matthew 11:28. Such confusion is abundant; Barth often slips into paraphrases of Scripture, where it is uncertain whether he is 'only' quoting it, or saying it 'himself'. In fact the same questions apply to Paul himself: his theology too is commentary, his voice too is riding on the authority invested in the prophets. His prophetic tone of assurance is also a sort of impersonation of another, prior voice. Barth's confusion of his own voice with Paul's is thus in keeping with the palimpsestic nature of Christian textual authority.

Barth's voice colludes not only with Paul's, and other scriptural voices, but with the modern authors he cites. Because his own style is influenced by them, and also because his quotations are built into the main body of the text, these other voices seem to merge with his own (an enactment of Bakhtin's account of dialogism). In this discourse the individual author is subsumed under the larger rhetorical tradition to which he subscribes.[44] Authorial autonomy and authority must be subverted in the communication of the Word. Barth confuses the Pauline voice (and other voices of religious authority) with his own in order to dislocate authority from the human, historical level and relocate it in God alone.

It should also be noted that Barth's commentary voice does not only consist in scriptural stylisation; it is also critical, ironic – its range is exceptional. (Balthasar's general assessment is certainly applicable to *Romans*: 'In Barth we

---

[44] 'The displacement of the self in the experience of listening for the Word of God is a hallmark of Barth's and Ricoeur's theological hermeneutics', says Wallace, and quotes Ricoeur: 'It was in fact Karl Barth who first taught me that the subject is not a centralizing master but rather a disciple or auditor of a language larger than itself' (Wallace, 1990, p.102; quoting Kearney, 'Dialogues with Paul Ricoeur', in *Dialogues with Contemporary Continental Thinkers*, Manchester University Press, 1984, p.27).

have a thinker…who tries to present the deepest drive of the Reformation in a way that can incorporate modern, Idealist, and existentialist thought, and yet at the same time is not averse to the earlier theological styles of the Fathers and Scholastics'.)[45] The idiom of post-Enlightenment critique is embraced, and even developed, rather than shunned. Because of its innate dialectic (of spirit and flesh, Yes and No), the theological voice is like a sponge: every idiom of worldly realism, every mode of critique, is of use. For in seeking to communicate the Word of God, this discourse must also give full expression to our human scepticism concerning it. To this end, Barth is at pains to incorporate the major modern voices of critical force, most clearly Marx and Nietzsche. Yet, crucially, it is not only secular suspicion that inspires Barth. Judeo-Christian tradition is innately critical, and – more unusually – self-critical. The prophets and psalmists are the master-critics of human folly, frailty, duplicity and illusion (87). And unlike modern ideologies, their message indicts us all; they resist the urge to exempt a righteous few from blame. The universalism of sin, and so of grace, is a Pauline theme that Barth, like Luther, makes much of. At the core of this pan-critical outlook is the doctrine of 'the infinite qualitative distinction between God and man', which Barth calls 'the theme of the Bible and the essence of philosophy [and the] *krisis* of human perception'(10). The insistence that God alone is righteous is the sternest warning against all religious and moral arrogance. It is the hard-core of critical thought, besides which all modern 'radicalism' is tame. Kierkegaard is credited with being the modern prophet of this theme.

Contrary to much of received opinion, the 'crisis' or negation of the human is not the last word, or even the dominant word, of the commentary. 'In the face of all the critical negations, we will all too easily miss the highly *positive* element in it…and read it as an essay in theological scepticism – as many of Barth's contemporaries did and as many readers continue to do today'.[46] Consistent positive statements are made about God and his knowability. For Barth (following Paul of course), the Gospel is an act of divine *power*. 'The Gospel of the Resurrection is the – 'power of God'…, His effective pre-eminence over all gods'(35); 'The power of God is power – "unto salvation"'(37). Yet this power is only known eschatologically, only to faith. Which is to say it is only known as a *rhetoric of power*. We cannot know this power except as it is proclaimed, asserted. (As we saw in Chapter Two, to call this power essentially rhetorical is not to discredit it but to insist upon its absolute otherness.) God's power is known to us only as a *voice* of power. 'The voice of God…is His *power*'(92). 'God speaks: and He is recognised as the Judge. By His speech and by His judgement a transformation is effected so radical that time and eternity…are indissolubly linked together'(77). Accordingly, the life of Jesus is characterised as 'humanity filled with the Voice of God [*Menschlichkeit voll redender Gottheit*]'(104). The passage which expands on this statement is a rhetorical climax; its text is Paul's first clear assertion that redemption comes through Jesus Christ (iii.24), and to this Barth reacts with almost ecstatic excitement. His attempted analysis is broken up by

---

[45] Balthasar, 1992, p.40.
[46] McCormack, 1995, p.245.

breathless praise. He then presents the Christ-event through the image from Dan. 2:24-35, of a single stone felling a mighty idol: '[I]n the hidden Life of Jesus we see also the stone...which smites the image upon its feet and...breaks it in pieces...Satan as lightning is fallen from heaven, his dominion ended; the Kingdom of God is at hand...'. He who sees all significance in the Christ event 'hears the creative Voice of God, and looks henceforward for no other, but awaits all from this redemption and from this Voice of God (Matt. xi. 1-4)' (104). In these images of divine power (or violence) Barth seeks to re-enact the cosmic exorcism effected in Jesus' words, in what amounts to a poetic theology of the Word.[47] His own rhetorical performance claims to participate in *the* rhetorical event of redemption.

We have seen that God is known in terms of power and voice. A third attribute can be added: God's authoritative utterance is one of *affirmation*. Affirmation means *saying Yes*, and Barth does not reduce it to a theoretical concept, a dead metaphor. Barth's sustained conception of God as the powerful Yes-Sayer (an extrapolation from 1 Corinthians 1:19) is of huge significance and influence: Jüngel declares that Barth's theology is reducible to 'a single word: the Yes that God says to himself and to the human race'.[48] Grace, he explains in his exegesis of iii.24, 'is altogether "Yes"; it is salvation, comfort, edification'(103). 'In one man, Jesus Christ, what was invisible becomes visible: in Him God utters His "Yes".' Human historical life is an endless 'see-saw of "Yes" and "No"'' beyond which God's Yes, to be confused with no human affirmation, is victorious (204). In contrast to his persistent misreading, Barth repeatedly emphasises that the (final, eschatological) dominance of 'Yes' is the whole point of this tortuous discourse, the beginning and end of his theme. Consequently, redemption is consistently envisaged as God's *speech-act*. A simplistic summary of the entire commentary would be to the effect of: We are redeemed by the power of God's 'Yes'. His forgiveness takes this form: despite our sin 'He continues to name us as his people in order that we may *be* His people... . Unlike any other verdict, His verdict is creative: He pronounces us, His enemies, to be His friends'(93). Our justification by grace is effected in God's act of declaration: 'He declares His decision to erect His justice by the complete renewal of heaven and earth. This declaration is *creatio ex nihilo*. When God speaks, it is done'(101-02). Because his 'verdict' contradicts human experience, its apprehension requires faith – which comes through *hearing*. 'The Kingdom of God has not "broken forth" upon the earth, not even the tiniest fragment of it; and yet, it has been *proclaimed*'(102). Theology has to exalt this 'rhetorical victory' above all else of more tangible and visible worth; it must assert the adequacy of a rhetorical apprehension of grace.

Because it is not of this world, the Word is known to us as a contradictory voice. Its expression therefore requires a particular grammar of inversion. In Barth's prose a negatively realistic statement, based on experience and observation, is characteristically followed by a contradictory counter-statement, introduced by a

---

[47] Milton, incidentally, uses the same image in *Paradise Regained*, to dramatise the victory of the Word: the Son repels Satan with the threat that his kingdom will be 'as a stone that shall to pieces dash/All monarchies besides throughout the world' (IV.149-50).

[48] Jüngel, 1986, p.18.

conjunction such as 'yet' or 'however'. This semantic movement is endowed with great significance by Barth; it is even a linguistic, or rhetorical, parable of redemption, a textual enactment of God's gracious inversion of the human situation. In his treatment of the text, 'But now apart from the law the righteousness of God hath been manifested'(iii.21), separate attention is given to the significance of the first two words. The phrase 'directs our attention to...the gospel of transformation, to the imminent Coming of the Kingdom of God, to affirmation in negation, to salvation in the world'(91). The contradictory conjunction unlocks the whole drama of faith. Barth is soon to fix upon one such conjunction as especially eloquent of this reversal of fortune: 'The righteousness of God is that "nevertheless" [*ist das* Trotzdem!] by which He associates us with Himself and declares Himself to be our God'(93). Similarly, the divine affirmation 'means that...the discord of human defiance is penetrated by the undertones of the divine melody "Nevertheless"'(95). Barth's discourse is analogous to the performance of a symphony wherein a recurrent motif is expressive of a contradictory and ultimately victorious force.[49] Elsewhere it is faith that is equated with this strangely singled-out word: 'Faith in Jesus, like its theme, the righteousness of God, is the radical "Nevertheless"'(99).[50] This rhetorical 'tune' is essential to Barth's representation of our redemption.

The Rhetorical Event of Faith

To acknowledge God's authority is also to be committed to its propagation; to dare to contribute one's voice to the cosmic declaration. As in an emotive sermon, the need for decision is repeatedly impressed upon the reader. 'Men must not be permitted to remain spectators, otherwise they will be unable to apprehend the conversion which God effects'(221). Yet when we proclaim our faith in God – as we must – we are in immediate danger of making a human possession of that faith. To proclaim a truly eschatological faith is an impossibility, but for the miracle of grace. Barth depicts this event dialogically: in confessing faith the believer's voice takes on an alien tone of authority. It also has the character of ventriloquism, or of vocal possession. In asserting with Paul that '*we have been discharged from the law*'(vii.6), 'we know not what we say, and we utter that which it is not lawful for us to utter':

> Nevertheless, we do make this assertion.... We pronounce that which should enter no human ear and proceed from no human mouth. The truth has encountered us from beyond a frontier we have never crossed; it is as though we had been transfixed by an arrow launched at us from beyond an impassable river.... It is not we who speak: Christ is the end of the law, the frontier of religion (238).

---

[49] The musical theme is a recurring one. In his commentary on John 1 he refers to 'the melody of triumph as the Word...comes into the world' (Barth, *Witness to the Word: a Commentary on John 1*, ed. by Furst, trans. by Geoffrey W. Bromiley, W. B. Eerdmans, Michigan, 1986, p. 66). We have also seen him liken the righteousness of God to a Bach fugue.

[50] Further examples in *Romans* p.79, p.123, p.137, p.211, p.392, p.405.

What is only true eschatologically must nevertheless find expression here and now. From around chapter five on, this is the basic drama of Barth's commentary: how can our confession of faith avoid the most despicable pretension? How dare we? The paradoxical solution is to *raise the stakes* of the religious claim; to insist, more boldly and naively than modern theology is accustomed to, that, in the discourse of faith, *God speaks through us*. More particularly, Barth's strategy is to raise the stakes of religious *assent*, of the act of proclaiming our faith. It is not a humanly defensible option to identify with the 'new man' of the Gospel, it is not a normal thing: it is arrogant nonsense – or, it is a function of God's will.

The act of confessing faith, of identifying with the Pauline 'we', is textually performed. This accounts for much of the unique force of Barth's commentary: it does not want merely to talk about eternity's invasion of time, the event of God's grace; it has to represent it, to enact it on the stage of the page.

> 'The Spirit himself beareth witness with our spirit that we are children of God'... . He speaks of us as – His children. We – God's children! Remember that, in daring this predication, we are taking the miraculous, primal, creative step which Abraham took; we are taking the step of faith, the step over the abyss from the old to the new creation, which God alone can take... . [W]e have dared to say it, when we have uttered the cry, *Abba, Father*... . Who dares to include himself amongst those that love God, for whom this hath been prepared? Yes, but who dares to exclude himself from their number? We have already included ourselves: we have uttered the word. There is – not, of course, as an experience – a seeing and hearing which puts all our questioning to silence, and which remembers only the decision which has been pronounced (299).

Barth seeks to express a moment of rhetorical possession by the Spirit. For in faith we defer to an alien rhetoric of authoritative certainty, we let it speak in us. There is an element of *inauthenticity* – 'we speak "as though" there had come into our heart what no human heart has contained'(299). The certainty and assurance of faith is imported, it is never 'our own voice'; it is known as an alien voice, an alien invasion, an arrow from 'the other side'. We have no experience of the truth we utter except through our rhetorical 'act'. There is a human speaking of which the real subject is God. '*Led by the Spirit* (viii.14), and crying, *Abba, Father* (viii.15), we declare ourselves to be – no, are declared to be – sons of God (viii.16) and heirs of His glory (viii.17)'(304).

To present the Word as alone authoritative entails the relativisation of all human rhetoric, including – paradoxically – the rhetoric of our proclamation. In chapter seven, Paul exhorts us to 'seriousness', which entails the exercise of authority, and here Barth adopts a corresponding tone of zeal:

> [A]s men greatly disturbed, we ought to stand up and demonstrate on behalf of this disturbance and against all brazen-faced human security. We ought seriously to strangle and exclude all opposition of men against men, and drive them to preferential respect for others; we ought to raise the standard of the dictatorship of genuine self-lessness. But can we maintain that the 'moment' of our authority, of our *seriousness*, is like that? Certainly not, for our authority is fashioned *according to*

this world, and partakes of its supremacy. And this is true of every known authority (456).

In a striking ambiguity of tone, the militant rhetoric is both genuinely intended, in as far as its reference is spiritual (i.e., to the authority of 'Christ in us'), and – at the same time – relativised, even satirised, in as far as its reference is human, worldly and 'ideological'.

Neither Barth's rhetoric nor Paul's is a direct expression of the Word of God. Yet the rhetorical authority that each assumes may have parabolic significance. Barth repeatedly alludes to the critical force of the Epistle – 'and where is it not polemical?'(536). In its task of pointing to divine agency, Pauline theology has to be '*in some sort the more bold*'(528). This boldness 'must be propounded from every possible standpoint. There must be sharp-shooting.... . There must be no yielding, no nervous anxiety about dangerous consequences!'(530). Our proclamation must be a rhetoric of strength, fighting talk. Yet, lest this polemical force be equated with that of the Word, it is at once relativized:

> And yet, though to speak about God is *bold*, we know very well that it is only *in some sort* bold.... . We know that human language can never break through to the absolute; for that would be the end of all things, and to that we can never be so bold as to set our hands. Side by side with those normal, well-regulated, bourgeois possibilities of life – no, not side by side with them, but in serio-comical fashion, hopefully in them *all* – there exists the...possibility of venturing, half seriously, half jocularly, upon an advance into the absolute (530).

Just when a rhetorical crusade seems to have been declared, an unsettling element of 'Dad's Army' is suddenly introduced. Our proclamatory purpose – in as far as it is ours – cannot be taken fully seriously: 'The seriousness of "dialectical" theology lies precisely in the fact that it takes very seriously the dissimilarity of its talk to divine talk, it takes seriously the ultimate lack of seriousness in all theology'.[51] Every human rhetoric of authority is dubious; it detracts from the otherness of the Word, makes of God's 'Yes' a human power of affirmation. Religion, even at its truest and most Pauline, is reliant upon human rhetoric; an emotive, strong, polemical form of discourse. But this is to speak 'after the manner of men'(220). *Pathos* belongs with *Eros* and *Bios*. We cannot speak in a celestial voice of authority; even Paul cannot. (In the third Preface Barth denies that 'the Spirit of Christ' speaks directly in the Epistle: instead, 'the whole is *litera*, that is, voices of those other spirits' (17).) In trying to express the import of the Word of God, '[w]e boldly employ...the language of religious romanticism, because it is impossible to describe the immediacy of divine forgiveness except by means of parables drawn from human immediacy.... . Men must not be permitted to remain spectators'(220). We can at best recognise the distance between our rhetoric and that to which it

---

[51] Bultmann, Rudolf, 'The Question of "Dialectic" Theology: a Discussion with Eric Peterson', in Robinson, 1968, p.262.

attempts to refer: 'It may then be that in our recognized inadequacy we encounter the truth'(273).

Barth's *Romans* commentary thus enacts the drama of dialectical theology. Firstly it identifies Christianity's truth with the authoritative Word. Yet as well as trying to express this authoritative rhetoric in a human theological rhetoric it also dwells upon the impossibility of this venture. This amounts to a new account of Christian proclamation as dialogical performance: the signification of the Word through the dramatic subversion of one's own discourse.

Barth's Response to Harnack

Faith, for Barth, requires dialogical expression (faith *is* dialogical; as its expression is all, or humanly all). Its dialogical structure constantly points to the agency and authority of the Word of God.[52] Instead of a single voice which credits and explains revelation, Barth presents us with the interaction of two voices; one of critical inquiry, even utter scepticism, and one of defiant faith, whose authority is presented as a function of the Word itself. Faith is entirely discredited as a human possibility, and affirmed as a divine reality. Without this contradictory dynamic, faith will always gravitate towards being just another possibility of human thought. Instead it is figured as the drama of the intrusion of the Word of God into the realm of human thought. Only through performing this conflict can theology impress us with the authority of the Word: its primary task. In this sub-section I briefly consider this dynamic in relation to Barth's response to one of his chief theological opponents.

In 1923 Barth publicly responded to an attack by Adolf von Harnack, 'the epitome of the culturally assimilated theologian'.[53] Harnack's complaint was that Barth dismissed historical criticism and thereby also the humane and enlightened form of faith that 'scientific' theology safeguards and promotes. In Kierkegaardian vein, Barth replies that this form of faith, which is humanly assured of its value, is the betrayal of the Gospel. What defines genuine faith is its absolute ungroundedness; because it is based in the Word alone, human understanding can have no purchase on it. Harnack objects that this concept of revelation is '*totally* unintelligible' and therefore impossible to believe. Barth ironically agrees: 'But is it not included...in the *concept* of revelation (and really not only in *my* concept!) that it is not possible to "believe" in it?"[54] Theology, Barth continues, must begin with Scripture, which is the 'unheard-of, unbelievable, and of course offensive'

---

[52] In *The Göttingen Dogmatics* he explains that our thought must be dialectical because God has addressed us. 'Dialectic means...thinking in such a way that there is dialogue. Two are needed for this. There must be two incompatible but inseparable partners in my thinking: a word and a counter-word... .' (Barth, *GD*, pp.309-310).

[53] Gorringe, 1999, p.4.

[54] Barth, 'An Answer to Professor von Harnack's Open Letter', in Robinson, J. (1968), *The Beginnings of Dialectical Theology*, vol. 1, trans. by K. R. Crim and L. De Grazia, John Knox Press, Richmond, Virginia, p.178.

witness 'that God himself has said and done something'.[55] 'Thus Scripture bears witness to revelation. It is not necessary to believe it; indeed one *cannot* believe it. But neither should one undermine the fact that it witnesses to revelation,...[to] God's possibility,...and this as *reality*.'[56] It thus belongs to our testimony to the *objective reality* of revelation that we insist upon its incredibility. There is a dialogical structure to this presentation of faith that directly follows Luther: we admit, 'with one voice', that it is unbelievable, yet with another voice, which corresponds to the Word, we *nevertheless* assert it.

> The *acceptance* of these incredible testimonies of the Scripture I call *faith*... . Let no one decieve himself here concerning the fact that this is an unheard-of occurrence, that the Holy Spirit must now be spoken of.[57]

As in *Romans*, the event of our confession of faith, in which faith consists, can only be seen as a function of the Holy Spirit. What 'goes on' in faith is something unique; it is not the formation of a conviction, opinion or theory. It can only be discussed in pneumatological terms.

Harnack ends the dialogue with Barth by consigning his theology strictly to the pulpit rather than the lectern: like Paul and Luther he offers himself as an object rather than a subject of scientific theology. Finally Harnack tells Barth that his dialectic 'leads us to an invisible point between absolute religious scepticism and naive biblicism'.[58] Though it means to be dismissive, this is in fact a reasonably good expression of the Barthian dialectic. For Barth's 'naive' eschatological realism entails a rigorously sceptical human realism concerning the *human* possibility of faith. To make the incomprehensible seem self-evident is 'worse than the worst and bitterest refusal to believe'.[59]

Central to the appeal of Barth's early theology is its Enlightenment-based impatience with religious mystification and sheer dishonesty; an urge to unmask and expose theological nonsense. (In the same way, as we began to see, Luther shows something of a proto-Enlightenment spirit.) He thus tells Harnack that he has more respect for atheism than for his 'simple gospel' – and this sentiment is indebted to Voltaire and Marx as well as Paul and the Reformers. What is so potent in Barth's early work is the way in which a thoroughly modern critical scepticism is used to radicalise, along Reformation lines, the nature of faith. As we shall now see, it is also used to radicalise the practice of dogmatic theology.

---

[55] Ibid., p.178.
[56] Ibid., p.179.
[57] Ibid., p.181.
[58] Von Harnack, Adolf, 'Postscript to my Open Letter to Professor Karl Barth', ibid., p.186.
[59] Barth, 'Answer to Professor von Harnack's Open Letter', ibid., p.180.

The Göttingen Dogmatics (and After)

Despite its formal development, Barth's theology is marked by a fundamental continuity of concern.[60] In *The Göttingen Dogmatics*, Barth's first work of dogmatic theology which consists of his lectures of 1924,[61] the attempted task remains: to ground faith and theology in the objectivity of divine authority, the actual agency of the Word. Instead of attempting a general exposition of this work, I am using it to extend my argument that, for Barth, faith consists in the distinctive dialogic in which the rhetorical authority of the Word is expressed.

The introductory section dispels any fear that the new dogmatic form precludes the rhetorical intensity and the dialectical force of *Romans*. Though dogmatics has a bad 'public image' ('might we not think of the dark and musty wigs of the 17th century on the one hand and head-shaking natural scientists on the other?'(4)), it is the unavoidable 'hard core' of all theology. For it is here, not in historical or practical theology, that 'the two-fold question arises: What are *you* going to say?...And *what* are you going to say?'(6). As in the second Preface of *Romans* the stakes of God-talk are raised: 'we have to consider the fact that "in some way" we have to speak about *God*. The [above] questions put a pistol at the breast of theologians and through them at that of the public'(6). Because its basic problem is our need to speak God's Word in its otherness, dogmatics retains the pathos of the dialectical approach.[62]

Dogmatics exists to reflect on and to regulate the human endeavour to speak of God on the basis of his own authoritative speaking: 'The phenomenon of Christian *speaking*...is as it were the *raw stuff* of dogma and dogmatics. As such it is our methodological starting point'(23-4): '*Christian preachers dare to speak about God*'(45). Barth emphasises at length the sheer presumption with which preachers 'make statements which demand *faith* from their hearers – an attitude which is obviously fitting only in relation to God. They make assertions about the final truth not only in existence but above it,...tossing out such words as eternity, assurance, victory, forgiveness, righteousness, Lord, and life, as though they could and should do so'(46). What then is the basis of this presumption? Barth answers this with reference to the church rather than the individual preacher:

> The Christian *church* dares to speak about God... . It dares to do this...because it finds in [its scriptural basis] an imperative to the effect that no matter what the cost,

---

[60] 'The ultimate purpose of so prophetic a thinker and preacher could never really change' (Balthasar, 1992, p.168). McCormack argues in more detail that there is 'a striking degree of continuity in Barth's work since 1916, and especially since the second *Romans*' (McCormack, 1995, p.245).

[61] *Unterricht in der Christlichen Religion, i, Prolegomena*, 1924, ed. by Hannelotte Reifen, TVZ, Zurich, 1985. ET: *The Göttingen Dogmatics: Instruction in the Christian Religion*, vol. 1, ed. by H. Reifen, trans. by G. W. Bromiley, W. B. Eerdmans, Michigan, 1991.

[62] Barth has transferred dogmatic thinking 'to the place previously occupied by dialectical thinking alone... . In this way Barth's radicalism was not dampened in the least by his 'turn to dogmatics''(McCormack, 1995, p.345). Ward argues that 'Barth's existentialism, and likewise his understanding of dialectic, remain fundamental for dogmatics. They provide the reason for dogmatic thinking itself' (Ward, 1996, p.96).

it must do so.... . By the presence of these writings, and at the very first partly by the oral proclamation of their authors, it felt itself enlisted in their host. The monuments of the witness of departed prophets and apostles were for it a command not to leave their places empty, to pass on their witness, itself to talk about God, always in the light of what they said, but precisely through this light with the knowledge, courage and authority to do so (53).

Permission and command to preach thus comes through a certain literary, or rhetorical, tradition which is deemed to constitute a *voice of authority*. To obey this voice is to propagate it, to re-perform it. He illustrates this in relation to Calvin, who is 'grasped and stilled and claimed...simply by the authority of the biblical books'. He becomes 'wholly voice and speech and persuasion...as though nothing were more self-evident than this torrential talk about God in spite of all the objections which might be urged against it, and which he himself knew well enough! Why was this? In the first instance we can find no other reason than this: Because he heard Moses, Jeremiah, and Paul speak about God, because he heard there the trumpet that summoned him to battle' (54-55). Like Calvin, the church as a whole cannot neutrally explain its proclamatory task: instead it 'refers to the text, to the authority with which the prophets and apostles talked about God and which demands that we do likewise. It dares to dare what they dared. Or rather, it does *not* dare *not* to do so. Here is the historical sequence or order in which Christian preachers place themselves'(55).

The supra-personal objectivity of faith here emerges as a *rhetorical-textual* reality. Faith means acknowledgement of the authority of this distinctive and objective rhetorical idiom. Further on Barth reflects on the privileged role of language in revelation. God uses human words to reveal himself, and because these remain human words he is *concealed* in his revelation. As McCormack observes, 'the complete inadequacy of human language for revelation is not set aside in the least. But in that the Word of God conceals Himself in human words, a relation of correspondence is established, an analogy between the Word and the words'.[63] Theology's subject matter is strictly limited to this linguistic or rhetorical idiom in which he is revealed and concealed. 'Protestantism meant originally to believe in the becoming-human of the Logos precisely in spoken human *words*'(33):

> The procedure of the Self-revealing God is a *dicere*; its content is *word*.... . No modern anti-intellectualism and anti-moralism may cause us here to put life, the irrational, the holy, etc., in place of the Word.... . It is for this reason that the testimony of the prophets and apostles comes to us in the form of *words*, and it is for this reason that permission and demand come to us – not to babble, not to mime, not to make music, but rather – to *speak* of God (62-63).

And apprehension of divine speech cannot be separated from a relationship of authority: 'God's address to us means directly the knowledge that God is almighty. Address here means claiming, commandeering, binding to faith and obedience.... .

---

[63] McCormack, 1995, p.341.

The act of the living God *is eo* ipso an act of lordship'(404). 'We cannot recognise God without accepting his authority'(172).

The Uprooting of Religious Subjectivity

Dogmatics is 'scientific reflection' (*'Wissenschaftliche Besinnung'*) on the principle of *Deus Dixit;* of the Word as the basis of faith. This entails a 'scientifically' rigorous opposition to any human, experiential grounding. 'It follows that if we are not to fall into the arms of Feuerbach at the very first step, that in this relation we must think of God as the subject'(11). In this work especially Feuerbach serves as the great warning figure; theology must above all become invulnerable to his critique if it is to overcome liberalism. Every possibility of its human and subjective foundation must be anticipated and precluded. Dogmatic thought must train itself in the insistence that its subject matter is God-in-his-revelation, and not the subjective apprehension of it, which 'can only be a shadow of revelation'(94). Our 'more or less vital religion and piety' is only 'a very special function of reason', it is only human. Above all, it must not detract from the subjecthood of God in revelation.

This insistence recurs like a refrain, in relation to every doctrine Barth considers. Though the doctrine of the Trinity is concerned with God's relationship to us, the subject of the doctrine is 'always solely *he*, never and nowhere *we*. Point by point we have seen that we must accept this "he not we" if we are to talk seriously about revelation'(134). In order to hold to the absolute sovereignty of the 'he', the subjective tendency that plagues religion must be rooted out like a pest (139). Religious experience, the staple of popular piety, is no sound basis for dogmatic theology: 'what personal experience says, dogmatics is supposed to put on the scales and test'(302). An aura of scientific precision is evoked, of clinical antidote to the excesses of 'religious feeling'.

> One cannot think dogmatically without a certain ruthlessness. The force that human thinking is achieving or seeking is that of which we read in Jer. 23:29 that it is like a fire, or like a hammer that smashes rocks. If that does not happen, if the pious words can slip through the sieve of dogmatics without being salted and sharpened and freighted, then something is wrong (304).

Dogmatics opposes the subjective tendency with *prophetic* force. It does so in order to establish the eschatological nature of faith: *'Deus dixit* is our confidence, not experience. We can only believe'(67). Yet it later emerges that even this is beyond us. *'Can* we believe, believe in *God*? Is not this something that is conceptually impossible? If we could have such a faith, would it not burn us like contact with a high-voltage circuit, but much more severely?'(124). Barth insists that revelation remains *hidden* to every human faculty:

> Just because revelation is given contingently in Jesus Christ, but given therefore in concealment, the faith that grasps it and affirms it is a leap in the dark and never ceases to be so. It is a psychological impossibility, just as revelation is a historical impossibility. It may be conceived – no, it may be asserted and described only as a

> miracle of the Holy Spirit…that forces us to do what we cannot do, that is, to believe in God, not because we have access to God but because he, the Holy Spirit, is himself God and creates access where there is none (197).

'The Holy Spirit…forces us', and he alone is 'the subjective possibility of revelation'. In relation to both *Romans* and Barth's reply to Harnack, I have suggested that faith emerges not as our possession but as *our possession by* an alien voice of authority. This is further developed in *The Göttingen Dogmatics*. What cannot be conceived can and must be *asserted*. What is outside of our experience must nevertheless be witnessed to. And, crucially, the locus of faith is, humanly speaking, this *act* of acknowledging and asserting the intrinsic authority of the Word. 'Act' may have reference not only to the realm of public expression, as opposed to inner experience, but also to the element of inauthenticity entailed in our assertion. For we employ a tone of confidence that is humanly unwarranted. 'No relativism, no scepticism, no personal timidity should prevent us from talking about God very naively, very definitely, and in the same matter-of-fact way as we talk about any other data. God is a datum in revelation by the Spirit'(331). Though, as flesh, we cannot believe in God in this 'matter-of-fact' way, such certainty is imported into our speech. '[T]here is in the relation of revelation a knowability of God which can be calmly asserted over against all historically or psychologically grounded scepticism because it is self-established'(336-37).

Let us consider a final instance of this dynamic from *The Göttingen Dogmatics*. How is it, he asks, that while most people do not believe, some do? It cannot be answered that only the latter perceive what is revealed, for revelation is always *hidden*; to believer as to nonbeliever. For this reason, believers should not 'commit the folly of trying to make a proof out of what they can only assert':

> If they are perspicacious…[believers will not say] that we need a particular organ for faith that the others do not have or have not developed sufficiently, whereas they themselves enjoy it. Finally, they will not insist on special experiences that they have had… . Do not they have to make a painful renunciation of all these things, and of all talk about their heart or mind or conscience, because they would be violating therewith their presupposition that revelation is *hidden*, and therefore their own thesis that *revelation* is hidden? Hence nothing seems left but a simple *Credo*, I believe (449-50).

This 'Credo', which entails a reference to the agency of God, 'is the only relevant answer to the question of why one believes. God wills it'(451). Here is one of Barth's clearest statements that, instead of being based in any form of experience, faith (from a human point of view) consists *only in the act of its assertion, only in the performance of the rhetoric of divine agency.*[64] This external act is always strange to us, outside of our 'inner being': 'Those who believe are astounding to themselves… . They can view their faith only as a miracle that they can only affirm…'(456). As in *Romans*, then, there is a 'dialogical' dynamic whereby faith's basis in the Word of God alone is rhetorically enacted.

---

[64] 'The proof of faith consists in the proclamation of faith. The proof of the knowability of the Word of God consists in confessing it' (*CD* 1.1, p.241).

In the first volume of his *Church Dogmatics*, Barth returns to this crucial question. Faith is certain knowledge of the Word of God. Yet it differs from all other certainty, or 'assurance', in that we cannot appeal to our experience in support of it. Instead this assurance has its basis in the Word of God, and is therefore a matter of *expectation* rather than possession.

> Regarded by itself [the believer's assurance] is baseless, without hold upon God, and, moreover worthless, alongside the other forms of human assurance, which have their seat not so strictly outside of man. It is more human, i.e. more unsure than all other human assurances, just because it is the assurance of expectation, this expectation. And yet 'unheard-of assurance'?... . Yes indeed...it is an assurance which bears in itself a metal which makes it superior to any other assurance...it is in its utter humanness an affirmation of 'unheard-of' assurance.
>
> Because surrounded by this ultimate lack of assurance, by the freedom of God, the assurance of our affirmation of the knowability of the Word of God cannot be great enough...we need not fear the danger of 'absolutising', so fearfully painted upon the wall at this stage by those who do not understand.[65]

Here again we see that the believer assumes an assurance that is humanly unwarranted. By admitting that its tone of authoritative certainty is humanly empty, faith performs its basis in the Word of God. The certainty of our confessional rhetoric does not belong to us – what possible grounds do we have for it? The utterance of faith must be understood sceptically – as a piece of rhetorical performance, ungrounded in our subjectivity – and *at the same time* pneumatologically – as rhetorical possession by the Spirit.

One could of course go on to trace this dynamic throughout the massive *Church Dogmatics*. Instead, finally in this chapter I shall offer an instance of it from one of his briefer later works: his lectures of 1946 subsequently published as *Dogmatics in Outline*. This work provides a useful sketch of his mature voice, with its ring of patriarchal confidence, its easy (over-easy?) authority. He is still concerned to reaffirm theology's basis in a rhetoric of objective authority and final certainty. In contrast to rational and experiential apologetics, theological evidence 'is not the evidence of my thoughts, or my heart, but the evidence of the apostles and prophets, as the evidence of God's self-evidence'.[66]

> Note well: in the whole Bible...not the slightest attempt is ever made to *prove* God.... . The Bible speaks of God simply as of One who needs no proof. It speaks of a God who *proves Himself* on every hand: Here am I, and since I am and live and act it is superfluous that I should be proved. On the basis of this divine self-proof the prophets and apostles speak. In the Christian church there can be no speaking about God in any other way.[67]

God's evasion of our proofs requires that we speak of him in a certain way; and this *way of speaking* is evident in the above: with a boldness that is almost

---

[65] Barth, CD 1.1, p.259.
[66] Barth, *Dogmatics in Outline*, trans. by G. T. Thomson, SCM Press, London, 1949, p.13.
[67] Ibid., p.38.

embarrassing Barth begins to impersonate the divine voice. In place of proofs we have a *style* of naive and confident assertion. Related to the bold simplicity of this tone of voice, Barth insists, is its joy: 'Where people believe, the urgent question is whether they do not speak joyfully and gladly also, just as the Bible has spoken and as in ancient and more recent times the Church has spoken and must speak'.[68] Such joy has a militant side to it: true monotheism means God's otherness from 'the ridiculous deities whom man invents. Once we have realised this, we can only laugh, and there is a laugh running through the Bible at these figures'.[69] Faith very largely consists in the imitation of the voice (or voices) of biblical witness and its rhetoric of cosmic confidence. Faith also entails a tone of *defiance*, against the power of unbelief within us, which is to be seen, in Lutheran fashion, as demonic temptation:

> We cannot deliver ourselves from pride and anxiety about life; but there will always be a movement of defiance, not least against ourselves. If we summarise all that opposes us as the power of contradiction, one has an inkling of what Scripture means by the devil. 'Has God really said...?' Is God's Word true? If one believes one will snap one's fingers at the devil.[70]

This dialogical agonistic representation of faith is of course modelled on Luther's. Barth too is concerned with faith's *tone of voice*. In correspondence to the 'style' of revelation, we must acquire a tone of confidence which is almost cavalier and triumphalist. It must reflect the absoluteness of Christ's victory over all other lordships and authorities. Because the powers of this world are defeated, however they rage on, 'we must cease to fear them any more. If you have heard the Easter message, you can no longer run around with a tragic face and lead the humourless existence of a man who has no hope. One thing still holds, and only this one thing is really serious, that Jesus is the Victor. We are invited and summoned...to live in thankfulness and not in fear'.[71] Faith corresponds to an attitude, a style of confident strength: 'We must not sit among [non-Christians] like melancholy owls but in a certainty about our goal, which surpasses all other certainty'.[72] As the Heidelberg catechism has it, we await Christ 'with head erect'.[73]

This rhetoric of confidence and authority relates to the heart of theology's content. Theological discourse must convey the central fact that the truth of revelation consists in its *authority*. Thus Barth concedes that life contains many 'revelations', such as love and beauty: 'But starting from Christian faith we must say of these revelations that they are lacking in a final, simply binding authority... All these revelations are notoriously devoid of any final, binding force.'[74] And this

---

[68] Ibid., p.31.
[69] Ibid., p.40.
[70] Ibid., p.20.
[71] Ibid., p.123.
[72] Ibid., p.132.
[73] Ibid., p.134.
[74] Ibid., p.83.

unique authority must find expression in theological rhetoric (for what existence does it have but the rhetorical?):

> [I]n each really Christian utterance there is something of an absoluteness such as cannot belong to any non-Christian language. The Church is not 'of the opinion', it does not have 'views', convictions, enthusiasms. It *believes* and *confesses*, that is, it speaks and acts on the basis of the message based on God Himself in Christ. And that is why all Christian teaching, comfort and exhortation is a fundamental and conclusive comfort and exhortation in the power of that which constitutes its content, the mighty act of God, which consists in the fact that He wills to be for us in His only-begotten Son, Jesus Christ.[75]

Christian discourse, including theology, is, for Barth, a *discourse of authority*; it exists 'in the power of that which constitutes its content'. It might be argued that dialogical performance is less of a concern to Barth's mature voice; he instead tends towards a stabler and more single voice, seemingly in danger of forgetting its human limitation. Yet it may also be shown that his mature dogmatics remains informed by the dialectical principle.

Like his Reformation predecessors, Barth's theology locates the truth of faith in the agency of the authoritative Word. Yet more than them he confronts the basic problem: no human rhetoric can adequately express the Word. His key discovery is that theology can criticise its own rhetoric while also affirming its rhetorical basis. Indeed there is a *symbiosis* between the affirmative and the critical: the affirmation of God's otherness is dependent upon critical vitality and vigilance. Barth learns this dynamic from Luther and Kierkegaard among others. Late in life he recalls the nature of Kierkegaard's influence on him.

> What attracted us particularly to him, what we rejoiced in, and what we learned, was the criticism, so unrelenting in its incisiveness, with which he attacked so much: all the speculation which blurred the infinite qualitative difference between God and man, all the aesthetic forgetfulness of the absolute claims of the Gospel... . [H]e became and was for us one of the cocks whose crowing seemed to proclaim from near and far the dawn of a really new day.[76]

This is a good example of the distinctive critical capacity that Barth finds within Protestant tradition, and of its indispensability to the proclamatory agenda.

---

[75] Ibid.

[76] Barth, 'A Thankyou and a Bow: Kierkegaard's Reveille', in *Canadian Journal of Theology*, vol. XI (1965), p.211.

Chapter 9

Barth and Nietzsche: Prophetic Rhetoric Regained

'[A] theology freed from ontology must take rhetoric seriously – theology must now choose a language, a style, rather than a philosophy.' (Webb, 1991, p.178).

Nietzsche and Barth have this in common: to think of them is not primarily to think of their specific arguments or conceptual coinage, but to think of a voice which has addressed one. Nietzsche's critique of Christianity, in common with his thought at large, is radically rhetorical; the central 'argument' is the very existence of this voice of self-determining strength, of new and creative authority.

Nietzsche's philosophical novelty is based upon a new attitude to rhetoric. In contrast to the Socratic and Enlightenment assumption, rhetoric is acknowledged to be the ineradicable basis of language and meaning: rational resistance is futile. An early study conceived of rhetoric as 'the essence of language. Language does not desire to instruct, but to convey to others a subjective impulse and its acceptance'.[1] This insight is at the root of his critique of conventional thought, and it is not an abstract insight but one acted upon, performed. Consequently, his identification of Christian morality with pathological weakness is dependent upon the voice which indicts it: such a critique must consist in a more compelling discourse. In this chapter I argue that Nietzsche's voice abstracts from the grammar of theological-prophetic discourse; he seeks to out-do it, to appropriate its rhetorical extremity, its pathos, which he sees as the rightful possession of self-determining man. His 'perspectivism' is to be seen in this light.

I then suggest that Barth's rhetorical theology is cognisant of Nietzsche's voice. Nietzsche's imitation of prophetic rhetoric can only be countered by genuinely prophetic rhetoric. This chapter entails a reading of Barth's early theology, especially his *Romans* commentary, as a response, a rejoinder, a riposte to the Nietzschean voice. It deals with a problematic of influence, abstraction and appropriation. Whereas Nietzsche critiques Christianity by apeing the prophetic voice, Barth critiques Nietzsche, and invents a distinctly modern theology, by counter-apeing the Nietzschean voice, which serves as a resource for the translation of prophetic speech into modern authorship.

The distinctiveness of Nietzsche's style has never ceased to attract comment. What is it about his insights, or his philosophical agenda that necessitates this rhetorical stridency, this stylistic extremity, this *voice*? In the words of one critic he 'make[s] his presence as an author literally unforgettable, to

---

[1] Cited in Lacoue-Labarthe, P., *The Subject of Philosophy*, ed. by Trezise, T., trans by Trezise et al., University of Minnesota Press, Minneapolis, 1993, p.23.

show that these views originate with him'.[2] But why is this stylistic exhibitionism necessary? Let us first consider this question in the context of his relationship to theology.

Nietzsche is adamant that his own critique of religion is unique; that it is not to be confused with the atheism of past philosophers. The death of God is only good news when we have appropriated his characteristics; otherwise his ghost haunts us, and our atheism is merely reactive. Such appropriation is, for Nietzsche, re-appropriation; a matter of reclaiming what truly belongs to us, what we falsely ascribed to God in a moment of ancient weakness. The second book of *The Will to Power* tells the story of this self-belittlement.

> In short, the origin of religion lies in the extreme feelings of power, which, being *strange*, take men by surprise... . [I]n so far as everything great and strong in man was considered *superhuman* and *foreign*, man belittled himself, – he laid the two sides, the very pitiable and weak side, and the very strong and startling side apart, in two spheres, and called the one 'Man' and the other 'God'.[3]

What we have discussed in relation to Barth and Kierkegaard as 'the God-man distinction' is thus the source of all error, the original sin against Man which now cries out for remedy. True philosophy constitutes a counter-history of the spirit: 'Man gradually takes possession of the highest and proudest states of his soul, as also of his acts and works'.[4] Nietzsche casts himself as the lone proclaimer of this movement. This determination to reclaim the characteristics of God is what sets his critique of Christianity apart. Merely to call God an oppressive superstition, a projection that may now be dismantled, or an error that we may now put behind us, is a comparatively straightforward position: instead of God and man, just man. Yet such atheism is abhorrent to Nietzsche. It is the acceptance of man as 'the very pitiable and weak side' of the above equation; it leads to the divinisation of the lowest common denominator of humanity, of the 'gregarious instinct';[5] it is spiritual lobotomy. The mainstream rejection of religion is condemned as mere nihilism, a failure of the human spirit. In *Thus Spake Zarathustra*, for example, 'humanist anti-religiosity is identified by Nietzsche with a bourgeois refusal of the great and noble, precisely of the *übermenschliche*, which Nietzsche in his notebooks identifies with the religious impulse itself. Refusal of God in the name of some sort of human normativity is *not* regarded by Nietzsche as critical'.[6]

What can it mean, then, for the characteristics of the old God to be reclaimed as the rightful possession of the new humanity? How can the Godness of God be preserved in his cancellation? What is the logic of this *Aufhebüng*? The primary problem is that the biblical God is defined *in distinction to man*: 'the infinite qualitative distinction' would seem to stand firmly in the way of

---

[2] Nehamas, A., *Nietzsche: Life as Literature*, Harvard University Press, Mass., 1985, p.37.

[3] *WP* vol., 2.1, pp.135-36.

[4] Ibid., p.137.

[5] Ibid., 2.2. p.275.

[6] Milbank, J., 'Problematising the secular: the post-postmodern agenda', in Berry, Wernick eds., 1992, p.33.

Nietzsche's project of re-appropriation. Yet Nietzsche translates the absolute difference between God and man into the absolute difference between *man* and man; between the higher and lower types of man (the gender-bias may as well stand in this instance). The dramatic distance between Creator and creature becomes (in one of Nietzsche's favourite phrases) 'the pathos of distance' between the master and servant classes: 'the chasm between man and man, class and class,...the will to be oneself and to distinguish oneself – that, in fact, which I call the *pathos of distance* is proper to all strong ages'.[7] Thus the passion with which he clings to the aristocratic principle is in a very real sense religious; it inherits the intensity of the God-relationship, or rather, from Nietzsche's viewpoint, this natural principle has hitherto been usurped by the fallacy of the God-relationship. The two principles, the God-man distinction, and the intra-human distinction, are thus mutually exclusive, they displace each other. Cf.: 'Europe has been dominated by men, with their 'equality before God', not sufficiently noble to see the radically different grades of rank...that separate man from man'.[8] And thus declares Zarathustra: 'So blinketh the populace – "there are no higher men, we are all equal; man is man, before God – we are all equal"'.[9]

For Nietzsche, then, we cannot simply 'drop' the pathos contained in the notion of divine creation (as common atheism does) but must re-claim it; the entire dialectic of God and man must be fitted into 'man', back where it belongs: 'in man, *creature* and *creator* are united: in man there is not only matter, shred, excess, clay, mire, folly, chaos; but there is also the creator, the sculptor, the hardness of the hammer...'.[10]

It thus follows that Nietzsche's 'noble virtues' are largely taken from the God onto whom they were projected (Nietzsche adapts the notion of projection from Feuerbach). The emergent Overman is not only free but sovereignly free; free for the creation of value. Like Jehovah's, this creative strength also manifests itself in the destruction of existing idolatrous values; 'he who hath to be a creator in good and evil – he hath first to be a destroyer, and break values in pieces'.[11] Nietzsche's ideal even incorporates a secularised version of grace: true virtue echoes the 'grand economy' of nature which 'is not afraid of high prices, of squandering';[12] according to Zarathustra, 'a gift-giving virtue is the highest virtue'. As Staten observes, 'Nietzsche manages to weave plausibly together the notions of compulsive gift-giving and hardness of heart'[13]– and I suggest that this pathos should be seen as biblically derivative.

The biblical God, then, is the measure, or the criterion, of what, when translated back into human terms, is truly valuable. This creates something of a methodological problem for Nietzsche, to put it mildly. We cannot help looking to

---

[7] *TI* 'Skirmishes in a war with the age' 37, p.93.

[8] *BGE* 3.62, p.84.

[9] *Zarathustra*, 'The Higher Man', 4, p.73.

[10] *BGE* 7.225, p.171.

[11] Z, 2, 34 'Self-surpassing' p.138.

[12] Quoted in Staten, 1990, p.10.

[13] Ibid., p.13.

God, from whom we must also learn to look away; he is both the model for all that is truly valuable and its perversion. We shall return to this ambiguity.

Promethean Perspectivism

Nietzsche is concerned both to analyse and to fill a perceived vacuum of authority; to confront a latent crisis of legitimation. Though religion lacks real credence, philosophy fails to replace it; and so Christian-based morality retains weary assent in the absence of any alternative. 'Now, admitting that faith in God is dead: the question arises once more: "who speaks?" My answer, which I take from biology and not from metaphysics, is: *"the gregarious instinct* speaks"... . People prefer to obey a law which is to hand rather than to *create* a new one, rather than to command themselves and others... .'[14] In analysing and exposing the vacuum of authority, he makes a bid to fill it: the new voice is itself the solution. Nietzsche presents us with a voice of authority which is consciously different from that associated with philosophy, based in a claim to universal to universal validity. '[W]here most philosophers write in an abstract, third-person "omniscient" voice, Nietzsche writes often in the first person...and there is no question whose opinion he is stating. His style draws attention to the author'.[15] His voice not only admits but insists that it has no justification outside of itself; it disdains to parade itself as 'objective truth'. Yet the type of authority that it *does* lay claim to is not lessened by this disavowal but radically, hyperbolically boosted: the authority is self-creative, sovereign, free, divine. Nietzsche's refusal of metaphysical foundationalism is not, as many critics assume it to be, the humble, unpretentious, pluralist (post-modern, feminist-friendly!) admission that his is only one perspective among others. In contrast to normal philosophy's 'pretended neutrality..., Nietzsche's shrill voice is modest in contrast', says one critic;[16] another thinks that his perspectivism anticipates 'the present recovery of silenced or marginalised voices'.[17] I suggest that this voice is not quite so humble or worthy. It is aping God, whose authority cannot, by definition, be validated by any external criteria, whose authority is unfounded because it is absolute, because the utterance itself is the creation of all value. The rejection of metaphysics is the precondition of the 'real task' which is 'to create values... . [T]he genuine philosophers are commanders and legislators; they say "Thus shall it be!" Whatever is and was becomes for them a means, a hammer';[18] it is the license, in other words, to play God.

Nietzsche's 'perspectivism', which has been hailed as the centre of his thought (and as the inspiration for postmodernism), should be seen as the

---

[14] *WP* vol.1, 2, pp.275-79.

[15] Solomon, in Solomon and Higgins, 1988, p.9.

[16] Magnus, S., *Nietzsche's Case: Philosophy as/and Literature*, Routledge, New York, 1993, p.18.

[17] Makarushka, I. S. M., *Religious Imagination and Language in Emerson and Nietzsche*, Macmillan, Basingstoke,1994, p.xii.

[18] *BGE* 6.211, p.152.

appropriation of the tradition of anti-apologetic theology discussed throughout my study. The 'new philosophers' heralded in *Beyond Good and Evil* are imitation incarnations of the Word of God. They are poetic creators of the truth they tell, their word shall have spontaneous authority to command. They are 'perspectivist' not in any weak relativist sense but in the sense that God's perspective is truth.

An important feature of Nietzschean 'noble virtue' is that it will not descend to self-justification. To attempt to prove the validity of one's position is a failure of taste, as well as logic. With the emergence of Socratic dialectics:

> a noble taste is vanquished, the mob comes to the top. Previously all such proffering of one's opinions was looked upon with suspicion. Honest things like honest men do not carry their reasons on their sleeve in such fashion... . That which needs to be proved cannot be worth much. Wherever authority still belongs to good usage, wherever men do not prove but command, the dialectician is regarded as a sort of clown.[19]

Nietzsche practically admits that this 'authentic' pathos is lifted from the Bible, or a certain strain within it. To the 'real' Jesus, 'dialectic is...quite absent, as likewise the idea that any faith, any "truth" can be proved by argument'.[20] And he argues against the desire, exemplified in George Eliot, to retain Christian morality without God:

> Christianity is a system, a complete outlook upon the world, conceived as a whole. If its leading concept, the belief in God, is wrenched from it, the whole is destroyed; nothing vital remains in our grasp... . Christian morality is a command, its origin is transcendental. It is beyond all criticism, all right to criticism,...it is true only on condition that God is truth.[21]

He admires this integrity (in the literal sense) that puts faith beyond rational criticism; he perceives that its meta-narrative can only be refuted by another, better, stronger one.

The project of human affirmation after God must take on the voice of authority that was once the preserve of Christian preaching. For such is the only historical precedent for a discourse of self-confident strength. '[I]n Germany there has only been one kind of public and approximately artistic discourse – that delivered from the pulpit';[22] 'We Germans are still young. Luther is still our last event; our last book is still the Bible.'[23] In connection with his own authorship he both acknowledges and parodies Luther: 'I can do nought else. God help me! Amen'.[24] Nietzsche's debt to Protestantism can hardly be overstated: 'his origins

---

[19] *TI*, 'The Problem of Socrates' 5, p.12.

[20] *AC* 32, p.170.

[21] *TI* 5, p.63.

[22] *BGE*, p.205.

[23] *GM*, 'Peoples and Countries' 6, p.218.

[24] *EH*, 'Why I Write' 2, p.60.

lay not in the clouds but in Protestant Christianity, of which he is manifestly an outcome'.[25]

Religious discourse has been both guardian and abuser of the true pathos. Yet this ambiguity can now begin to end; for the appropriate voice has at last emerged which can affirm human life with the passion hitherto wasted on God. The argument against religion must take a new aesthetic or rhetorical turn, in which the superiority of this new voice is performed. This assumption of superiority is the novelty of his attack on Christianity: 'No one hitherto has felt Christian morality beneath him'.[26] The nonsense of doctrine and ritual is irrelevant besides the deficiency of the Christian ideal. Though this may be theoretically argued (and he is not entirely averse to philosophical argument), it is style rather than content which takes centre stage. The real critique consists not in this or that argument (which will never be wholly original) but in a voice which is no less intense, no less compelling, no less *interesting* than any theological voice from the past. *Humanity's* truth must be proclaimed from the rooftops; this, the true Evangel, must out-evangelise the Gospel. Unless we dare to speak with authority – in this, prophetic, sense – our 'critique' is merely reactive and does not deserve to succeed. Thus Staten:

> Nietzsche's discourse on power is itself an exercise of power. Because Nietzsche appeals to no instituted authority or canons of demonstration, the constative value of his discourse depends entirely on the persuasiveness of its claim to autarky, or, more precisely, on its enactment of the motions of that very power concerning which it speaks. Where there is no appeal to some additional authority, only the discourse *of* power can be a discourse *on* power.[27]

Nietzsche's style is often called 'prophetic', as if he is in the same club as the biblical prophets. Yet what sense does it make to speak thus, to invoke this model of authority? What, in other words, is the *logic* of prophetic speech? We began to consider this question in Part One. Prophetic speech represents an authority of which it is the only present manifestation. Yet if this authority is real, why is it not directly, extra-linguistically coercive? Why does it rely upon a *rhetoric* of authority? The drama of the prophetic voice requires a narrative foundation. The grammar of biblical prophetic speech corresponds to the narrative of God's revelation in the form of human weakness. By inverting the Christian narrative, Nietzsche invents his own account of the need for such a voice. It is the story of the attainment of power by the weak. This constitutes a sort of Fall, in which everything is turned upside-down. The slaves have poisoned 'the very springs of life',[28] so that true strength is weakened, Samson-like. 'The corruption, the ruination of higher men...is in fact the rule: it is dreadful to have such a rule always before one's eyes'.[29] The easy objection to this is that if *ressentiment*

---

[25] Hollingdale, R. J, 'The Hero as Outsider', in Magnus and Higgins, 1996, p.82.

[26] *EH* 3, p.66.

[27] Staten, H., *Nietzsche's Voice*, Cornell University Press, New York, 1990, p.33.

[28] *GM*, quoted in Solomon and Higgins, 1988, p.30.

[29] *BGE* 9.269, p.244. Deleuze thinks that 'one of the finest remarks in *The Will to Power* is:

triumphs, then surely it is the true strength, and Nietzsche fuels this objection by admiring, in spite of himself, the cunning and resilience of the ascetic will (he is particularly fascinated by Pascal). We are asked to believe that true strength is in perpetual danger of extinction and requires a desperate, polemical defence – which now takes the form of Nietzsche's own discourse. This position is only intelligible as an abstraction from the logic of biblical prophecy, in which God's strength is hidden in the form of weakness, and revealed only in this instance of rhetorical strength.

Despite the self-contradiction in his position, Nietzsche insists, with admirable determination, that it is justified by its poetic force. 'Only as an aesthetic phenomenon is the existence of the world justified', he declared early on[30], and he is similarly confident that the story he tells is justified by the rhetorical-aesthetic force of its telling. It is not the rational but the *pathetic* weakness of modern Christianity that discredits it. Zarathustra says of Christians: 'They would have to sing better songs for me to learn to have faith in their Redeemer; and his disciples would have to look more redeemed!'[31]. Barth may be seen as taking this challenge seriously.

Barth's Theology as a Response to Nietzsche

In response to Nietzsche's 'prophetic' mode of attacking Christianity, Barth rediscovers the prophetic mode of proclaiming it. Only authentic prophetic speech is capable of exposing the illogic of its imitator and of retaking the rhetorical highground.

After Nietzsche, then, theology must show that *it* is the supreme discourse of human affirmation, that *its* story of our liberation cannot be indicted by any other. Of course it can only respond by re-telling its own (Christological) story, rather than arguing on neutral ground. Yet it can perform its task of self-explication in such a way as to deflate the rhetorical pathos of its opponent, take the wind out of his sails, expose his pretension. Secular reason (of which Nietzsche's 'unreason' is a strange form) cannot be rationally refuted, only out-narrated; out-*orated* .[32] And so I will show that Barth is concerned to out-do Nietzsche at his own rhetorical game (which is really theology's own rhetorical game).

The stylistic intensity of Barth's *Romans* commentary may be seen to relate to Nietzschean vitalism, to be a rival form of '*über*-discourse'. Barth is certainly influenced by Nietzsche's voice. From the Prefaces alone there are indications that he conceives of himself as something of a theological Nietzsche, as a polemical presence to be reckoned with, a critical force, a disturbing enlightener. 'This is a critical work', announces the second Preface, 'in the full and most serious meaning

---

'the strong always have to be defended against the weak' (Deleuze, 1983, p.58).

[30] *BT*, quoted in Lavrin, 1971, p.33.

[31] *Z* 204, quoted in Solomon and Higgins, 1988, p.150.

[32] 'Out-narration' is the coinage of Milbank, discussed in the next chapter (Milbank, 1990, p.330).

of the word "critical"'.[33] Which is what? He tells us indirectly: it has been 'rightly pointed out that the book may exercise a fatal influence upon immature minds. And yet, the man who makes this criticism ought seriously to reflect whether the persistent covering up of the dangerous element in Christianity is not to hide its light under a bushel'. Its light is dangerously bright: this contests the secular image of en*light*enment as a smooth growth, naturally liberating, unambiguously desirable. Real enlightenment, he agrees with Nietzsche, is dangerous, problematic, a scandal to the 'enlightened classes'; it is necessarily polemical, aggressive, at odds with the civil discourse of liberalism. Barth's discourse is not satisfied to be labelled as 'critical', for it is determined to redefine that category, to challenge our assumption that we know what 'critical' means. Even the criticism that comes from the Church, 'however transcendent it may be, is human, all too human; for it is a 'beyond' which still remains in this world' (428).

Barth's first Preface almost invites accusations of Nietzschean arrogance in its suggestion that this work is written before its time; that 'this book must – wait'(3). The fifth Preface reflects upon the ironic success that the book has already met with. He fears that in writing against 'human – too human – vapourings...especially...religious vapourings' he has merely served a peculiar cultural need: 'I had set out to please none but the very few, to swim against the current, to beat upon doors which I thought were firmly bolted. Was I altogether deceived?'(22). Like Nietzsche, his fear is of *being understood*,[34] of being assimilated into the existing categories rather than revealing their inadequacy. In Barth's case this means breaking down existing habits of thought for the sake of a new hearing of the Word. 'We must not shrink from being the Church Militant', this Preface concludes – and there is a Nietzschean element in Barth's militant tendency; almost 'theologising with a hammer'. Balthasar suggests that *Romans* 'is like "dynamite", and comes dangerously close to Nietzsche. The people to whom Paul wrote his letter seem to have been "very free spirits" who, like Nietzsche, are beyond free thinking "liberalism"'. Perhaps still with Nietzsche in mind, Balthasar concludes that in *Romans* 'Barth's Christian radicalism is "*überchristlich*", and thus is unchristian'.[35]

Webb devotes a chapter of his study of Barth's 'rhetorical theology' to the Nietzschean affinity, explaining that Nietzsche's 'is a style that bears an uncanny resemblance to Barth's, qualifying as one of the rhetorical precedents for *Romans*'.[36] The classical trope of hyperbole (extremity, exaggeration, *übertreibung*) is identified as the key stylistic link, and, Webb argues, there is a common rationale to its use; both men see themselves as responding to a situation of crisis. The religious and cultural situation is such that one has to shout – not so as to be heeded by one's contemporaries but so as to speak 'across' them, towards the future. 'Given the metaphor of crisis, Barth has no choice but to write in a style

---

[33] Barth, *Romans*, p.13. (Subsequent references to *Romans* will follow in text).
[34] 'Every deep thinker is more afraid of being understood than of being misunderstood' (Nietzsche, quoted in Lavrin, 1971, p.46).
[35] Balthasar, 1992, p.71.
[36] Webb, S. H., *Re-figuring Theology: the Rhetoric of Karl Barth*, State University of New York Press, 1991, p.92.

many will perceive as being too turbulent, profuse and distorted – in a word, exaggerated'.[37] Although this stylistic, and tropological, affinity is certainly present, it is not a matter of Barth's passive acceptance of Nietzsche's rhetorical method but of his *critical* response to it. And this process of critical response to Nietzsche, I am suggesting, is determinative of Barth's rhetorical theology. Webb quotes the following passage from *The Will to Power* in which Nietzsche warns the rulers of Europe that 'we immoralists' are the strongest power of the day:

> A powerful seduction fights on our behalf, the most powerful perhaps that there has ever been – the seduction of truth – 'Truth'? Who has forced this word on me? But I repudiate it; but I disdain this proud word: no we do not need even this; we shall conquer and come to power even without truth. The spell that fights on our behalf, the eye of Venus that charms and blinds even our opponents, is *the magic of the extreme*, the seduction that everything extreme exercises: we immoralists – we are the most extreme.[38]

What response can there be to a rhetoric of absolute extremity, which identifies truth with its own capacity for excess? It must be a consciously *rhetorical* response, or it abandons the field to Nietzsche's voice and retreats to the discredited strongholds of metaphysics, hiding in the pretence of objectivity, of 'non-rhetorical' discourse. I suggest that theology is uniquely able to respond with a rhetoric which 'contains' Nietzschean extremity in both senses; it possesses it as a resource, and it orders it, submits it to the discipline of its grammar. Of course on one level any critic can accuse Nietzsche of indisciplined ranting, of indulging in 'mere rhetoric'. But all such criticism will have a smack of *ressentiment*, for the neutral academic voice has been rendered suspect, and its sensible complaints can only contribute to Nietzsche's case. The rhetorical highground remains his; the more he is indicted by soberer philosophers, the greater his *poetic* victory.

Staten continues his analysis of Nietzsche's discourse 'on and of' power with the observation that 'the power of a discourse is ultimately dependent on an audience; the only power in Nietzsche's writing is whatever power is felt as power by some actual audience at some moment in history'. Unlike physical force, which manifests itself irresistibly, unambiguously:

> Nietzsche, as a writer, no matter how powerful, necessarily depends for his effect on the at least provisional receptiveness of his audience. And since his power or authority depends in large part on the self-assurance of his power communicated in the tone and mode of his utterance, the audience that will not listen not only refuses the utterance itself but also saps its energy at the source, weakens it, not only depriving it of its effect, but altering its constitution, its tone and mode.[39]

The Nietzschean enchantment[40] is broken by refusing to listen to him in the way that he requires, by refusing to take his voice seriously. Yet, as Hamburger

---

[37] Ibid., p.99.

[38] Ibid., p.94.

[39] Staten, 1990, pp.33-34.

[40] W. B. Yeats calls Nietzsche, approvingly, 'the strong enchanter'. Conversely, Nietzsche

perceives, this refusal is hard-won, an accomplishment of readership: 'the "Dionysian Imperialism", the bragging and self-dramatisation,...the self-propelled rhetoric and hyperbole...call for readers truly Nietzschean in their readiness to fight back, to discriminate and deflate; and, more than any other writer of his time, Nietzsche might have served, and can still serve, to create such readers'.[41] The force of his style is thus 'negatively edifying'; reading him can teach one the resilience needed to 'deflate' his pathos, to break the spell. Yet I suggest that in order to be fully free of his spell we require an alternative idiom of extremity, a contrary rhetoric of power. Barth, in *Romans* and beyond, may be seen as providing this and as offering a reading of Nietzsche which renders him unimpressive, even ridiculous. Only a stronger rhetoric has the right to call Nietzsche's empty. His power to impress and to compel is only neutralised, or exorcised, by an alternative rhetoric of authority. And the Christian idiom of rhetorical authority is sufficiently different: authority is located outside of the individual author, in a tradition and community of discourse. Also, of course, it has in Christ a *supra-rhetorical* basis.

Despite the debt to Nietzsche's authorship, then, Barth presents us with a rhetoric which has a distinctly alternative logic. This is most clearly evident from the nature of the genre within which he works in *Romans*: he is writing a commentary on an existing text. Barth's discourse is ordered, structured, constrained – not only by the text itself but by the history of its exegesis, the weight of which is practically unparalleled. In taking on this formal constraint, his authorship is as unfree (in one sense) as is possible. Nietzsche's authorship, in contrast, eschews dependence upon other texts, even upon the existing typology of authorship; the formal distinction between philosophy and poetry is defied. In *Thus Spake Zarathustra* he even inverts the logic of biblical commentary – he refers to the New Testament in order to demonstrate his freedom from it (which is rather a typical contradiction). Yet the greater 'freedom' of Nietzsche's authorship may conversely be seen as a measure of his isolation. What 'constrains' Barth is his implication in a *community* of authorship; his voice is determined by both the 'mighty voice of Paul' (*Romans*, p.2) and the voices of his previous exegetes. Also and ultimately, of course, by the voice of God, which is expressed in the latter voices but not without remainder. As we saw in Chapter Eight, the 'voice' of Barth's text is made up of a plurality of voices, all of which are secondary to *the* (humanly inexpressible) Voice. Nietzsche's voice, on the other hand, is singular, non-dialectical; it claims rigid identity with the process of redemptive utterance. Furthermore, Barth is bound not only by the community of textual tradition but by the concrete community of the church, just as the form of the original epistle is determined by its recipients. What is the community of readership that Nietzsche posits? An 'élite' of disaffected intellectuals nurtured on Romanticism. His rhetorical context is more historically limited, more *dated*.

---

calls Christianity an enchantment to be broken, the Circe of thinkers, eg. *EH* 'Why I am a Fatality', 7, p.139.
[41] Hamburger, Michael: 'A Craving for Hell; on Nietzsche and Nietzscheans', *Encounter* 1962, p.44.

Barth is able to lay claim to a voice of authority without sharing Nietzsche's hubristic excess. He is rooted in a tradition in which prophetic imitation is not merely a mark of Romantic egotism. He is primarily a hearer, a receiver; his word, his text, precedes him.

Heroic Obedience

Barth celebrates the 'unfreedom' of the commentary form. It is used as a parable of the 'unfreedom' of obedient faith. His theology makes a virtue of such constraint. The true interpreter 'dares to accept the condition of utter loyalty' to his author (18). This is a very Barthian pathos, consistent throughout his theology – of *daring* to obey: he elsewhere calls Christian love 'a venture of *submission*'.[42] The quasi-military discipline of exegetical obedience is also that of faith itself; and throughout his theology such submission is presented as heroic, even *übermenschliche*.

The Nietzschean pathos of heroic daring is thus applied to the very un-Nietzschean ideal of submission. This inversion repeatedly informs Barth's rhetoric. Barth is *defiantly obedient*, he defies the equation of obedience with weakness and unfreedom, he is unrepentantly penitent. In its awareness that it flouts the first rule of modern humanism, Christian obedience entails its own sort of defiance. When, in *Romans*, we hear that 'Christianity displays a certain inclination to side with those who are immature, sullen and depressed, with those who "come off badly" and are, in consequence, ready for revolution'(463), we are meant to acknowledge that Nietzsche's 'authority' is being blankly defied. The appeal of the Nietzschean ideal is acknowledged and refused – and, most interestingly, *appropriated*. I am suggesting that Barth shows a consistently 'post-Nietzschean' sense of faith as the 'scandal' of affirming what seems to be weakness, of advocating faith *even after* its identification with *ressentiment*: this significantly affects the rhetoric of Christian proclamation, and thus the 'sensibility' of faith itself. In *The Church Dogmatics* Barth still has Nietzsche in mind as he articulates the nature of Christian vocation; we are called to be 'sheep among wolves... This is not a very heroic or comforting aspect of Christian existence. There is nothing here for Nietzsche.'[43]

In Chapter Eight we have seen Barth depict Pauline faith as heroic strength only to deny that any human pathos corresponds to the agency of God. The pathos of Romantic individualism, then, is both accentuated and inverted. *Here* is the truly rare nobility, the true daring – where all individual qualities are negated and forgotten in obedience to the new Subject. Barth insists that faith is acknowledgement of the agency of God; it is where he alone is great, 'and not man, not even Christian man... . The dignity of solitude comes to [the individual] only if and in so far as he sacrifices his isolation, the tragically guilty magnitude of his standing on his own feet, his "I am that I am"'.[44] This implicit criticism of

---

[42] Barth, *Ethics*, p.457. In Christian life, he later says, one is 'free for the venture of relying both in life and death on God' (*CD* 4.3 pt2, p.554).

[43] Barth, *CD* 4.3 pt.2, p.630.

[44] Barth, *The Resurrection of the Dead*, trans. from *Die Auferstehung der Toten* (1924) by

Nietzsche also reflects his influence, and that of Romantic individualism generally. The expression of faith has recourse to 'the language of religious romanticism' in its simultaneous construction and demolition of a human ideal. Similarly, *The Göttingen Dogmatics* endows the 'venture' of proclamation with 'heroic' pathos. 'How lonely are those who dare to speak about God, removed from the broad way of the many, or even the quiet paths of the finest and noblest among us'.[45] Such are both indifferent to the pathos of nobility, *and* endowed with a sort of '*uber-Edelkeit*'.

For Barth, theology is constantly on guard against romantic pretension; it entails endless ambiguity and irony towards its own pathos (all *pathos* is ultimately implicated with *eros* and *bios* – 501). It does not take its own rhetoric fully seriously, because it recognises the inadequacy of all human expression, rhetorical as well as conceptual. Barth's ability to be detached from his own rhetorical pathos is an important mode of his celebrated capacity for self-irony.[46] We shall presently suggest that such is lacking in Nietzsche.

Overcoming Man: The New Subject

We have noted Barth's conception of theology as '*über*-discourse', as going beyond 'criticism', or free-thinking radicalism. The Nietzschean *form*, because applied to faith, implies a criticism of Nietzsche's substance: it is this discourse *and not his* that points beyond the *Allzumenschliches*, beyond good and evil, towards the transvaluation of values; this that heralds the twilight of the idols, the revaluation of all values, the true daybreak.

This, and not Nietzsche's, is the true discourse of man's overcoming. 'Man is something that must be overcome'. In these words of Frederick Nietzsche one could gather up the whole truth about our existence which Jesus...'brought to light... The old human must disappear in the face of the divine new.'[47] *The Göttingen Dogmatics* continues this theme: 'man suffers from the fact that he is something that has to be overcome and cannot be overcome':

> [T]he contradiction inherent in the human situation cannot be overcome because it is man's own act. Overcoming it would mean removing the subject that causes it.... . In keeping with this is the truth that in revelation we always have to do with the fact that God becomes the subject. God overcomes the contradiction by himself becoming man and by creating faith and obedience in us by his Spirit (75).

The Nietzschean motif of man's overcoming is appropriated and re-rooted in the theologic of divine subjectivity. And in the process Nietzsche's account of this phenomenon is exposed as vacuous, as yet another all-too-human endeavour. Much of the relevance of Nietzsche to Barth's theology lies in his concern, especially evident in *Zarathustra*, with the new, eschatological subject. Such is the Overman;

H. J. Stenning, Hodder and Stoughton, London, 1933, p.21.

[45] Barth, *GD*, p.49.

[46] See e.g. Frei, H., 'Karl Barth: Theologian', in Frei, 1993, *passim*.

[47] Barth and Thurneysen, *Come Holy Spirit, Sermons*, 'Jesus and Judas', p.125.

he is 'not yet', not to be identified with the higher type of man: though Nietzsche-Zarathustra heralds his advent, the full-scale creation of values is not yet possible. In the light of theological grammar, Nietzsche's eschatological subject is a mere postulsation. 'The word "overman"...names no more than an ill-defined hope that remains in the subjunctive.... But what right does Nietzsche have to posit such an eternal ground?' [48]

The new, redeeming subjectivity that Nietzsche desperately tries to 'conjure up' is, in Christianity, already the case, a reality, a *fait accompli*. It is Christ, who not only will but *has* come. There is a fundamental *difference of direction*; the locus of Nietzschean assurance is radically future, and only future. In Christian eschatology the 'not yet' is substantiated by an 'already', and by reference to the agency of another subject. There is a common image which nicely illustrates this 'difference of direction'. Zarathustra announces his love for 'the great despisers because they are great adorers, and arrows of longing for the other shore'.[49] For Barth the truth is not in our striving forward, 'arrow-like': instead 'the truth has encountered us from beyond a frontier we have never crossed; it is as though we had been transfixed by an arrow launched at us from beyond an impassable river' (*R*, 238). The eschatological gulf can only be overcome from 'the other side' and by means of the agency of another. (Nietzsche often uses another arrow image, to similar effect: 'the struggle against Christianity produced in Europe a magnificent tension of soul...; with such a tensely strained bow one can now aim at the furthest goals'.)[50] For Barth, Nietzsche becomes the latest exponent (and the apotheosis) of the problematic that humanism cannot solve: man must be overcome, yet overcoming the human contradiction 'would mean removing the subject that causes it'.

Barth's theology is significantly determined by this rhetorical surpassing of humanist affirmation. Faith's subject-matter is the achieved certainty of redemption: the Resurrection, a past event, is the seal of God's eschatological Yes. And, as we have previously discussed, this *tone of voice* of superior assurance, of confidence, of *über*-affirmation, is at the heart of Barth's theology.

The Christian account of man's overcoming exposes Nietzschean teleology as one-dimensional. In the Christian account, future hope is also past accomplishment; and, because of divine agency, man's overcoming is not down to man (but up to God). In *Romans*, Barth accordingly insists that Nietzsche's pseudo-eschatology is merely human, is 'on this side': 'Is there born of woman any Super-man who is not with Christ under the law as long as he liveth?'(238). Barth ironically consigns Nietzsche to the dustbin of *religious* history. For if religion is subject to the crisis of divine judgement, so is anti-religion; there is no intrinsic advantage in either by which one may evade the divine critique:

> [A]ll the protestations against religion from Nietzsche down to the most degraded and loud-voiced anticlericals, the whole anti-theological romanticism of aestheticism, socialism and the Youth Movement...are incompetent to provide

---

[48] Harries, K., 'The Philosopher at Sea', quoted in Magnus, 1994, p.181.
[49] 'Zarathustra's Prologue', 4, p.9.
[50] *BGE*, Preface, p.3.

security.... . So long as [they] fail to draw attention to that which lies beyond them,
and so long as they attempt their own justification, either as faith, hope, and charity,
or as the enthusiastic and dionysiac gestures of the Anti-Christ, they are assuredly
mere illusion (136).

The 'enthusiastic and dionysiac gestures of the Anti-Christ' suggests a rather
tedious adolescent performance. Barth's rhetoric divests the Promethean of its
romantic pathos: because God is our creator, who 'holds us over the abyss of
nothing', there is 'no occasion to oppose him as Prometheus opposed Zeus'.[51] Such
is neither rare nor dangerous but merely ordinary: it is *obedience* which is unusual,
daring, exciting. (There is a similar rhetorical strategy in G. K. Chesterton: 'people
have fallen into a foolish habit of speaking of orthodoxy as something heavy,
humdrum and safe.   There never was anything so perilous or so exciting as
orthodoxy... .'[52] Similarly, 'the land of anarchy' is devoid of adventures, 'But a
man can expect any number of adventures if he goes travelling in the land of
authority...[and the] forest of doctrine and design'.[53] This relates to a theme in
Barth: the Christian will be 'like a child in a forest, or on Christmas eve;...life in
the world...will be an adventure'.[54]

There is a comic element to the Promethean mistake; there is cause to deride
it as well as to condemn it. Barth's essay-length foot-note on Nietzsche in *C.D.* 3.2
has an element of mockery, as well as of stern rebuke, as if to a wayward child.
(The atheist, he says elsewhere, is like 'a naughty child that screams and scolds its
mother – but the mother is still there'.)[55] Christianity is unimpressed by
Nietzsche's ideal, it tells him that he too is confronted by the Gospel. 'Dionysius-
Zarathustra, it says, is not a God but a man, and therefore under the cross of the
Crucified and one of His host'.[56] The pathos of isolation (which Barth here sees as
the Nietzschean motif) is disturbed and shattered, and – again – *rendered futile* by
the existence of the Gospel: 'The fellow-man has returned whom Zarathustra had
escaped or to whom he merely wanted to be a hammer, and he has returned in a
form which makes...all hammering futile'.[57] In this last image of futile
hammering, the Nietzschean hero begins to seem like a child playing with a plastic
hammer. And an unhappy child: Nietzsche's isolation from his fellow man is
fruitless and sad.

Nietzsche is, for Barth, exceptionally representative of the dominant
tradition of modern secular thought: he alone gives full voice to its hidden logic.
The Gospel must be reasserted 'in self-evident antithesis not only to him, but to the
whole tradition on behalf of which he made this final hopeless sally'.[58] His lonely
madness is the natural expression of all opposition to Christianity since the

---

[51] Barth, *Ethics*, p.118.
[52] Chesterton, G. K., *Orthodoxy*, Doubleday, New York, 1959, p.101.
[53] Ibid., p.157.
[54] Barth, *CD* 3.3, p.242.
[55] Barth, *Prayer and Preaching*, p.30.
[56] Barth, *CD* 3.2, p.241.
[57] Ibid.
[58] Barth, *CD* 3.2. p.241.

Renaissance. Barth uses frequent pejorative terms – 'frenzied...outburst', 'angrily uncertain' – which refer to his final madness, and base his entire thought in 'the nervous violence of ill-health'. Yet this is not merely an argument *ad hominem*; in a sense Barth is *pro homini*: Nietzsche is credited with stating his case 'with unequalled logic and perspicacity. And in his refusal to evade its deepest root and supreme consequence, in his enthusiastic acceptance of them, he resolutely and passionately and necessarily rejected, not a caricature of the Christian conception of humanity, but in the form of a caricature the conception itself.'[59] There is real admiration for this 'integrity', this daring to go all the way. Though it is excessive, frenzied, 'over the top' ('Goethe was on the same path as Nietzsche, an exponent of the same "I am", but he knew when to stop'), this neurotic excess is also unprecedented fidelity to the logic of humanism; 'he trod the way of humanity without the fellow-man to the bitter end'. Barth unmasks Nietzschean pathos (diagnosing it in genealogical fashion) as the latent madness of modern humanism.

Nietzsche emerges as one who takes both his rhetoric and himself too seriously. He is incapable of self-irony, and thus of self-criticism: 'Nietzsche, despite what is constantly said about him, is in some very deep sense incapable of irony'.[60] In his discourse there is no distance between the author and his subject matter, all is on the same level. In Christianity true seriousness is (on one level) removed from the realm of our doing and saying – our redemption is not at stake, not in question, not reliant upon our speech or action: 'Only this one thing is really serious, that Jesus is the Victor'.[61] In relation to the Word, Christian discourse can only be relatively serious. This makes it more capable of self-irony, lightness, playfulness, gaiety. By contrast, Nietzschean gaiety is false and laboured; it is forced gaiety. We *have to* laugh because truth demands it, man's auto-redemption depends on it; it is jollity at gun-point. In Christianity laughter is a symptom of man's *release* from the problem of redemption, a sign of our achieved freedom, not a necessary attitude for its achievement.

In conclusion we return to our primary point. Nietzsche fails, or refuses, to understand the prophetic logic of Christian rhetoric (and thus of Christian faith). The rhetoric of obedience, of submission to God, does not have the servile character of ordinary worldly obedience. Instead it *participates* in the divine authority it both acknowledges and represents. Central to Barth's conception of faith is its prophetic representation of divine majesty. It plays a constructive and creative part in the event of the Word. Even in its abasement before God it participates in the authority it acknowledges; for that authority is realised in its performance. This logic is essentially Christological: the obedience of the Son co-exists with his exaltation. God hides and reveals his glory in the form of weakness – more precisely in the form of the weakness of prophetic rhetoric.

This very anti-Nietzschean dynamic can be further demonstrated with reference to the section on divine providence in *CD* 3.3. Christian obedience is the 'antithesis of sentiment and resentment'; it is participation in the eschatological

---

[59] Ibid., p.231.
[60] Staten, 1990, p.45.
[61] Barth, *Dogmatics in Outline*, p.123.

subject. Barth depicts this in a rhetoric of extreme submission that would make Nietzsche flinch: 'The Holy Spirit rules the Christian in a conflict in which the Christian's own spirit is beaten' (255). Yet the sustained militaristic rhetoric might also provoke Nietzsche's admiration – perhaps there *is* something here for Nietzsche. The Christian is initiated into the creative will of God; in prayer he 'acquires a share in the universal lordship of God' (284). 'Within the creaturely movement of faith, obedience and prayer there moves the finger and hand and sceptre of the God who rules the world'. I suggest that in passages such as these Barth still has the Nietzschean critique in mind: he refutes it through a rhetoric of participation in the creative authority of God; the performance of such a rhetoric disables Nietzsche's charges of resentment and weakness. At times Nietzsche seems to acknowledge that Christian rhetoric is a manifestation of strength rather than weakness; he can't help admiring Pascal. As if in response, Barth makes explicit the element of creative strength within the Christian rhetoric of obeisance.

Nietzsche and Rhetorical Violence

Nietzsche's defenders remain troubled by his violence. Despite the 'embarrassing militarised language', says Solomon, it should not be assumed that Nietzsche advocates mere barbarism. Indeed, 'The warrior imagery may be misleading... . [O]ut of the hundred plus names that appear in *Beyond Good and Evil*, for example, a full ninety percent are writers and artists, not führers and Homeric heroes'.[62] Is he only an advocate of rhetorical rather than actual violence, then? Danto argues that his violence is a means to being remembered. 'If one's writings are...meant to hurt, the aphorism is a natural, obvious form to use, for piercing like a dart the defences of reason it lodges inextricably in the mind...'.[63] He cites Nietzsche's boast: 'Unconcerned, mocking, violent – thus does wisdom want us: She is a woman, and always loves only a warrior'.[64] The logic of this textual violence, and its relationship to actual violence, demands reflection.

   Nietzsche's discourse relies on rhetorical violence because it is (pseudo-) prophetic; it represents an absent authority. Yet this absent authority is his ideal of natural human strength. Natural strength resembles God even in its present weakness; it has an otherworldly and exclusively eschatological character. Unless natural strength is absent, or weak, Nietzsche's discourse becomes redundant. If it was actually strong and presently in power, what need would it have of Nietzsche speaking up for it? Because Nietzsche wants to be a prophet, the power he proclaims has to be presently weak, even though this power is 'natural strength'. He has to invent the unlikeliest of stories: the cause of 'natural strength' relies upon the literary output of a lone scholar. This absurdity is only comprehensible as secularised prophecy.

---

[62] Solomon, 1998, p.6.

[63] Danto, Arthur, 'On *The Genealogy of Morals*', in ibid., p.14. The *Genealogy* is a trap of disguised violence, 'a kind of literary camouflage for the sharpened stakes of aphorism he has concealed for the unwary' (p.18).

[64] Preface to *GM*, quoted in ibid., p.12.

Nietzsche's neo-prophetic rhetoric constitutes a demand that theology offer an account of its own rhetoric. How does it differ from his? We have previously argued that rhetorical violence within the Christian idiom is prevented by its Christological basis from being the ideology of actual violence. We have also seen, through various examples, how Christian discourse acknowledges its own limitation and attempts to signify the Word *through* self-criticism. Nietzsche's discourse, as we have seen, lacks these Christological and dialogical safeguards, and so his rhetoric is implicated in the economy of violent actuality. He cannot be defended against political 'misreadings' of his thought. Instead, fascism is perhaps the most coherent reading of him available.[65] And of course he is not alone in lacking the 'safeguards' of Christian discourse: all secular rhetorics of authority have their logical representative in him.

Nietzsche thus serves as an important warning figure for my theological approach, as well as an inspiration to it. His work and its reception reminds us that the realm of rhetorical violence is not necessarily, not 'naturally' distinct from that of actual violence. Nietzsche reminds Protestant discourse of its proximity to violent normality, and so of its redeeming difference.

---

[65] 'Nazism was heir to a philosophical legacy…, the importance and dimensions of which have, I believe, been underestimated. Hitler might have called Himmler 'our Ignatius Loyola', but this did not mean that he had not also read Nietzsche, after his own fashion…' (Lacoue-Labarthe, 1990, p.102).

Chapter 10

After Barth

'What if by talking about Christianity as a religion these [nineteenth-century] theologians had already ceased to speak of Christianity and hence were unable to communicate the faith authoritatively to those on the outside? What if the only relevant way of speaking of Christianity was from within?'[1]

This final chapter is not a survey of all that has gone on in theology since Barth. Through a reading of a major theological trend, heavily indebted to Barth, it relates my argument to the recent theological climate. As we shall see, Barth's legacy has contributed to a significant shift in theology away from liberal foundationalism; from the attempt to base faith in the discourse of the rational human subject. 'Postliberal' theology, at its height in America in the 1980s, developed Barth's insistence that theology's foundation lies within itself, within its own distinctive linguistic practice. It helped to keep 'liberalism' and 'apologetics' under suspicion, dirty words almost. Yet I suggest that there is a striking omission within this and other related schools of academic theology: the problem of rhetorical authority is evaded. It fails to *perform* this problem, which is the central performance of Protestant discourse. Despite respect for Barth, it has inadequate grasp of 'dialectical theology', which I suggest remains the blueprint for theology's contemporary possibility, for it enables theology to be both critical and affirmative of its own basis. Now as for Barth, the priority is to affirm faith's basis in the divine utterance, and to show how this affirmation contains its own critical resources.

The term 'postliberal' strictly refers to the theological method advocated by George Lindbeck, in that he coined the term (in his influential book of 1985, *The Nature of Doctrine*). Yet because of his reliance upon the work of others – such as the hermeneutical theory of his colleague Hans Frei and the brand of philosophical theology influenced by Wittgenstein – it is possible to refer to a cluster of theological approaches under this umbrella heading. Placher, for example, expresses his sympathy with 'what Lindbeck had named "postliberal theology"', and then applies the term to the work of Frei, Hauerwas and others.[2]

Postliberal theology can be characterised in terms of its affinity with, and its difference from, liberal theology. Like liberal theology, it borrows from such disciplines as philosophy, language theory, sociology, and literary criticism in order to talk about Christian faith. And also like liberal theology it is wary of

---

[1] Barth, 'Evangelical Theology in the Nineteenth Century', in Barth, *The Humanity of God*, p.30-31.
[2] Placher, W. C., *Unapologetic Theology: a Christian Voice in a Pluralistic Conversation*, The John Knox Press, Louisville, Kentucky, 1989, p.2.

deviating from academic rhetorical propriety. Unlike liberal theology, however, it is wary of the apologetic impulse. It accepts Barth's protest that theological liberalism (or 'modernism', or 'revisionism') reduces Christianity to liberal-humanist platitudes. This entails philosophical nonfoundationalism, which 'announces that no final justification or explanation is available for certainties to be established'.[3] It may even go by the name of 'nonfoundational theology'.[4] In explicit contrast to the tenor of modern theology, it often defines the theological task as 'self-description': it may also be called 'descriptive theology'. It thus celebrates the unfounded particularity of the Christian 'idiom', or 'narrative', 'mythos', 'grammar', or even 'language-game' – I suggest that all these terms are indicative of its rather awkward attitude to the question of Christianity's *truth-claim*. As one critic comments, such theology fails to 'reconcile its intratextual hermeneutics with its relativist notion of truth'.[5] It respects, though at a sober distance, the temerity of Karl Barth, who is credited with securing theology's autonomy from secular methodology. Yet, except in fleeting bursts, it does not resemble Barth stylistically: it generally conforms to the rhetoric of academic liberalism – which I shall suggest is more problematic than it acknowledges. Though these theologians assume 'the Barthian mantle', observes Wallace, it is questionable 'whether Barth's thought can be harnessed in the service of [their] relativist understanding of theological truth-claims'.[6]

     In relation to the various strands of postliberalism that I address, my argument is essentially the same. Such theology gives insufficient account of why this idiom, the Christian, is inhabited in the first place, spoken from within. In the absence of the apologetic option (of proving the reasonability of Christianity), what is the logic of theological discourse? On what authority, if not universal rationality, does theological discourse speak? (All other disciplines in reality assume some form of universal rationality, however hard it is postmodernly critiqued.) These are basic, almost simplistic questions, yet they abide. I have already sketched out my 'answer' in my reading of Protestant tradition: theology addresses the question of truth through its dialogical performance of a rhetoric of authority. This performance is at odds with academic discourse. (For example, Barth's *Romans* is excessively based in rhetorical performance to count as academic discourse today.) Postliberal and postmodern theology not only shies away from this performance (which is probably inevitable in the academy), it also shies away from reflecting on its foundational role in Protestant tradition. If it wants to retain its academic voice and status, theology should at least reflect on the rhetorical performance it thereby renounces.

---

[3] Ward, G. J., 'Karl Barth's Postmodernism', *Zeitschrift für Dialektische Theologie*, 1998, 14.1, pp.32-51, p.39.
[4] See Thiel, J. E., *Nonfoundationalism*, Fortress Press, Minneapolis, 1994, p.51; and Thiemann, R. F., *Revelation and Theology: the Gospel as Narrated Promise*, University of Notre Dame Press, Indiana, 1985, pp.72-74.
[5] Wallace, M. I., *The Second Naivety: Barth, Riceour and the New Yale Theology*, Mercer, Macon, Georgia, 1990, p.88).
[6] Ibid., p.109.

Theology as Description

In the introduction to *Types of Christian Theology*, Hans Frei asks how we can come to read Scripture as a text as opposed to a historical source. In this context, he suggests, 'the closest discipline to theology is not history at all...[but]...a certain kind of social anthropology that bears some relationship to a kind of literary inquiry also'.[7] For Christianity is not an abstract system but a social reality, a 'really discernible community with varying features...'.[8] Following Ricoeur he advocates a hermeneutic of *restoration* rather than suspicion: 'Rather than *explaining* the culture that one looks at, one tries to *describe* it'.[9] Such a notion is indebted to what anthropologist Clifford Geertz calls 'thick description': in order to be understood, a culture's own (practice-based) 'language' must be learned. 'I'm suggesting very simply that the Church is like that – a culture, not only of course for the observer but also for the agent, the adherent, who would understand it'.[10]

In much recent theology there is a surprising degree of consensus for this self-understanding. For Thiemann, for example, 'Nonfoundational theology is located squarely within the Christian tradition and community and seeks to "re-describe" the internal logic of the Christian faith.'[11] This, and the accompanying metaphor of 'grammar' are the theological projects most consistently proposed after 'foundationalism': the categories of narrative and intratextuality are largely dependent on this sociological model. In such approaches, the old questions as to the truth and reference of religious language are referred to the fact that such language is integral to the life of the confessing community. It just happens that assertions about God and invocations of him are practical, sociological facts. This hermeneutic is also indebted to Wittgenstein, who is often invoked by postliberals, though perhaps rather selectively. (A case can be made from his fragmented religious reflections that Wittgenstein was attracted to Christianity's basis in a rhetoric of authority; thus his opposition to rational apologetics and preference for 'Hebraic style').[12] Thiemann cites his maxim 'Don't ask for the meaning; look for the use',[13] and Frei in the above passage notes Geertz's debt to 'what Wittgenstein called a language game'. Elsewhere he observes: 'Clifford Geertz calls culture an "acted document", and the term applies also to religion'.[14]

Paul L. Holmer's book *The Grammar of Faith* (1978) was influential in bringing the category 'grammar' to the attention of theology. He complains of the 'immense conceptual confusion' arising from theology's attempt to explain itself in

---

[7] Frei, H., *Types of Christian Theology*, ed. by George Hunsinger and William C. Placher, Yale University Press, Mass., 1992, pp.11-12.

[8] Ibid., p.12.

[9] Ibid., pp.12-13.

[10] Ibid., p.13.

[11] Thiemann, 1985, p.75.

[12] See Rhees, R., *Reflections of Wittgenstein*, Blackwell, Oxford, 1981, pp.116-17, p.123, p.175).

[13] Thiemann, 1985, p.56.

[14] Frei, "'The Literal Reading' of Biblical Narrative in Christian Tradition: Does it Stretch or Will it Break?', in McConnell ed., 1986, p.71.

the terms of secular thought, and he turns to 'grammar' as a means to clarity. Thus '[t]here is merit to the notion projected by Ludwig Wittgenstein that theology is the grammar of faith'.[15]

> The point is that the language of faith is not an artificial and contrived tongue. People speak in this way and in conjunction with Apostles, saints, and the proposers of law and gospel. *Faith, hope, grace,* and other words become internal to one's life and its vicissitudes. Fairly soon, that language of faith is extended to all of one's planning, judging, wishing, and even the remembrance of things past.[16]

Because religious language is integral to an actual form of life, theoretical inquiry as to its validity is misplaced. Bultmann's charge that the mythological language of the New Testament is obsolete overlooks the fact that meaning relates to linguistic use. As long as primary Christian speech exists, religious language and concepts are – by virtue of being used and founded in communal 'life-forms' – *already* meaningful. Theology should be the 'maintenance' of their primary use; the grammar of this *living* language. As Hauerwas says, Holmer's point is that 'we must be de-schooled from the presumption, fostered by much of modern theology, that there is something wrong with first-order religious speech'.[17]

Yet it soon emerges that, for Holmer, theology also has a *rhetorical* task: to convey the *glamour* of this 'grammar'. The theology of which he speaks 'is infinitely more glorious...than the term grammar might suggest'.[18] It is not finally concerned with rules about the arrangement of words and the structure of sentences but with 'the whole of human life itself'. There is thus 'nothing small or piddling about it at all. On the contrary, it is histrionic and magnificently dramatic...';[19] 'Instead of assuming that there are thoughts...for which the Biblical text is but an approximate and local expression...let us really give honour to the text once more!'[20] Underlying this grammatical approach, then, is a large and poetic claim for the rhetorical grandeur and for the *authority* of this idiom. ('Drama' is often used almost as a code for 'rhetorical authority'.) 'What could be more exciting and more stimulating? It is as if there has been an invasion by the Almighty and a whole new quality of life can now ensue... . There is high drama here. Theology has a right to create fervor, to elicit a hymnody, to cause rejoicing'.[21]

Familiarity with the Christian idiom confers a new rhetorical ability, Holmer explains – this is what faith *is*: 'People become Christian by obeying the first-person language of the Bible and making themselves at home in it'.[22] This internalisation of biblical rhetoric is of greater account than mere acquaintance

---

[15] Holmer, P. L., *The Grammar of Faith*, Harper and Row, San Francisco, 1978, p.17.
[16] Ibid., p.99.
[17] Hauerwas, S., 'Making sense of Paul Holmer', in *Wilderness Wanderings: Probing Twentieth Century Theology and Philosophy*, Harper Collins, Colorado, 1997, p.145.
[18] Ibid., p.22.
[19] Ibid.
[20] Ibid., p.47.
[21] Ibid., p.35.
[22] Ibid., p.193.

with a particular narrative. Unlike Dostoyevsky's novels for example, the Biblical stories 'are linked up with worship and the quality of one's life':

> The use of the word *God* is thereby being taught to us, and this makes those stories quite different from even the most serious fiction. *God* becomes a concept, not just a name; for he is more like a Mighty Ruler, a King of Kings, Almighty and Everlasting, than he is like King George the Fifth. He is King and kingly, not Zossima or Natasha.
> Theology in this context is being learned. For after a while we know how to use the word God in responsible and patterned ways. A way of speaking is born in us, and with it comes also a way of thinking.[23]

The differentness of 'God' from a fictional character lies in the fact that this (narratively contextualised) 'concept' is idiomatic of *authority*. Also, to know God is inextricable from 'a way of speaking' that we acquire: a way of speaking related to the acknowledgement of divine authority – such could serve as a definition of faith. Grammatical competence, then, is also, indeed especially, a matter of *tone*. We learn to speak of God's redemption with a certain triumphalism (boasting in him). We learn to testify to 'good news'. We learn to speak of ourselves, and of humanity, with humility and realism.

D. Z. Phillips points out 'an oscillation in Holmer's work between theological and philosophical concerns'.[24] He notes 'a tension between conceptual analysis...and the theological desire to guard a gospel; a desire which leads him sometimes to use language which is at home within the Faith as if it were an external experiential confirmation of that Faith'.[25] He concludes that 'it is clear that Holmer is doing far more than informing himself and his audience of theology's proper task. He is also engaged in the task himself'. Phillips warns against persistent confusion: despite his entire thesis, Holmer at times seems to revert to experiential apologetics. Yet if his work is to count as *Christian theology*, the theologian is necessarily involved in something more than grammatical clarification. He performs his acknowledgement of this idiom's authority. By this criterion, Phillips' own work does not qualify as theology in the strict sense. Indeed Phillips admits as much. His work, he says, is 'not that of a Christian philosopher or a Christian scholar. Hopefully it is the work of a philosopher endeavouring to become clear about a cluster of beliefs which have been and are extremely important in the lives of men and women'.[26] Yet theology has only limited cause to be grateful for Phillips' 'justification' of its language. For theology must 'justify' religious language in another sense from the analytic: by its own rhetorical practice.

It emerges from Holmer's book that the attempt to limit theology to 'self-description' and 'grammatical clarification is rather paradoxical. For – according to

---

[23] Ibid., p.201.
[24] Phillips, D. Z., *Faith After Foundationalism*, Routledge, London, 1988, p.239.
[25] Ibid., pp.241-42.
[26] Ibid., p.95.

its own grammar – theology is implicated in the articulation of a universal truth-claim.

Hans Frei: Barthian Modesty

We have already noted Frei's debt to an anthropological model of religion, which informs his notion of theology as description. Yet still more significant is his debt to Barth. His new, corrective approach to the interpretation of Scripture may be seen as an attempt to safeguard Barth's redirection of theology. In an early essay he reflects on Barth's Herculean achievement: 'Barth contravened the whole tendency of modern theology...';[27] he 'turned his back on by far the largest part of the modern theological tradition with its anthropological starting point and logic'.[28] The key to this defiant stand is that he thinks from *within* the Christian idiom, rather than first seeking to establish anthropologically either the possibility or the necessity of what it proclaims.

In another early essay he expresses his underlying conviction 'that the story of modern Christian theology (beginning with the end of the seventeenth century) is increasingly, indeed, almost exclusively that of anthropological and Christological apologetics...'.[29] The focus of such apologetics, he says, has been anthropology: 'Bultmann's famous dictum that all theological assertions are anthropological assertions is a summary of the largest part of the theological household's convictions – Barth aside'.[30] He agrees with Barth that:

> ...it is not the business of Christian theology to argue the *possibility* of Christian truth any more than the instantiation or *actuality* of that truth. The possibility follows logically as well as existentially from its actuality. Hence I should want to draw a sharp distinction between the logical structure as well as the content of Christian belief, which it is the business of theologians to describe and not to explain or argue, and the totally different logic of *how one comes to* believe...on which the theologian has relatively little to say... .[31]

Here, as in the previously cited essay, it emerges that the unapologetic task of description is rooted in a very Barthian assertion of the objective 'actuality' of Christian truth. The same point emerges in another essay on Barth: it is his prophetic boldness, his 'astonishing confidence and ego strength', that secures the possibility of theology as description.[32] I am suggesting that this dynamic be more

---

[27] Frei, H., 'Karl Barth: Theologian' (1968), in Frei, 1993, p.170.

[28] Ibid., p.174.

[29] Frei, 'Remarks in Connection with a Theological Proposal' (1968), ibid., p.27.

[30] Ibid., p.28.

[31] Ibid., p.30. The Preface to his work of the same year, *The Identity of Jesus Christ*, makes the same point: 'The order of belief is logically a totally different matter from that of coming to believe or the apologetic justification of Christianity' (Frei, 1975, p.xii).

[32] Frei, 'Eberhard Busch's Biography of Karl Barth', in Frei, 1992, p.151). Here he also cites the view of Maurice Wiles that Barth 'is best read as a poet among theologians', concluding that in a sense 'he was indeed a poet, setting forth mimetically a world of

openly acknowledged: the rejection of apologetics is a function of a theology of proclamation. Yet Frei does not want such issues to distract from the sober exposition of faith's content, professing disinterest in 'how one comes to believe'. At the end of this essay, though, he briefly considers the problem.

> To the pilgrim – and who isn't? – the possibility of [Christianity's] truth is not often a matter of the evidence for it, but of the surprising scramble in our understanding and life that this story unaccountably produces: Understanding it aesthetically often entails the factual affirmation and existential commitment that it appears to demand as part of its own storied pattern.[33]

He seems to be talking about an impression of authority, mediated aesthetically. But, typically of his rather cautious brand of theology, he does not develop the thought.

Frei's hermeneutical work, beginning with *The Identity of Jesus Christ*, attempts to put his conception of theology as description into practice. He opposes the liberal supposition that the meaning of the Gospel must be interpreted according to extra-scriptural categories. Instead, we should not look beyond the Gospel stories for 'the essence of Chrisitianity': these narratives, told in this way, are what the meaning and truth of the faith consists in. He draws on that school of literary criticism, 'New Criticism', which locates the meaning of a text in its formal structure: as Hunsinger says, he 'breaks with liberalism by a formalist turn'.[34]

The Identity of Jesus Christ is based in the insistence that the question of who Jesus is can only refer to what is narrated in the gospels. This insistence is firmly based in his rejection of apologetics, here characterised as the tendency of theologians to demonstrate 'the credibility or (in our day) the "meaningfulness" of Christianity to their sceptical or confused contemporaries'.[35] This tendency leads to 'distortions of Christ's identity', which is the title of part three of the book. To 'explain' Christ as either a mythological figure or a mere mortal is simply to go against the text. Orthodoxy consists above all in adherence to the literal sense of the biblical narrative (which he is careful to distinguish from its historical truth). Theology must not seek to explain in what sense this story is *true*: its discourse is 'purely formal and descriptive'.[36] Frei's approach may be seen as an 'emergency measure' to counter the dominance of liberal hermeneutics in theology and so to reassert a traditional christological basis for theology. As Ford observes, Frei's emphasis on the unsubstitutable identity of Jesus Christ is 'guarantee of Christian particularism'.[37]

---

discourse' (p.162).

[33] Ibid., p.44.

[34] Hunsinger, George, 'Hans Frei as Theologian: the Quest for Generous Orthodoxy', *Modern Theology* 8 (1992) pp.103-28, p.109.

[35] Frei, 1975, p.xi.

[36] Ibid., p.42.

[37] Ford, D. F., 'Hans Frei and the Future of Theology', *Modern Theology* 8.2 (1992), p.206.

Frei's hermeneutical theory has been called 'modest',[38] and I suggest that his entire approach is excessively modest to stand in the tradition of Barth (who could not boast that modesty was among his virtues).[39] Indeed Frei is himself aware of this: in his Preface to *The Eclipse of Biblical Narrative* he wonders whether Barth would approve of the book: 'In his hands theology becomes an imperious and allegiance-demanding discipline, and he might well have rejected out of hand the external treatment it receives in this essay'.[40] Despite an element of false modesty this seems a genuine admission that Barth has a larger conception of theology than description; that for Barth it must be a discourse invested with the authority of proclamation. As Placher observes of Frei's method, 'truth questions remain after the hermeneutical task is complete'.[41] We shall return to Frei's hermeneutical theory, and its relationship to 'truth questions', in the context of a consideration of Lindbeck's 'proposal'.

George Lindbeck: Intratextuality

Lindbeck acknowledges a considerable debt to Frei. In the Foreword to *The Nature of Doctrine* he singles out the influence and inspiration of his Yale colleague – with good reason, as we shall see.

In *The Nature of Doctrine* Lindbeck sets out his influential proposal for 'theology in a postliberal age' which culminates in the 'intratextual' method. The main body of the book argues for a 'cultural-linguistic' theory of religion, in place of the 'experiential-expressive' theory that dominates modern theology and religious studies. He is thus in the first place promoting a general theory of religion rather than a specific approach to Christian theology: 'although the argument of the book is designed to be doctrinally and religiously neutral, it is prompted by convictions about the kind of theological thinking that is most likely to be helpful to Christians and perhaps others in the present situation'.[42] This equivocal tone surfaces throughout the book, as we shall see.

He identifies three 'familiar theological theories of religion and doctrine'; the cognitivist, which identifies doctrines with truth-claims about objective realities; the 'experiential-expressive', which 'interprets doctrines as noninformative and nondiscursive symbols of inner feelings, attitudes, or existential orientations'; and, most popularly, a combination of the two.[43] He proposes instead a 'regulative' conception of doctrines as 'comunally authoritative

---

[38] Schwartzentruber, P., 'The Modesty of Hermeneutics: the Theological Reserves of Hans Frei', *Modern Theology* 8 (1992), pp.181-95, *passim*.

[39] 'Only those are modest who have reason to be, he would sometimes say with his Basel accent' (Jüngel, 1986, p.17).

[40] Frei, 1974, p.viii.

[41] Placher, 1989, p.46.

[42] Lindbeck, George A., *The Nature of Doctrine: Religion and Theology in a Postliberal Age*, SPCK, London, 1984, p.10.

[43] Ibid., p.16.

rules of discourse, attitude, and action'.[44] This conception belongs to a 'cultural-linguistic' approach to religion, which stresses the way in which 'religions resemble languages together with their correlative forms of life and are thus similar to cultures (insofar as these are understood semiotically as reality and value systems – that is, as idioms for the construction of reality and the living of life)'.[45] In this alternative, 'religions are seen as comprehensive interpretative schemes, usually embodied in myths or narratives and heavily ritualised, which structure human experience and understanding of self and world'. Such a scheme is *religious* 'when it is told with a particular purpose or interest'. A religion is an objective social idiom: '[l]ike a culture or language, it is a communal phenomenon that shapes the subjectivities of individuals rather than being primarily a manifestation of those subjectivities'. Wittgenstein's famous insight that 'there is no such thing as a private language' is enlisted in this subjection of the subjective to the social and linguistic, and his notion of a 'language-game' is applied to a religious tradition. From this it follows (in terms similar to Holmer's) that:

> ...to become religious involves becoming skilled in the language, the symbol system of a given religion. To become a Christian involves learning the story of Israel and of Jesus well enough to interpret and experience oneself and one's world in its terms. A religion is above all an external word, a *verbum externum*, that molds and shapes the self and its world, rather than an expression or thematization of a preexisting self or preexisting experience.[46]

In the case of the major monotheistic religions, such an externality largely takes the form of a story, enshrined in a canonical text; thus does 'intratextuality' become the form of intra-semiotic fidelity.

It hardly needs saying that there are theological problems here, or at least begged questions. So far, as with D. Z. Phillips, we have at best an assurance that religious truth-claims are not the nonsense they appear to logical positivists, that they belong to life-forms which may be *no less valid* than any other. How, then, can Lindbeck extricate his thesis from a relativist dead-end and address the problem of religious truth claims? It would seem that the cultural-linguistic approach can say nothing as to the truth of a religion, for '[o]ne language or culture is not generally thought of as "truer" than another, much less unsurpassable, and yet that is what some religions claim to be'.[47] Yet towards the end of the book Lindbeck claims that his model supplies a fresh perspective on the question of truth, an alternative to the cognitivist and to the experiential-expressivist approaches Truth is primarily a matter of 'categorical adequacy' and of internal coherence.[48]

Although truth-claims must primarily be considered intrasemiotically, Lindbeck does not entirely neglect the awkwardly obvious question: how can we

---

[44] Ibid., p.17.
[45] Ibid., p.18.
[46] Ibid., p.34.
[47] Ibid., p.46.
[48] Ibid., p.48.

judge between semiotic systems? He acknowledges that his position may seem to imply relativism and fideism, but denies this is necessarily so. His position, he explains, does not deny the existence of 'universal norms of reasonableness'; only the possibility that 'these can be formulated in some neutral, framework-independent language'.[49] In order to define such 'norms' he returns to the metaphor of grammar. In language the best grammar is that which allows the most to be said; in a way that is ultimately elusive it underlies the creative power of speech and thought.

> Thus reasonableness in religion and theology, as in other domains, has something of that aesthetic character, that quality of unformalizable sklll, which we usually associate with the artist or the linguistically competent... . In short, intelligibility comes from skill, not theory, and credibility comes from good performance, not adherence to independently formulated criteria.[50]

This appears to be hint that the only viable 'truth-criterion' in theology consists in skilful rhetorical performance. He then suggests that 'the reasonableness of a religion is largely a function of its assimilative powers', of its ability to make sense of life for its adherents, even in the face of cultural change.[51] Like Kuhn's scientific paradigms, religions are tested through history by a sort of rational criterion, which is in a sense '*über*-rational', as it transcends any particular account of reason. This criterion is not ideal: it 'does not enable individuals to decide between major alternatives on the basis of reason alone, but it does provide warrants for taking reasonableness in religion seriously...'.[52] This criterion of assimilative power is theologically problematic in seeming to equate religious truth with success. Also, it is rather brave to develop such an argument in an age when religion (in the West) seems to have *lost* most of its assimilative power, to be unable to cope with new realities. Is not secular liberalism the supreme 'assimilator'? In a sense, surely, it is *nothing but* assimilation.

Lindbeck's final chapter (which is heavily indebted to Frei) is a call for intratextual practice; yet, in keeping with his 'neutrality', for intratextuality as a general practice: each religion should be 'intra' its own respective text. The scriptural (canonical) text is *the* text, the criterion of the community's meaning: 'Intratextual theology redescribes reality within the scriptural framework rather than translating Scripture into extrascriptural categories. It is the text, so to speak, which absorbs the world, rather than the world the text'.[53] As a theologian, Lindbeck calls for Christians to inhabit the world of the Bible. But for 'Lindbeck the neutral', the Bible is not *the* text, but *a* '*the* text'. Because of his neutrality, he cannot perform the intratextuality he himself calls for. He earlier argued that 'one can no more be religious in general than one can speak language in general';[54] yet

---

[49] Ibid., p.130.
[50] Ibid., pp.130-31.
[51] Ibid., p.131.
[52] Ibid.
[53] Ibid., p.118.
[54] Ibid., p.23.

it surely makes no more sense to be intratextual in general. There is a confusion of rhetorical motives here. The wider cultural environment, he says, benefits from religions being true to themselves rather than seeking to adapt: '...the West's continuing imaginative vitality and creativity may well depend on [it]'.[55] But this is a quintessentially liberal concern – 'the future of the arts', and irrelevant to the *theological* case for intratextuality, which could only be made intratextually. His conclusion decrees that 'those of postliberal inclinations...will argue for intratextuality on both religious and nonreligious grounds: the integrity of the faith demands it, and the vitality of Western societies may well depend in the long run on the culture-forming power of the biblical outlook in its intratextual, untranslatable specificity'.[56] The two-prong tactic obscures the fact that the only reason for *being* intratextual is the belief that it is an expression of God's sovereign will. To exalt the (alleged) by-product of cultural fertility is to confuse the issue. The real theological task is to practice intratextuality in such a way that it seems inherently compelling.

In an article of 1986 Lindbeck invokes Barth in his intratextual manifesto, admitting that the piece is 'more about the theological situation in which we find ourselves than it is about Karl Barth'.[57] Barth is heralded as a champion of the integrity and sufficiency of the biblical text; as a proto-intratextualist. Lindbeck notes that as early as 1916 he was exhorting Christians to live in 'the strange new world within the Bible' and opposing the alien frameworks of liberalism. Barth's cause must always be taken up afresh, for the Bible's 'captivity to establishment culture or anti-establishment counter-culture continues',[58] now as in the time of the Reformation. Indeed the situation seems to be worsening: 'This loss of intratextuality is perhaps a more serious part of the global crisis than are the social, economic, and political problems to which we more commonly advert'.[59] As in *The Nature of Doctrine*, general, humanistic grounds for intratextuality accompany the theological case.

At one point in this essay Lindbeck acknowledges that something more is required of theology than mere familiarity with, and close reading of the Bible: 'Close reading of Holy Writ and attentive listening to God's Word are not identical. The hearing...does not happen, so Christians believe, except in the power of the Holy Spirit'. And in order to illustrate this distinction, he offers a comparison:

> Contrast reading a book by an author one supposes dead, and then reading the same book with the knowledge that, whoever the author is, she is the one who observes what one does and will decide one's future. The second reading will be more, not less, rigorous than the first, but in a drastically different way.... One will try to look at oneself and one's world through her eyes so that one can behave appropriately. [60]

---

[55] Ibid., p.127.
[56] Ibid., p.134.
[57] Lindbeck, 'Barth and Textuality', *Theology Today*, vol. 43.3 (1986), p.361.
[58] Ibid., p.365.
[59] Ibid., p.372.
[60] Ibid.

This seems to be a clue as to the role of authority in intratextuality (rather similar to the clue we found in relation to Frei). This (rather terrifying) authoress is in a position of absolute power over us and we read her text accordingly. Intratextual practice surely depends upon the belief that this text has authority over all secular 'texts', or interpretative frameworks. There is a further hint to this effect in his tribute to Barth's achievement 'in almost single-handedly recovering for theology that ancient understanding of the Bible as matrix and norm in which the church can be renewed, and in which Christians can learn to agree to disagree, not in permissive pluralism, but within the singular and authoritative universe of biblical discourse which is the Word of God'.[61] Why is this 'universe' authoritative? We cannot expect a reason why (such would be self-defeating), yet it ought to be more clearly admitted that Lindbeck's intratextuality, like Frei's hermeneutic, can only be based in the assertion of the text's authority. (Sommerville offers a critique of Lindbeck from a similar perspective. His conception of theology 'falls into the category of philosophy; it is only reflection upon religion and is not "religion" itself. All this goes back to the fact that religion engages with power, while philosophy stops at the level of truth claims.... . Religion is a kind of response to a kind of power... . Knowing the idiom does not make a person religious; only responding to a statement or proclamation could do that... . If one's religion doesn't include a sense of urgency and maybe even compulsion, it won't hold our own attention very long, and it won't excite anyone else's curiosity'.)[62]

Narrative and Authority

As is already evident, narrative is one of the dominant categories of nonfoundational theology. For Thiemann it 'provides an organising image for a theology concerned to reassert the primacy of God's identity for the theological task'.[63] Lindbeck's conception of intratextuality demands that every human story is subsumed into the overarching biblical story. And Frei is largely responsible for the trend: as we have seen, he seeks to base theology in the 'literal sense' of scriptural narrative. In this sub-section I suggest that a proper understanding of the role of narrative entails attention to the scandal of authority that *this* narrative entails.

Many exponents of narrative theology cite Auerbach's *Mimesis, or the Representation of Reality in Western Literature*. In his Preface to *The Eclipse of Biblical Narrative*, Frei names Auerbach alongside Barth and Gilbert Ryle as his work's chief influences.[64] Auerbach's insight is that its distinctive narrative form is basic to the Bible's function as religious text. Unlike the narrative world of the *Odyssey*, the biblical story is involving of its audience in an absolute and exclusive way; it demands to be taken as *the* story.

---

[61] Ibid., p.376.
[62] Sommerville, C. J., 'Is Religion a Language Game? A Real World Critique of the Cultural-Linguistic Theory', in *Theology Today* 51.4 (1995), pp.598-99.
[63] Thiemann, 1985, p.84.
[64] Frei, 1974, p.vii.

The Bible's claim to truth is not only far more urgent than Homer's, it is tyrannical – it excludes all other claims. The world of the Scripture stories is not satisfied with claiming to be a historically true reality – it insists that it is the only real world, is destined for autocracy... . The Scripture stories do not, like Homer's, [seek to] please and enchant us – they seek to subject us... . Far from seeking, like Homer, to make us forget our reality for a few hours, [the biblical text] seeks to overcome our reality – we are to fit our own life into its world, feel ourselves to be elements in its structure of universal history.[65]

Frei quotes this passage, and his comments on it clearly influence Lindbeck's notion of intratextuality.[66] Yet throughout postliberal theology there is insufficient reflection on Auerbach's major point: the distinctiveness of the biblical narrative is its claim to authority, a claim that is in one sense violent.

In *Barth and God's Story*, David Ford puts Barth's use of narrative in the context of 'the "scandal" of his theology...for most post-Enlightenment world-views [which consists] in his claim that history is a predicate of revelation and that a subject-centred must give way to a christocentric anthropology'.[67] Ford quotes telling remarks from *The Church Dogmatics* which reveal Barth as a narrative theologian before his time: 'When the Bible speaks of revelation it does so in the form of narrating a story or a series of stories'; 'Dogmatics is therefore much less a system than the narration of an event'.[68] There is ample evidence to this effect in Barth's later work: 'Who and what Jesus Christ is, is something that can only be told, not a system that can be considered and described'; 'The Bible tells the story of God; it narrates His deeds... . The Bible proclaims the significance and the importance of this working and acting, this story of God, and in this way it proves God's existence, describes His being and His nature... . And so the Bible is not a philosophical book but a history book, the book of God's mighty acts, in which God becomes knowable by us'.[69]

With reference to his presentation of certain doctrines, Ford shows how 'Barth insists on taking the story as his criterion of reality, whatever common sense might object'.[70] And in his conclusion he returns to this crucial point: the overwhelmingly biblical basis of Barth's theology entails a 'scandal of particularity'; 'His chief way of expressing this is through the dominance of one story over all others, with the guarantee of the story being the presence of Christ'.[71] What emerges from this as basic to Barth's method is not narrative *per se* but the boldness with which Barth privileges *this* story. The theological re-telling of the story must convey, not least stylistically, the scandal of its claim to authority. To tell this story requires a distinctive manner of speech, based in a pneumatological

---

[65] Auerbach, 1968, p.14-15.

[66] Frei, 1974, p.3.

[67] Ford, D., *Barth and God's Story: Biblical Narrative and the Theological Method of Karl Barth in The Church Dogmatics*, Verlag Peter Lang, Frankfurt, 1985, p.13.

[68] Ibid., p.24 (from *CD* 1.1, p.362 and p.321).

[69] Barth, *CD* 2.2, p.188; *Dogmatics in Outline*, p.38.

[70] Ibid., p.40.

[71] Ibid., p.182.

account of proclamation. Ford concludes that Barth's is the supreme attempt to 'present the God of the storytellers'.[72] Yet storytelling *per se* does not settle the question of Barth's theological style. For Barth, theology is *a certain presentation* of God's story, whose style must correspond to the authority of its content. The 'truth' of this story, and its authority over all other stories, is dependent upon the voice which proclaims it to be so. Biblical narrative is an empty category without the Word-inspired voice, or rhetorical style, which re-tells it as authoritative, as a story uniquely charged with truth.

The postliberal emphasis upon the Bible, and the essential content of Christianity, as *narrative* requires supplementation. Theology's concern is the Bible (and the wider textual tradition) not as narrative but as *the narrative contextualisation of the Word* – of a rhetoric of authority which theology itself participates in. The pre-eminent status of the Christian text is dependent upon the forms of prophetic, psalmic and apostolic speech which 'perform' the absoluteness of this narrative's claim. Without this emphasis it remains unclear how this story is qualitatively distinct from all others, how it bears an identification with truth. A remark of Wittgenstein expresses this crucial combination of narrative and imperative: 'Christianity offers us a historical narrative and says: now believe! But not, believe this narrative with the belief appropriate to a historical narrative, rather, believe, through thick and thin...'.[73] Faith is hardly a conventional response to a narrative. The postliberals, however, evade the awkward fact of the authoritative context of this 'narrative': 'One reason for the popularity of the concept of narrative is that it brackets the question of truth: accurate historical reports and the purest fictions are both narratives. Attention to narrative...offers theologians a chance to duck awkward questions about the *truth* of the stories'.[74]

Frei and Lindbeck, and others, agree that theology should describe how the Christian 'text' is supreme for faith, insisting that we cannot for a moment stand outside of this idiom in order to justify it. While accepting that it cannot be extratextually justified, I am suggesting that it is nevertheless possible to reflect on the nature of the intratextual commitment, and that such reflection may illuminate the Christian conception of truth, the logic of faith. I have suggested that the descriptive theological practices of both Frei and Lindbeck are founded in the (Barthian) presupposition of the *authority* of this idiom. As Thiel says, their theories 'are but nuanced depictions of the priority, and hence authority, of the Christian message of graceful salvation for the practice of theological reasoning'.[75]

I suggest, then, that postliberal theology fails, albeit consciously, to reflect on its own presupposition. A consequence of this omission is that the categories of narrative and intratextuality fail to acknowledge the sheer scandal of the *a priori* commitment to the authority of this 'text'. It belongs to the logic of Reformation faith that we submit to the authority of this idiom *in spite of* our rational

---

[72] Ibid., p.136 (quoted from Wicker, 1975, p.4).

[73] Wittgenstein, Ludwig, *Culture and Value*, ed. by G. W. von Wright, trans. by Peter Winch, Chicago, 1980, p.32, quoted in Whittaker, J. H. W., 'Christianity is not a Doctrine', in Bell ed., 1988, p.57.

[74] Green, G., 'Fictional Narrative and Scriptural Truth', in Green ed., 1987, p.80.

[75] Thiel, 1994, pp.77-78.

tendencies. The pathos of this conflict is neglected by recent postliberalism at least as much as it was by liberalism. It may have become an academic maxim that 'there's no such thing as universal rationality', but it may not be entirely in theology's interests to aver. For in the reality of faith, common sense continues to object to the irrationality of the intratextual mode of thought. It is thus misleading to present this commitment as no less reasonable than any other 'construal' of the world.

Furthermore, it belongs to the logic of this idiom that we can never sufficiently inhabit it, make it the criterion of our life and thought. (This point is half acknowledged by Lindbeck. Even for mature Christians, he says, the process of conformity to the 'externum verbum' has just begun: 'They have only begun to confess Jesus as Lord, to speak the Christian language, the language of the coming kingdom'.)[76] For Luther, Kierkegaard and Barth, as we have seen, faith entails the agonistic struggle to assert the Word's supremacy: its authority is known through its dialogic encounter with 'the flesh', and most obviously with reason. To inhabit the Christian idiom, or to absorb the story, is always to struggle to do so; its authority over the believer is not a sociological fact but a matter of constant rhetorical construction. In Barth's words, 'To recognise God once more as God is an ability won only in fierce inner personal struggle'.[77] The postliberal position often seems to give the very un-Barthian impression that faith is a human *possibility*.

John Milbank: 'Out-narrating'/Out-orating

As a coda to 'postliberalism' I want to advert briefly to Milbank's 'postmodern' thesis in *Theology and Social Theory*. What I am chiefly taking from his book (partly against its author's intention) is the insight that the postmodern situation, in which Christianity emerges as one historically contingent *mythos*, is of positive value in revealing the rhetorical nature of Christian truth. I then want to suggest that this postmodern approach shares some of the problems of the postliberals, and that it raises questions about the limits of academic theology.

Milbank is developing a radically nonfoundational theology in relation to social theory. For in contemporary theology, he declares, foundationalism largely abides in this form. His nonfoundationalist project entails, of course, the rejection of theological liberalism. His anti-apologetic credentials are thus displayed from the first, and in no uncertain terms:

> If my Christian perspective is persuasive, then this should be a persuasion intrinsic to the Christian logos itself, not the apologetic mediation of a universal human

---

[76] Lindbeck, 1984, p.60. Cf. Hunsinger: 'The truths of Christian theology shape our experience by contradicting it' (Hunsinger, George, 'A Response to William Werpehowski', *Theology Today* 43 (1986), pp.354-60, p.357).

[77] Barth, 'The Righteousness of God' (1916), in *The Word of God and the Word of Man*, p.24.

reason... . What follows is intended to...restore in postmodern terms, the possibility
of theology as a meta discourse.[78]

Theology is 'a meta discourse', along the lines of social theory: 'if truth is social it
can only be through a claim to offer the ultimate "social science" that theology can
establish itself and give any coherent content to the notion of "God"'.[79] It is
through refusing to submit to the terms of humanist discourse that theology can,
through its defiantly alternative mode of speech, relate 'the word of the creator
God'. As critics have noted, Milbank's opening is significant as rhetorical
performance. Loughlin observes that 'Milbank's story begins with a rousing call to
arms – full of bravado, setting straight off into enemy territory'; and that the book
as a whole tells the heroic story of theology's restoration to supremacy. He
wonders whether this boldness entails the return of 'the tyranny of a master
narrative'.[80]

As a postmodern, Milbank embraces the historicist revolution from which
Christianity emerges as one unfounded and contingent cultural construct among
others. Yet as a theologian with claims to orthodoxy, he strongly contests the
dominant account of 'secular reason' which claims to be a value-free and post-
metaphysical mode of knowledge: instead it is 'a kind of reinvented paganism'.[81] It
is Nietzsche who has spawned this modern heresy; he 'has become the only true
master of suspicion: the thinker of a 'baseless suspicion' which rests, unlike the
sociologies of Marx, Freud and sociology, on no foundationalist presuppositions'.[82]
Such thought, Milbank contends, is implicated in an anti-Christian narrative, in a
nihilist pathos: it is even equated with 'the devil'.[83] The task of its exorcism is
beyond the powers of the rational Enlightenment. To counter the *mythos* founded
on Nietzschean suspicion 'one cannot resuscitate liberal humanism, but one can try
to put forward an alternative *mythos*, equally unfounded, but nonetheless
embodying an 'ontology of peace', which conceives differences as analogically
related, rather than equivocally at variance'.[84] If radical historicism is accepted, all
'post-metaphysical' discourse is rhetorically charged. There is no neutral
deconstruction of human motivation; all such discourse necessarily submits to a
pathos which is finally religious – or pagan. The post-Nietzschean triumph of
historicist relativism, or 'difference', is not value-free. That Nietzsche is its
founder is no accident, from which it may recover. It is founded on an ontology of
violence, on a *belief* in chaotic power as the most fundamental cosmic 'fact'. (As

---

[78] Milbank, John, *Theology and Social Theory: Beyond Secular Reason*, Blackwell, Oxford,
1990, p.1. He says elsewhere that with the ending of modernity, theology 'no longer has to
measure up to accepted secular standards of scientific truth or normative rationality'
(Milbank, 'Postmodern Critical Augustinianism...', in *Modern Theology* 7.3 (1991), p.225.
[79] Ibid., p.6.
[80] Loughlin, G., 'Christianity at the End of the Story or the Return of the Master-Narrative',
Modern Theology 8.4 (1992), pp.365-84, p.367.
[81] Milbank, 1992, p.2.
[82] Ibid., p.278.
[83] Ibid., p.296.
[84] Ibid., p.279.

Kerr observes, his thesis resembles that of Girard in its identification of the secular with violence.)[85]

Milbank's basic question (as it emerges in chapter 11) can be put thus: on what grounds can we counter the nihilist relativism that has replaced metaphysical tradition? He insists that only theology can 'refute' it without retreating to discredited foundations. MacIntyre is charged with making such a retreat – into the ancient notion of social order grounded on virtue.[86] Only Christianity can answer Nietzsche, for its basis is openly rhetorical: 'the Fathers and the scholastics understood the beliefs grounding their ethics as matters of persuasion, or of faith. These positions of faith could not be dialectically inferred or called into question but were, rather, "rhetorically" instilled';[87] 'a theological perspective (whether that of Augustine or Aquinas, or Barth)...speaks in modes beyond the point where dialectics leaves off, namely, in terms of the imaginative explication of texts, practices and beliefs'.[88] MacIntyre still seeks arguments against nihilistic secular reason. 'But my case is that it is only a *mythos*, and therefore cannot be refuted, but only out-narrated, if we can persuade people – for reasons of "literary taste" – that Christianity offers a much better story'.[89]

What is this story? He characterises the Christian *mythos* as that of the 'ontological priority of peace over conflict', which is the dynamic of Augustine's *City of God*, and the opposite of Nietzschean critique. Yet this 'ontology' is distinct from the philosophical variety. It is not a pseudo-scientific claim about 'Being', but a way of expressing the crux of the Christian plot: 'it explicates the beliefs implicit in this narrative... . [T]his principle is firmly anchored in a narrative, a practice, and a dogmatic faith, not in universal reason'.[90] This is repeated towards the close of the book; 'I do not think there is any way of demonstrating this ontological priority of peace... . But it follows as an explication of the doctrine of creation'.[91]

In the beginning of the final chapter he sketches out three 'counter' categories in which 'to think a Christian theology, and at the same time to think theology as a social science': a 'counter-history' of ecclesial origins, a 'counter-ethics' of the different practice entailed, and a 'counter-ontology' which undergirds theology's difference. I suggest that all of these categories may be seen as subject to another: 'counter-rhetoric'. The entire theological undertaking has a different logic from humanist discourse; its criterion of persuasion is wholly other. It is a truth-discourse which defies the presuppositions of humanist argumentation, rejecting a conception of rhetoric that is rooted in the seemingly reasonable. Milbank often emphasises that Christianity sides with a rhetorical as opposed to a dialectical approach; this validates his resistance to apologetics. He explains that

---

[85] See Kerr, Fergus, 'Rescuing Girard's Argument?', *Modern Theology* 8.4 (1992), pp.385-99.
[86] Ibid., pp.327-28.
[87] Ibid., p.328.
[88] Ibid.
[89] Ibid., p.330.
[90] Ibid., p.390.
[91] Ibid., p.432.

Christianity 'from the first took the side of rhetoric against philosophy and contended that the Good and the True are those things of which we "have a persuasion, pistis, or faith"';[92] 'Hence the relationship of God to the world becomes, after Christianity, a rhetorical one, and ceases to be anything to do with "truth", or, in other words with the relation of reality to appearance'.[93] We have seen that secular reason cannot be refuted, only 'out-narrated', and it would seem that this also means 'out-*orated*'.[94]

Milbank's alternative to foundationalism (and nihilism) emerges as a narrative, rhetorical and aesthetic account of faith.[95] The unprovable superiority of the Christian story must be powerfully and persuasively told, or performed. And this performance, Milbank insists, takes the form of the historical community of witness. Siding with Hauerwas' notion of narrative theology, Milbank argues that the metanarrative, which alone has foundational status, embraces the history of the Church – this social event interprets and critiques all else. Here he departs from Frei's and Lindbeck's account of narrative and performance. That of Hauerwas 'is at once simpler, and more drastically profound: for him Bible-Church constitute a single, dynamic "inhabited' narrative"'.[96]

Underlying Milbank's position is a half-concealed theology of proclamation. The introductory section talked of theology's task as articulating again 'the word of the creator God'. Towards the end it is announced that theology's task is 'to tell again the Christian *mythos*, pronounce again the Christian *logos*, and call again for Christian *praxis* in a manner that restores their freshness and originality'.[97] And between, as we have seen, rhetorical performance is repeatedly preferred to abstract notions of 'truth'. But, as we have also seen, the practice of the church, or the 'community' is consistently identified as the locus of the Christian performance of difference. He wants proclamation to be embedded in the witnessing practice of the community. How, though, and in what particular community? 'What Church *is* this?' asks one critic.[98] Can Christianity's truth be read off from the actual difference of some community's identity and practice? The attempt to do so would surely flounder in ethical argument, as Milbank is aware: 'I am not concerned to provide an "ethics"...but rather to describe a supra-ethical religious affirmation which recasts the ethical field in terms of a religious hope'.[99] He almost sounds like a good Barthian here, a theologian of God's transcendent

---

[92] Ibid., p.398.
[93] Ibid., p.430.
[94] Hauerwas supplements the phrase differently: to out-narrate must also mean 'to out-sing the world' (Hauerwas, S., 'Creation, Contingency, and truthful Nonviolence: a Milbankian Reflection', in *Wilderness Wanderings: Probing Twentieth Century Theology and Philosophy*, Harper Collins, Colorado, 1997, p.193).
[95] The aesthetic element is emphasised by Coles: 'Unwilling to appeal to foundations, his strategy is aesthetic' (Coles, R., 'Storied Others and Possibilities of Caritas: Milbank and Neo-Nietzschean Ethics, *Modern Theology* 8.4 (1992), pp.331-51, p.331.
[96] Milbank, 'Critical Study of Hauerwas', *Modern Theology* 4.2 (1988), pp.211-16, p.212.
[97] Milbank, 1992, p.381.
[98] Nichols, 1992, p.329; see also Flanagan, in ibid., p.336.
[99] Milbank, 'Enclaves, or Where is the Church?', *New Blackfriars* 73 (June 1992), p.343.

'Yes'. For surely this 'religious affirmation' is understood as a reflection of the Word (which is not a word he favours). We have already seen how this is true for Augustine, whose 'ontology of peace' should be understood in terms of a theology of the Word.

Though insistent that faith has no foundation but its own rhetorical performance, Milbank is keen to avoid advocating a 'rhetoric of authority' in the narrow sense he associates with Protestant neo-orthodoxy. So he invests heavily in nonverbal communication, in the community's existence *as* communication. He wants this to be understood as the locus of the authoritative rhetorical performance that defies nihilism. But, rather paradoxically, his own rhetorical practice has to work hard to this end. Despite his own logic, he has to construct a post-Nietzschean theological voice: this emerges as a more obvious locus of 'performance' than any communal practice it talks about.

Ironically then, Milbank's position ends up endowing the theological voice with excessive weight – significantly, he subsequently acknowledges this:

> Today, theology is tragically too important. For all the current talk of a theology that would reflect on practice, the truth is that we remain uncertain as to where today to locate true Christian practice... . [Consequently] the theologian feels almost that the entire ecclesial task falls on his own head: in the meagre mode of reflective words he must seek to imagine what a truly practical repetition [of Christian practice] would be like. Or at least he must hope that his merely theoretical continuation of the tradition will open up a space for wider transformation.[100]

As the articulator and expositor of the fragmented witness of the 'community', this sort of theology makes an implicit claim to be the ultimate discourse, the gatherer-together of the performed Word. In a critique of Radical Orthodoxy, the school rooted in Milbank's work, Steven Shakespeare is suspicious of this passage: 'The humble tone masks an unprecedented self-importance. The (radically orthodox) theologian is the true continuation of the Church, and therefore is the true continuation of Christ's incarnation. Surely no liberal theologian could place more weight on their own individual experience and insight!'[101] There is insufficient account of the limitation of this theological voice in relation to the Word. Though he occasionally makes a gesture towards dialectical theology,[102] the principle is not central to an account of theology as 'explication of Christian practice'.[103]

---

[100] Milbank, *The Word Made Strange*, Blackwells, Oxford, 1998, p.1.

[101] Shakespeare, S., 'The New Romantics: A Critique of Radical Orthodoxy', *Theology*, SPCK, May-June 2000, p.173.

[102] The Church, he suggests, has the character of 'an encated, serious fiction... . We can only be *persuaded* that this is indeed the blood of Christ if we are also persuaded by the performance (despite the performance) and persuaded by the preacher (despite the preacher)' (Milbank, 'Enclaves', p.342); 'The community is what God is like, and he is even more like the ideal, the goal of community implicit in its practices. Hence he is also unlike the community...' (Milbank, 'Postmodern Critical Augustinianism', *Modern Theology* 7:3, April 1991, p.228).

[103] Ibid., p.228.

There is a related problem surrounding the question of rhetorical violence. Responding to the book Graham Ward comments: '[t]here is, then, a necessary idealism, a necessary "violence" one might say, as Milbank retells the history of ideas within the Christian superstory'.[104] Though postmodernism is critiqued as essentially violent, there would also seem to be a form of violence in Milbank's conception of persuasion: he 'hopes for the rhetorical victory' of the ontology of peace. Ward wonders how Milbank's 'ontology of peace' squares with both the violence entailed in its promotion and the violence of revelation itself – 'for could not the incarnation, the resurrection, and Christ's miracles be described as violences?'[105] Milbank replies that the Church's task of persuasion does *seem* to require a form of violence: 'Certainly, to be persuaded is to be forced, is to succumb to what is taken to be superior power. This power is "violent" (arbitrary, domineering) unless what is persuasive has the force of "truth" and one is "truly" persuaded'.[106] This of course begs the question: how can we tell mere violent persuasion from truth? His point seems to be that *from a human perspective* Christian rhetoric will always appear to be implicated in the general violence of persuasion, yet *from an eternal perspective* the ontology of peace is not contaminated by this necessity. There seems a contradiction that remains insufficiently tackled in Milbank's work between the peaceful praxis of the community (relating to the 'ontology of peace') and the rhetorical violence in which the discourse of this community must consist.

Ultimately, Milbank shares the same problem as the postliberals. Theology can only make a half-turn away from liberalism or modernism, unless it understands *itself* in terms of performance; dialogical performance of the rhetoric of divine authority. But can academic discourse really accommodate this possibility?

---

[104] Ward, G. J., 'John Milbank's Divina Commedia', *New Blackfriars* 73 (1992), p.312.
[105] Ibid., p.317.
[106] Milbank, 'Enclaves, or Where is the Church?', *New Blackfriars* 73 (June 1992), p.348.

Conclusion

My study has sought to reassess the role of 'authoritative rhetoric' in Protestant tradition. It has argued that the Protestant account of Christianity's truth is rooted in its rhetorical performance of divine authority. Against the assumptions of recent thought, it has sought to affirm this basis, and so to defend this rhetorical idiom from charges of authoritarianism. My defence has taken various forms, used various arguments. In Part One I have proposed that the distinction between rhetorical and actual violence remains a fundamental condition of the possibility of Christian discourse, and so of faith. In Christ, the rejection of violence is also the *defeat* of violence, which Christian witness re-presents. This seeming contradiction is very basic to Christianity. I also introduced, partly in relation to Augustine, the notion of dialogism within the Christian rhetoric of authority, whose full significance is developed in Protestant thought and literature.

In Part Two I have given an (incomplete, of course) account of Protestantism as a rhetorical phenomenon – as it emerges in Luther and is renewed in Kierkegaard and Barth. Each appeals to the Word's authority as the basis of faith. Yet within this proclamatory logic, I have argued, is a critical mechanism which maintains the otherness of the Word. We see this first in Luther's dialogism, his notion (and performance) of the alien Word. I then showed how this dynamic – of dialogical proclamation – is basic to the Protestant poetics of both Herbert and Milton, though in very different ways. I then discussed the impact of the Enlightenment on this rhetorical tradition. In Kierkegaard, it is on the defensive against the dominant discourses of human reason. His resistance to secular thought entails a rediscovery of the dialogical conception of faith.

In Chapter 7, I called a new and surprising witness for the defence of my rhetorical tradition: Romantic thought. Along with its Modernist supplement, it serves as a warning against the secularisation of prophetic speech. In Nietzsche we have perhaps the clearest modern counterpoint to the Christian idiom; his thought serves as a mirror in which it may view its own uniqueness (inverted, perverted). All secular rhetorics of authority (meaning all secular accounts of truth) tend towards self-righteous violence, for they lack awareness of their own limitation. Karl Barth is the modern master-exponent of the dialogic structure of faith; the notion that God's Word resists human appropriation. Using Nietzsche, and others, Barth presses modern 'suspicion' into the service of faith. It is *through* self-criticism that theology undercuts its own human basis and performs the otherness of the Word. My last chapter has discussed the limited nature of Barth's reception, and hinted at a critique of tendencies within contemporary Christian theology.

The problem with theology is that it wants to exist. I mean, to exist as a fully respectable form of academic discourse. This makes it very hard for Protestant theology especially to remain true to its inheritance. For it has its basis in a highly rhetorical form of discourse, an intense verbal performance, a dramatic rather than abstract account of truth. The discourse of faith involves two voices, for it expresses the Word of God's encounter with human resistance. Theology in its purest form is simply a reflective expression of this *agon*. Yet academic theology has effectively severed links with the performative, agonistic discourse of faith, in which the authority of the Word of God is presented by means of this dialogical performance. It chooses to speak as other human sciences do, with a single and secure voice; it locates its difference in its subject-matter alone, not in its form. Is it not enough that we speak about *this* (theology says) – surely it would be going too far to talk about this *and* to do so in a peculiar voice? But what if the subject-matter is falsified by being talked of in a 'normal' voice, what if the subject-matter is inseparable from a peculiar, distinctive way of speaking? Academic Protestant theology should be aware that it is a contradiction in terms, that its performance goes against its basis. For its basis is a *different* performance, a rhetorical performance of authority (by dialogical means), such as cannot be allowed in the academic arena.

The danger in academic theology is that it wants *not* to be a contradiction in terms. It wants to be like the other human sciences (but rather grander because of its subject-matter). This involves redefining its subject-matter so that its own role and status are not jeopardised, but rather enhanced. So Christianity becomes essentially a practice, an embodied narrative, a cultural-linguistic life-form, or a supreme piece of 'theory', and theology becomes its articulate voice, its expositor. The last thing academic theology wants to admit is that Christian faith is essentially a *discourse*, a form of *rhetorical* performance, and that theology in the fullest sense is involved in this, is simply the discourse of faith at its most reflective and intellectually open. For, if this is the case, then *academic* theology is relegated to the sidelines, to the wings. Its own discourse is exposed as limited, secondary: reflection on a form of speech which it is itself incapable of by definition, proclamation and performance being incompatible with the contemporary academy. Academic theology does not want to be sidelined in this way: it wants the limelight, like a literary critic with pretensions to original genius.

Consequently, because it casts doubt on the academic voice, Protestant tradition has become marginal to academic fashion, an irrelevance or embarrassment rather than an inspiration. If we are to take seriously the idea that theology in the highest sense is concerned with communication of the Word of God, then we are very soon aware of the inadequacy of academic discourse. If, on the other hand, we decide that such a theology is logocentric or authoritarian (or whatever), and that theology's true concern is exposition of the community's practice, or outwitting contemporary philosophy, then the academic arena will suit us very well.

Within the academy, Protestant theology cannot perform its own rhetorical particularity, its dialogical drama. But it can reflect on it, and this, I suggest, is the most that academic Protestant theology can do; be the literary criticism of 'confessional', performative theology. If it wants to do more, it must renounce the safety of the polite measured voice of humanist inquiry, and get performing.

Bibliography

Primary Works

Aristotle, *On Rhetoric: a Theory of Civil Discourse*, trans. by George A. Kennedy, Oxford University Press, 1991.

Augustine, *Concerning the City of God against the Pagans*, trans. by H. Bettenson, intro. by J. O'Meara, Penguin, Middlesex, 1984. (*De Civitate Dei*, ed. J. E. C. Welldon, SPCK, London, 1924).
- *Confessions*, trans. by H. Chadwick, Oxford University Press, 1991 (Latin text: ed. James O'Donnell, Clarendon 1992).
- *On Christian Doctrine*, ed. and trans. by R. P. H. Green, Oxford University Press, 1995.

Bakhtin, Mikhail M., *Speech Genres and Other Late* Essays, trans. by V. W. McGee, ed. by C. Emerson and M. Holquist, University of Texas Press, Austin, 1981.
- *The Dialogic Imagination: Four Essays*, ed. by M. Holquist, trans. by C. Emerson and M. Holquist, University of Texas Press, Austin, 1986.
- *Philosophy of the Act*, trans. by V. Liapunov, ed. by M. Holquist, Texas University Press, Austin, 1993.
- *The Bakhtin Reader: Selected Writings of Bakhtin, Medvedev and Voloshinov*, ed. by P. Morris, Edward Arnold, London, 1994.

Barth, Karl, *The Word of God and the Word of Man*, trans. from *Das Wort Gottes und Theologie* (1925) by D. Horton , Hodder and Stoughton, London, 1928.
- *Der Römerbrief*, 2nd edn., 1922, Theologischer Verlag Zurich, Zurich, 1940. ET: *The Epistle to the Romans*, trans. from the 6th edition by E. C. Hoskyns, Oxford University Press, 1933, 1968.
- *The Resurrection of the Dead*, trans. from *Die Auferstehung der Toten* (1924) by H. J. Stenning, Hodder and Stoughton, London, 1933.
- *Credo: a Presentation of the Chief Problems of Dogmatics with Reference to the Apostles' Creed; 16 Lectures Delivered at the University of Utrecht in 1935*, trans. by J. Strathearn McNab, Hodder and Stoughton, London, 1936.
- *The Holy Ghost and the Christian Life*, trans. by R. Birch Hoyle from lectures delivered at Elberfeld on October 9th, 1929, Muller Press, London, 1938.
- *Dogmatics in Outline*, trans. by G. T. Thomson, SCM Press, London, 1949.
- *The Church Dogmatics*, ed. by G. W. Bromiley and T. F. Torrance, T & T Clark, Edinburgh, 1956-1969.
- *From Rousseau to Ritschl, being the translation of Die Protestantische Theologie Im 19. Jahrhundert*, ed. by J. McIntyre and A. McIntyre, trans. by B. Cozens, SCM Press, London, 1959.
- *Theology and Church*, trans. from *Die Theologie und die Kirche* (1928) by Pettibone Smith, SCM, London, 1962.
- *Evangelical Theology: an Introduction*, trans. by G. Foley, Weidenfeld Nicholson, London, 1963.
- *Prayer and Preaching*, trans. by B. E. Hooke, SCM Press, London, 1964.
- 'A Thank you and a Bow: Kierkegaard's Reveille', in *Canadian Journal of Theology*, vol. XI, 1965.

- *The Theology of Schleiermacher: Lectures at Göttingen, Winter Semester of 1923/4*, ed. by D. Ritschl, trans. by G. W. Bromiley, T & T Clark, Edinburgh, 1982.

- *Witness to the Word: a Commentary on John 1*, ed. by Furst, R. T., trans. by G. W. Bromiley, W. B. Eerdmans, Michigan, 1986.

- *Unterricht in der Christlichen Religion, i. Prologomena, 1924*, ed. H. Reiffen, Theologischer Verlag, Zurich, 1985. ET: *The Göttingen Dogmatics: Instruction in the Christian Religion*, vol. 1., ed. by H. Reifen, trans. by G. W. Bromiley, W. B. Eerdmans, Michigan, 1991.

- *The Theology of Calvin*, trans. by G. W. Bromiley, Eerdmans, Michigan, 1995 (Theologischer Verlag Zurich, 1922).

Barth, Karl and Eduard Thurneysen, *Come Holy Spirit: Sermons 1920-1924*, trans. by G. W. Richards, T & T Clark Edinburgh, 1934.

- *God's Search for Man: Sermons*, trans. by George W. Richards, T & T Clark, Edinburgh, 1935.

- *Revolutionary Theology in the Making: Barth/Thurneysen Correspondence, 1914-1925*, trans. by J. D. Smart, Epworth, London, 1964.

Boethius, *The Consolation of Philosophy*, trans. by V. E. Watts, Penguin, London, 1969.

Brunner, Emil, 'The Epistle to the Romans by Karl Barth: an Up-to-date, Unmodern Paraphrase', in Robinson ed., *The Beginnings of Dialectical Theology*, 1968.

Bultmann, Rudolf, 'New Testament and Mythology', *in Kerygma and Myth: a Theological Debate*, vol. 1, ed. by H. W. Bartsch, trans. by R. H. Fuller, SPCK, London, 1953.

-'Karl Barth's *Epistle to the Romans* in its Second Edition', in Robinson ed., *The Beginnings of Dialectical Theology*, 1968.

- 'The Question of 'Dialectic' Theology: a Discussion with Peterson', in Robinson ed., *The Beginnings of Dialectical Theology*, 1968.

Carlyle, Thomas, *On Heroes, Hero-Worship and the Heroic in History*, ed. by C. Niemeyer, University of Nebraska Press, 1966.

Castiglione, Count Baldassare, *The Book of the Courtier*, trans. by Sir Thomas Hoby, ed. by Virginia Cox, Everyman, London, 1994.

Celsus, *On the True Doctrine: a Discourse Against the Christians*, ed., trans. by R. Joseph Hoffmann, Oxford University Press, 1987.

Donne, John, *Complete Poetry and Selected Prose*, ed. J. Hayward, Bloomsbury, London, 1929.

Eliot, T. S., *After Strange Gods; a Primer of Modern Heresy*, Faber, London, 1933.

-*The Use of Poetry and the Use of Criticism; Studies in the Relation of Criticism to Poetry in England*, Faber, London, 1933.

- *Notes Toward the Definition of Culture*, Faber, London, 1948.

- *The Sacred Wood*, Methuen, London, 1950.

Girard, René, *Violence and the Sacred*, trans by P. Gregory, The Johns Hopkins University Press, Baltimore, 1977.

-'To Double Business Bound': Essays on Literature, Mimesis and Anthropology*, Johns Hopkins University Press, Baltimore, 1978.

- *The Scapegoat*, trans. from *Le Bouc Emissaire* by Yvonne Freccero, The Athlone Press, London, 1986.

- *Things Hidden Since the Foundation of the World*, with J. Oughoulian and G. Lefort, trans. from *Des Choses Cachées Depuis la Fondation du Monde* by S. Bann and M. Metteer, The Athlone Press, London, 1987.

- *Job, The Enemy of his People*, trans. by Y. Freccero, The Athlone Press, London, 1987.

Gogarten, Friedrich, 'The Holy Egoism of the Christian: an Answer to Julicher's Essay "A Modern Interpreter of Paul"' (1920), in Robinson ed., 1968.

- 'Between the Times' (1920), ibid.
- 'The Crisis of our Culture', ibid.
- *Christ the Crisis*, trans. from *Jesus Christ Wende der Welte* by R. O. Wilson, SCM Press, London, 1970.

Harnack, Adolf von, 'Fifteen Questions to those who are Contemptuous of the Scientific Theology', in *Die Christliche Welt*, 1923, in Robinson ed., *The Beginnings of Dialectical Theology*, 1968.
- *Liberal Theology at its Height, Selected Writings*, ed. by M. Rumscheidt, Collins, London, 1988.

Hazlitt, W., *Selected Writings*, ed. by R. Blythe, Penguin, Middlesex, 1987.

Hegel, G. W. F., 'The Tubingen Essay', in Hegel, *Three Essays 1793-1795*, ed. and trans. by P. Fuss and J. Dobbins, Notre Dame, Indiana, 1984.

Herbert, George, *The English Poems of George Herbert*, ed. Patrides, C. A. Everyman, London, 1974.
- *The Country Parson, The Temple*, ed. by J. N. Wall Jr., SPCK, London, 1981.

Hobbes, Thomas, *Leviathan*, ed. with an intro. by C. B. Macpherson, Penguin, Middlesex, 1978.

Homer, *The Iliad*, trans. by Robert Fagles, Penguin, Middlesex, 1990.

Jülicher, Adolf, 'A Modern Interpreter of Paul', in Robinson ed., *The Beginnings of Dialectical Theology*, 1968.

Kierkegaard, Søren, *On Authority and Revelation: The Book on Adler, or a Cycle of Ethico-Religious Essays*, trans. by W. Lowrie, Harper & Row, New York, 1955.
- *Edifying Discourses, a Selection*, ed. by Holmer. P. L., trans. by D. F. and L. M. Swenson, Collins, London, 1958.
- *The Point of View for my Work as an Author: a Report to History and Related Writings*, trans. by W. Lowrie, Harper & Row, New York, 1962.
- *The Last Years: Journals 1853-5*, ed. and trans. by R. Gregor Smith, Collins, London, 1965.
- *The Sickness Unto Death*, ed. and trans. by Howard V. Hong and Edna H. Hong, Princeton University Press, 1980.
- *Fear and Trembling* and *Repetition*, ed. and trans. by Howard V. Hong and Edna H. Hong, Princeton University Press, 1983.
- *Philosophical Fragments*, ed. and trans. by Howard V. Hong and Edna H. Hong, Princeton University Press, 1987.
- *Either/Or*, 2 vols, ed. and trans. by Howard V. Hong and Edna H. Hong, Princeton University Press, 1990.
- *For Self-Examination and Judge for Yourself*, ed. and trans. by Howard V. Hong and Edna H. Hong, Princeton University Press, 1990.
- *Concluding Unscientific Postscript to Philosophical Fragments*, ed. and trans. by Howard V. Hong and Edna H. Hong, Princeton University Press, 1992.
- *Kierkegaard: a Selection from his Journals and Papers*, ed. by Hannay, Penguin, London, 1996.

Louth, A. ed., *Early Christian Writings: the Apostolic Fathers*, trans. by M. Staniforth, Penguin, London, 1987.

Luther, Martin, *Commentary on the Epistle to the Galatians*, trans. by Middleton, E., James Clarke, London, 1956.
- *The Bondage of the Will*, trans. by J. I. Packer and O. R. Johnston, James Clarke, London, 1957.
- *Sermons I, Works vol. 51*, ed. and trans. by Doberstein, J. W., Fortress, Philadelphia, 1959.
- *Martin Luther, Selections from his Writings*, Dillenberger ed., Doubleday, New York, 1961.

- *Documents of Modern History*, ed. by Rupp and Benjamin Drewery, Edward Arnold, London, 1970.

- *A Compendium of Luther's Theology*, ed. Kerr, Doubleday, New York, 1978.

- *Table Talk*, trans. by W. Hazlitt, Harper Collins, London, 1995.

Milton, John, *Complete Poetry and Selected Prose*, ed. by E. H. Visiak, Nonesuch Press, London, 1938.

- *Paradise Lost*, ed. by S. Elledge, Norton Critical Edition, New York, 1993.

Montaigne, Michel de, *An Apology for Raymond Sebond*, trans. and ed. by M. A. I. Screech, Penguin, Middlesex, 1987.

Nietzsche, Friedrich, The Complete Works, 18 vols, ed. by O. Levy, trans. by H. Zimmerman, T. N. Foulis, London, 1914.

- *Thus Spake Zarathustra* (1883-5), trans. R. J. Hollingdale, Penguin, 1961.

- 'The Birth of Tragedy' (1872), in *The Birth of Tragedy and the Case of Wagner*, trans. Walter Kaufman, Vintage, New York, 1967.

- *The Antichrist* (1888), in Twilight of the Idols and The Anti-Christ, trans. R. J. Hollingdale, Penguin, Harmondsworth, 1968.

- *The Will to Power*, trans. Walter Kaufman and R. J. Hollingdale, Vintage, New York, 1968.

- *Beyond Good and Evil* (1886), trans R. J. Hollingdale, Penguin, Harmondsworth, 1973.

- *Daybreak* (1881), trans. R. J. Hollingdale, Cambridge University Press, 1982.

- *Ecce Homo* (1888), trans. R. J. Hollingdale, Penguin, Harmondsworth, 1992.

- *On the Genealogy of Morals* (1887), trans. Douglas Smith, Oxford University Press, 1996.

- Twilight of the Idols or How to Philosophize with a Hammer, trans. D. Large, Oxford University Press, 1998.

Noyes, R. ed., *English Romantic Poetry and Prose*, Oxford University Press, 1956.

Pascal, B., *Pensées*, trans. with an introduction by A. J. Krailsheimer, Penguin, Middlesex, 1976.

Plato, *Phaedrus*, trans. by W. Hamilton, Penguin, Middlesex, 1977.

- *Gorgias*, trans. by R. Waterfield, Oxford University Press, 1994.

Pound, Ezra, *Literary Essays of Ezra Pound*, ed. T. S. Eliot, Faber, 1954.

Robinson, J. M. ed., *The Beginnings of Dialectical Theology*, vol. 1, trans. by K. R. Crim and L. de Grazia, John Knox Press, Richmond, Virginia, 1968.

Sidney, Philip, *Selected Prose and Poetry*, ed. R. Kimbrough, Wisconsin Press, 1983.

Stevenson, J. and Frend, W. H. C. ed., *A New Eusebius*, SPCK, London.

Swift, Jonathan, *Gulliver's Travels and Selected Writings in Prose and Verse*, ed. by John Hayward, Random House, 1949.

Tillich, Paul, 'Critical and Positive Paradox: a Discussion with Barth and Gogarten', in Robinson ed., *The Beginnings of Dialectical Theology*, 1968.

Windeatt, B. A. ed., *The Book of Margery Kempe*, Penguin, London, 1985.

Yeats, W. B., *Explorations*, Macmillan, London, 1962.

- *Selected Criticism*, ed. by A. N. Jeffares, Macmillan, London 1964.

- *The Poems, a New Edition*, ed. by R. J. Finneran, Macmillan, London, 1983.

Secondary Material

Alter, R. (1990), The Art of Biblical Poetry, T & T Clark, Edinburgh.

Auerbach, E. (1968), *Mimesis: The Representation of Reality in Western Literature*, Princeton University Press, New Jersey.

Aulen, G. (1931), *Christus Victor*, trans. by A. G. Herbert, SPCK, London.

Austin, J. L. (1975), *How to Do Things with Words*, Oxford University Press.

Balthasar, H. U. (1982), *The Glory of the Lord: a Theological Aesthetics*, 7 vols., ed. by Joseph Fessio and John Riches, trans. by Erasmo Leiva-Merikasis, T & T Clark, Edinburgh.

- (1988), *Theo-Drama: Theological Dramatic Theory*, trans. by G. Harrison, Ignatius, San Francisco.

- (1992), *The Theology of Karl Barth: Exposition and Interpretation*, trans. by E. T. Oakes, Communio Books, San Francisco.

Barrett, L. (1988), 'Theology as Grammar: Regulative Principles or Paradigms and Practices?', *Modern Theology* 4.2 (Special Issue: George Lindbeck's *Nature of Doctrine*), pp.155-72.

Bauckham (1993), *A Commentary on the Book of Revelation*, Cambridge University Press.

Bell, R. H. ed. (1988), *The Grammar of the Heart: New Essays in Moral Philosophy and Theology*, Harper and Row, San Francisco.

Berkouwer, G. C. (1956), *The Triumph of Grace in the Theology of Karl Barth*, trans. by Harry B. Boer, Paternoster Press, London.

Berlin, I. (1993), *The Magus of the North: J. G. Hamann and the Origins of Modern Irrationalism*, Fontana, London.

Biggar, N. (1993), *The Hastening That Waits: Karl Barth's Ethics*, Oxford University Press.

- ed., (1988), *Reckoning with Barth: Essays in Commemoration of the Centenary of Karl Barth's Birth*, Mowbray, Oxford.

Bloom, A. (1987), *The Closing of the American Mind; How Higher Education has Failed Democracy and Impoverished the Souls of Today's Students*, Simon and Schuster, New York, 1987.

Bloom, H. (1987), *Ruin the Sacred Truths; Poetry and Belief from the Bible to the Present*, Harvard, New Jersey.

Bossy, J. (1985), *Christianity in the West 1400-1700*, Oxford University Press.

Boyle, M. O. (1983), *Rhetoric and Reform: Erasmus' Civil Dispute with Luther*, Harvard University Press, Mass.

Brown, A. (1999), *The Life of W. B. Yeats, a Critical Biography*, Blackwell, Oxford.

Brown, P. (1967), *Augustine of Hippo*, Faber, London.

- (1988), *The Body and Society: Men, Women and Sexual Renunciation in Early Christianity*, Faber, London.

Buber, M. (1968), *Biblical Humanism*, ed. Nahum N. Glatzer, Macdonald, London.

Burke, K. (1970), *The Rhetoric of Religion: Studies in Logology*, University of California Press.

Burrell, D. B. (1992), 'An Introduction to *Theology and Social Theory*', *Modern Theology* 8.4 (Milbank special edition), pp. 319-30.

Busch, E. (1970), 'Dialectical Theology: Karl Barth's Reveille', *Canadian Journal of Theology* 16, pp. 165-75.

- (1976), *Karl Barth: his Life from Letters and Autobiographical Texts*, trans. by John Bowden, SCM Press, London.

Capps, D. and Dittes, J. E. ed. (1990), *The Hunger of the Heart: Reflections on the Confessions of Augustine*, Society for the Scientific Study of Religion, Monograph Series no. 8, West Lafayette, Indiana.

Certeau, M. de (1992), *The Mystic Fable*, vol.1, trans. by Michael B. Smith, University of Chicago Press.

Chesterton, G. K. (1959), *Orthodoxy*, Doubleday, New York.

Clark, K. and Holquist, M. (1984), *Mikhail Bakhtin*, Harvard University Press, Mass.

Coles, R. (1992), 'Storied Others and the Possibilities of Caritas: Milbank and neo-Nietzschean Ethics', *Modern Theology* 8.4 (Milbank special edition), pp. 331-45.

Connor, S. (2000), *Dumbstruck; a Cultural History of Ventriloquism*, Oxford University Press.

Corns, T. N. ed. (1993), *The Cambridge Companion to English Poetry, Donne to Marvell*, Cambridge University Press.

Cunningham, D. S. (1990), *Faithful Persuasion: In Aid of a Rhetoric of Christian Theology*, Notre Dame University Press, Indiana.

Danielson, D. ed. (1997), *The Cambridge Companion to Milton*, Cambridge University Press.

Deleuze, G. (1983), *Nietzsche and Philosophy*, trans. by H. Tomlinson, Athlone Press, London.

Dorsch T. S. ed. and trans. (1965), *Classical Literary Criticism*, Penguin, Middlesex.

Douglas, M. (1978), *Purity and Danger, an Analysis of Concepts of Pollution and Taboo*, Routledge and Kegan Paul, London.

Dumouchel, P. ed. (1987), *Violence and Truth: On the Work of René Girard*, Athlone Press, London.

Ellul, J. (1985), *The Humiliation of the Word*, trans. J Main Hanks, Eerdmans, Michigan.

Entzminger, R. L. (1985), *Divine Word: Milton and the Redemption of Language*, Duquesne Univerity Press, Pittsburgh.

Evans, G. R. (1992), *Problems of Authority in the Reformation Debates*, Cambridge University Press.

Evans Pritchard, A. (1976), *Witchcraft, Oracles and Magic Among the Azande*, Clarendon, Oxford.

Fenn, R. (1990), 'Augustine: Death Anxiety and the Power and Limits of Language', in Capps and Dittes eds. (1990), *The Hunger of the Heart: Reflections on the Confessions of Augustine*, Society for the Scientific Study of Religion, Monograph Series no. 8.

Fish, S. E. (1978), *The Living Temple; George Herbert and Catechizing*, University of California Press.
    - (1997), *Surprised by Sin, the Reader in Paradise Lost*, second edition, Macmillan, London.

Ford, D. (1985), *Barth and God's Story: Biblical Narrative and the Theological Method of Karl Barth in* The Church Dogmatics, Verlag Peter Lang, Frankfurt.
    - (1985), 'The Best Apologetics is Good Systematics: a Proposal about the Place of Narrative in Christian Theology', *Anglican Theological Review* 67, pp. 232-54.
    - (1986), Review of Lindbeck, *The Nature of Doctrine*, *Journal of Theological Studies* 37, pp. 227-82.
    - (1992), 'Hans Frei and the Future of Theology', *Modern Theology* 8.2, pp. 203-14.

Forsyth, N. (1987), *The Old Enemy: Satan and the Combat Myth*, Princeton University Press, New Jersey.

Frazer, J. (1996) *The Golden Bough: a Study in Magic and Religion*, Penguin, Middlesex.

Frei, Hans W. (1974), *The Eclipse of Biblical Narrative*, Yale University Press, New Haven.
    - (1975), *The Identity of Jesus Christ: the Hermeneutical Bases of Dogmatic Theology*, Philadelphia University Press.

- (1986), 'The 'Literal Reading' of Biblical Narrative in Christian Tradition: Does it Stretch or will it Break?', in McConnell ed., *The Bible and Narrative Tradition*, Oxford University Press, New York.

- (1992), *Types of Christian Theology*, ed. by G. Hunsinger and W. C. Placher, Yale University Press, Mass.

- (1993), *Theology and Narrative, and Narrative: Selected Essays*, ed. by George Hunsinger and William C. Placher, Oxford University Press.

- (1993), 'Conflicts in Interpretation', in *Theology Today* 49.3, pp. 344-56.

Frye, N. (1990), *Words with Power: being a Second Study of the Bible and Literature*, Harcourt Brace Jovanovich, New York.

Garrett, S. R. (1989), *The Demise of the Devil*, Fortress Press, Mass.

Gorringe, T. (1998), *Against Hegemony: The Theology of Karl Barth in Context*, Cambridge University Press.

Gouwens, D. J. (1996), *Kierkegaard as Religious Thinker*, Cambridge University Press.

Green, G. ed. (1987), *Scriptural Authority and Narrative Interpretation*, Fortress, Philadelphia.

Greenblatt, S. (1980), *Renaissance Self-fashioning: from More to Shakespeare*, University of Chicago Press.

- (1988), *Shakespearean Negotiations: the Circulation of Social Energy in Renaissance England*, Clarendon, Oxford.

Hamilton, D. B. and Strier, R. eds. (1996), *Religion, Literature and Politics in Post-Reformation England, 1540-1688*, Cambridge University Press.

Hannay, A. ed. (1998), *The Cambridge Companion to Kierkegaard*, Cambridge University Press.

- (1991) *Kierkegaard,* Routledge, London.

Hauerwas, S. M., (1997), *Wilderness Wanderings: Probing Twentieth Century Theology and Philosophy*, Harper Collins, Colorado.

Hobson, T. W., (2001), 'Another Dome, Another Scam: Martin Luther and the National Lottery', *Modern Believing*, April 2001.

Holmer, P. L. (1966), 'Theology and Belief', *Theology Today* 22.3, pp. 358-71.

- (1978), *The Grammar of Faith*, Harper and Row, San Francisco.

Holquist, M. (1990), *Dialogism: Bakhtin and his World*, Routledge, London.

Hunsinger, G (1991), *How to Read Karl Barth: the Shape of his Theology*, Oxford University Press.

- ed. (1976), *Karl Barth and Radical Politics*, Westminster Press, Philadelphia.

- (1992), 'Hans Frei as Theologian: the Quest for Generous Orthodoxy', *Modern Theology* 8.2, pp. 103-28.

Jasper, D. ed. (1993), *Postmodernism, Literature and the Future of Theology*, Macmillan, London.

- (1993), *Rhetoric, Power and Community: an Exercise in Reserve*, Macmillan, London.

Jüngel, E. (1989), *Theological Essays*, 2 vols, trans. with an intro. by J. R. Webster, T & T Clark, Edinburgh.

- (1986), *Karl Barth, A Theological Legacy*, trans. by Garrett E. Paul, Westminster Press, Philadelphia.

Kadai, H. O. ed. (1967), *Accents in Luther's Theology: Essays in Commemoration of the 450th Anniversary of the Reformation*, Concordia, St. Louis.

Kennedy, G. A. (1980), *Classical Rhetoric and its Christian and Secular Tradition from Ancient to Modern Times*, University of North Carolina Press, Chapel Hill.

- (1990), '"Truth" and "Rhetoric" in the Pauline Epistles', in Warner ed., 1990.

Kenner, H. (1960), *The Invisible Poet; T. S. Eliot*, Allen, London.

Kermode, F. (1979), *The Genesis of Secrecy: On the Interpretation of Narrative*, Harvard University Press.

Kerr, F. (1992), 'Rescuing Girard's Argument?', *Modern Theology* 8.4, pp. 367-78.

King, J. N. (1982), *English Reformation Literature; the Tudor Origins of the Protestant Tradition*, Princeton University Press.

Knott, J. R. (1980), *The Sword of the Spirit: Puritan Responses to the Bible*, Chicago University Press.

Kolakowski, L. (1978), *Main Currents of Marxism, Its Origins, Growth and Dissolution; 1, The Founders*, trans. by P. S. Falla, Oxford University Press.

Kraus, H. (1986), *Theology of the Psalms*, trans. by Keith Crim, Augsburg Press, Mass.

Lacoue-Labarthe, P. (1993), *The Subject of Philosophy*, ed. by Trezise, trans. by Trezise et al., University of Minnesota Press, Minneapolis.

Lane Fox, R. (1986), *Pagans and Christians*, Viking, London.

Lash, N. (1976), *Voices of Authority*, Sheed and Ward, London.

- (1979), *Theology on Dover Beach*, Darton, Longman and Todd, London.

- (1986), *Theology on the Way to Emmaus*, SCM Press, London.

- (1992), 'Not Exactly Politics or Power?', *Modern Theology* 8.4 (Special Edition on John Milbank's *Theology and Social Theory*), pp. 353-64.

- (1996), *The Beginning and End of 'Religion'*, Cambridge University Press.

LaValley, A. J. (1968), *Carlyle and the Idea of the Modern: Studies in Carlyle's Prophetic Literature and its Relation to Blake, Nietzsche, Marx and Others*, Yale University Press, New Haven.

Lavrin, J. (1971), *Nietzsche: a Biographical Introduction*, Studio Vista, London.

Liftin, D. (1994), *St. Paul's Theology of Proclamation: 1 Corinthians 1-4 and Greco-Roman Rhetoric*, Cambridge University Press.

Leibrecht, W., (1966), *God and Man in the Thought of Hamann*, trans. by J. H. Stam and M. H. Bertram, Fortress, Philadelphia.

Lindbeck, G. A. (1984), *The Nature of Doctrine: Religion and Theology in a Postliberal Age*, SPCK, London.

- (1986), 'Barth and Textuality', in *Theology Today* 43, pp. 361-76.

Lindhart, J. (1986), *Martin Luther: Knowledge and Mediation in the Renaissance*, Edwin Meller, Lewiston.

Loughlin, G. (1992), 'Christianity at the End of the Story or the Return of the Master-Narrative', *Modern Theology* 8.4 (Milbank special edition), pp. 365-84.

Louth, A. ed. (1987) *Early Christian Writings: the Apostolic Fathers*, trans. by M. Staniforth, Penguin, Middlesex.

Magnus, B. and Higgins, K. M. (1996), *The Cambridge Companion to Nietzsche*, Cambridge University Press.

Magnus, S. and M. (1993), *Nietzsche's Case: Philosophy as/and Literature*, Routledge, New York.

Makarushka, I. S. M. (1994), *Religious Language in Emerson and Nietzsche*, Macmillan, Basingstoke.

Mark, J. (1985), 'The Challenge of Nietzsche's Atheism', *Theology* 88, pp. 272-81.

Matheson, P. (1998), *The Rhetoric of the Reformation*, T & T Clark, Edinburgh.

McConnell, F. ed. (1986), *The Bible and Narrative Tradition*, Oxford University Press.

McCormack, B. L. (1995), *Karl Barth's Critically Realistic Dialectical Theology: its Genesis and Development, 1909-1936*, Clarendon Press, Oxford.

McWilliam, J. ed. (1992), *Augustine: From Rhetor to Theologian*, Wilfrid Laurier University Press, Ontario.

Meynell, H.A. ed. (1990), *Grace Politics and Desire: Essays on Augustine*, University of Calgary Press, Canada.

Milbank, J. (1990), *Theology and Social Theory: Beyond Secular Reason*, Blackwell, Oxford.
- (1991), "'Postmodern Critical Augustinianism": A Short Summa in Forty Two Responses to Unasked Questions', *Modern Theology* 7.
- (1992), 'Enclaves, or where is the Church?', *New Blackfriars* 73, pp. 341-50.
- (1992), 'Problematising the Secular: the Post-Postmodern Agenda', in Berry, Wernick ed. 1992.
- (1997), *The Word Made Strange: Theology, Language, Culture*, Blackwell, Oxford.
Monk, R. (1990), *Wittgenstein: the Duty of Genius*, Jonathan Cape, London.
Morson, G. S. (1986), *Bakhtin: Essays and Dialogues on his Work*, University of Chicago Press.
- and Emerson, C. (1990), *Mikhail Bakhtin: the Creation of a Prosaics*, Stanford University Press, California.
Nehamas, A. (1985), *Nietzsche: Life as Literature*, Harvard University Press, Mass.
Nichols, A. (1992), '*Non tali auxilio*: John Milbank's Suasion to Orthodoxy', *New Blackfriars* 73, pp. 203-11.
Niditch, S. (1996), *Oral World and Written Word; Ancient Israelite Literature*, John Knox Press, Kentucky.
Oberman, H. A. (1981), *Masters of the Reformation: the Emergence of a New Intellectual Climate in Europe*, trans. by D. Martin, Cambridge University Press.
- (1982), *Martin Luther: Man Between God and the Devil*, Fontana, London.
- (1994), The Impact of the Reformation, T & T Clark, Edinburgh.
Ong, W. J. (1967), *The Presence of the Word: Some Prolegomena for Cultural and Religious History*, Yale University Press, New Haven.
- (1982), *Orality and Literacy: the Technologizing of the Word*, Methuen, London.
Osborne, S. (1997), *Tertullian, the First Theologian of the West*, Cambridge University Press.
Palmer, R. ed. (1990), *Studies in the Literary Imagination: Bakhtin and the Languages of the Novel*, Georgia State University Press.
Patrides, C. A. (1974), '*A Crown of Praise*: The Poetry of Herbert', *The English Poems of George Herbert*, Everyman, London.
Patterson, D. (1988), *Literature and Spirit: Essays on Bakhtin and his Contemporaries*, University Press of Kentucky, Lexington.
Pattison, G. (1997), *Kierkegaard and the Crisis of Faith: an Introduction to his Thought*, SPCK, London.
- (1988), *The End of Theology – and the Task of Thinking about God*, SCM, London.
Paulin, T. (1996), *Writing to the Moment; Selected Critical Essays 1980-1996*, Faber and Faber, London.
Paxson, J. J. (1994), *The Poetics of Personification*, Cambridge University Press.
Pelikan, J. ed. (1968), *Interpreters of Luther*, Fortress, Philadelphia.
Perelman, C. (1979), *The New Rhetoric and the Humanities: Essays on its Rhetoric*, Reidel, Boston.
Phillips, D. Z. (1988), *Faith after Foundationalism*, Routledge, London.
- (1998), 'Lindbeck's Audience', *Modern Theology* 4.2 (1988) (Special Issue: George Lindbeck's *Nature of Doctrine*), pp. 133-154.
Placher, W. C. (1987), 'Paul Ricoeur and Postliberal Theology: A Conflict of Interpretations?', *Modern Theology* 4.1, pp. 35-52.
- (1989), *Unapologetic Theology: a Christian Voice in a Pluralistic Conversation*, John Knox Press, Louisville, Kentucky.

Poland, L. (1990), 'The Bible and the Rhetorical Sublime', in Martin Warner ed., *The Bible as Rhetoric: Studies in Biblical Persuasion and Credibility*, Routledge, London, 1990.

Polman, A. D. R. (1961), *The Word of God According to Augustine*, W. B. Eerdmans, New York.

Reé, J. and Chamberlain J. eds. (1997), *Kierkegaard: a Critical Reader*, Blackwell, Oxford.

Rhees, R. (1981), *Reflections of Wittgenstein*, Blackwell, Oxford.

Richter, D. H. (1990), 'Dialogism and Poetry', in Palmer ed. (1990), *Studies in the Literary Imagination: Bakhtin and the Languages of the Novel*, Georgia State University Press.

Ricoeur, P. (1986), *The Rule of Metaphor: Multi-disciplinary Studies in the Creation of Meaning in Language*, trans. by R. Czerny, K. McLaughlin and J. Costello, Routledge and Kegan Paul, London.

Robbins, G. (1951), *The T. S. Eliot Myth*, Henry Schuman, New York.

Roberts, R. H. (1991), *A Theology on its Way?: Essays on Karl Barth*, T &T Clark, Edinburgh.

Robinson-Hammerstein, H. ed. (1989), *The Transmission of Ideas in the Lutheran Reformation*, Irish Academic Press, Dublin.

Ross, D. (1995), *Aristotle*, Routledge, London.

Rowse, A. L. (1977), *Milton the Puritan; Portrait of a Mind*, Macmillan, London.

Schwartzentruber, P. (1992), 'The Modesty of Hermeneutics: the Theological Reserves of Hans Frei', *Modern Theology* 8, pp. 181-94.

Scubla, L. (1987), 'The Christianity of René Girard and the Nature of Religion', trans. by R. Anspach, in Dumouchel 1987, pp. 160-78.

Scribner, R. W. (1989), 'Oral Culture and the Transmission of Reformation Ideas', in Robinson Hammerstein ed. (1989), *The Transmission of Ideas in the Lutheran Reformation*, Irish Academic Press, Dublin.

Shakespeare, S. (2000), 'The New Romantics: A Critique of Radical Orthodoxy', *Theology*, SPCK, May-June 2000.

Shuger, D. K. (1988), *Sacred Rhetoric: the Christian Grand Style in the English Renaissance*, Princeton University Press, New Jersey.
    - (1996), 'Subversive Fathers and Suffering Subjects; Shakespeare and Christianity', in Hamilton and Strier ed., Religion, Literature and Politics in Post-Reformation England, 1540-1688, Cambridge University Press.

Solomon, R. C. and Higgins, K. M. ed. (1988), *Reading Nietzsche*, Oxford University Press.

Sparn, (1989), 'Preaching and the Course of the Reformation', in Robinson-Hammerstein, H. ed. (1989), *The Transmission of Ideas in the Lutheran Reformation*, Irish Academic Press, Dublin.

Spence, S. (1988), *Rhetorics of Reason and Desire*, Cornell University Press, New York.

Staten, H. (1990), *Nietzsche's Voice*, Cornell University Press, New York.

Steiner, G. (1992), *Heidegger*, Fontana, London.

Stock, N. (1985), *The Life of Ezra Pound*, Penguin, Middlesex.

Taylor, C. (1979), *Hegel and Modern Society*, Cambridge University Press.

Thiel, J. E. (1994), *Nonfoundationalism*, Fortress Press, Minneapolis.

Thiemann, R. F. (1985), *Revelation and Theology: the Gospel as Narrated Promise*, University of Notre Dame Press, Indiana.
    - 'Response to George Lindbeck', *Theology Today* (1986-87), pp. 377-82.

Updike, J. (1976), *A Month of Sundays*, Penguin, Middlesex.
    - (1986), *Roger's Version*, Penguin, Middlesex.

Wallace, M. I. (1990), *The Second Naivety: Barth, Riceour and the New Yale Theology*, Mercer, Macon, GA.

Ward, G. J. (1992), 'John Milbank's Divina Commedia', *New Blackfriars* 73, pp. 309-18.

- (1995), *Derrida and the Language of Theology*, Cambridge University Press.
- (1998) 'Karl Barth's Postmodernism', *Zeitschrift für Dialektische Theologie* 14.1, pp. 32-51.
Warner, M. ed. (1990), *The Bible as Rhetoric: Studies in Biblical Persuasion and Credibility*, Routledge, London.
Waswo, R. (1987), *Language and Meaning in the Renaissance*, Princeton University Press, New Jersey.
Watson, J. R. ed. (1983), *An Infinite Complexity; Essays on Romanticism*, Edinburgh University Press.
Webb, S. H. (1991), *Re-figuring Theology: the Rhetoric of Karl Barth*, State University of New York Press.
Westra, H. J. (1990), 'Augustine and Poetic Exegesis', in Meynell ed. (1990), *Grace Politics and Desire: Essays on Augustine*, University of Calgary Press.
Wilding, M. (1993), 'John Milton: the early works', in *The Cambridge Companion to English Poetry, Donne to Marvell*, ed. by T. N. Corns, Cambridge 1993.
Wilken, R. L. ed. (1984), *The Christians as the Romans Saw Them*, Yale University Press.
Williams, R. (1984), '"Religious Realism": On Not Quite Agreeing with Don Cupitt', *Modern Theology* 1.1, pp. 3-23.
- (1999), *On Christian Theology*, Blackwell, Oxford.

Index